BACK O' CAIRNS

D0727526

THE FRONTISPIECE

THE FRONTISPIECE overleaf, which shows typical figures in the rush to the Palmer goldfields, is a rendering by CLEM SEALE based on the original murals in the West Coast Hotel, Cooktown, by the wandering artist GARNET AGNEW. Here are the swagman miner and his Chinese counterpart. Here, too, are men at work, with rifle ready beside them, and one who bit the dust from bullet, spear, or tomahawk, or simply perished on the track from fever, thirst, or privation, as so many did. Then there are the inevitable hold-up men and confidence men and card-sharpers who preyed on the successful diggers returning loaded with gold to the "roaring city" of Cooktown. The lady in the piece is the notorious "Palmer Kate", the price of whose favours was an ounce of gold, with a fight first to win a kiss.

The drawing "Gold!", on the title page, is of a well-known prospector, Billy Weiss, when he found a golden gully running into the Palmer.

Back o' Cairns

ION IDRIESS

Angus&Robertson
An imprint of HarperCollins*Publishers*

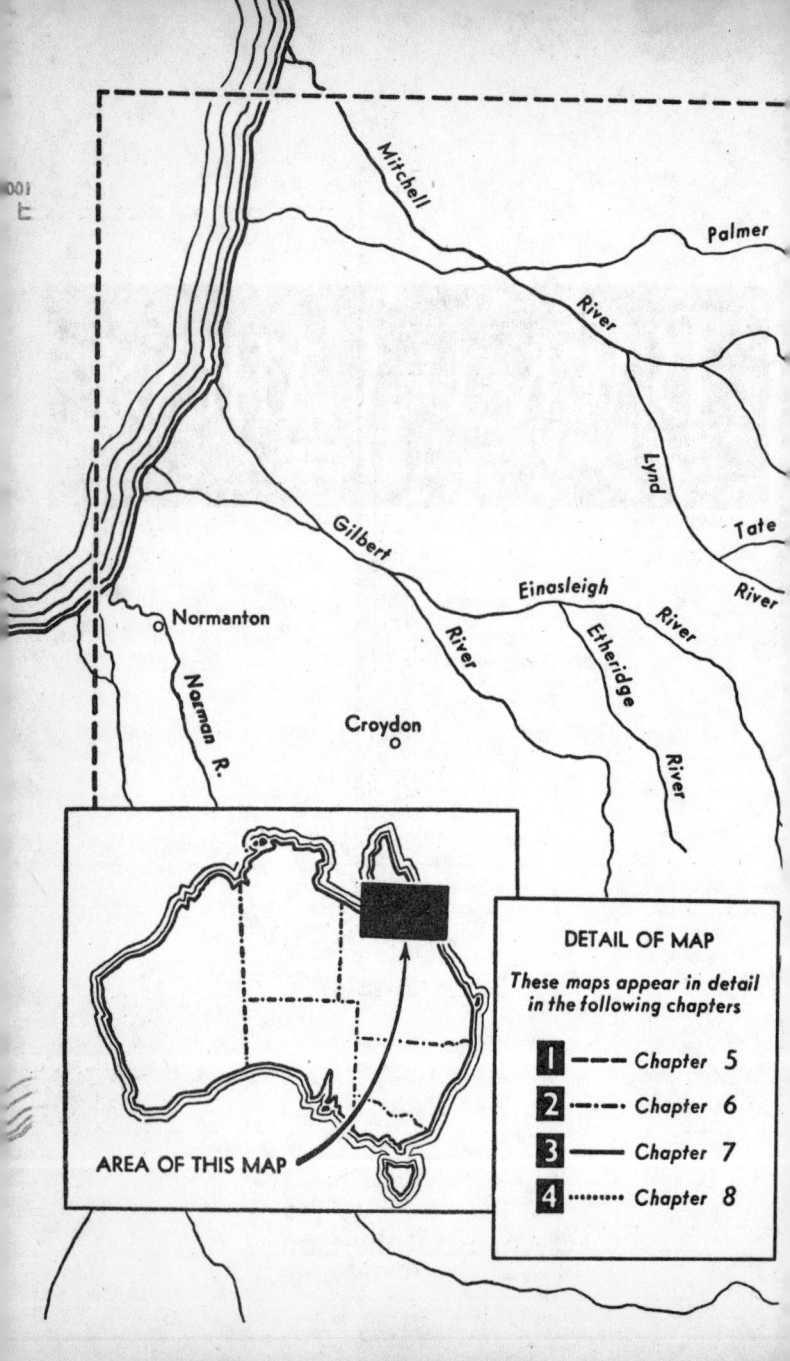

Mitchell

Palmer

River

Lynd

Tate

River

Gilbert

Einasleigh

Normanton

River

Etheridge

River

Norman R.

Croydon

DETAIL OF MAP

These maps appear in detail in the following chapters

1 --- *Chapter 5*
2 -·- *Chapter 6*
3 — *Chapter 7*
4 ······· *Chapter 8*

AREA OF THIS MAP

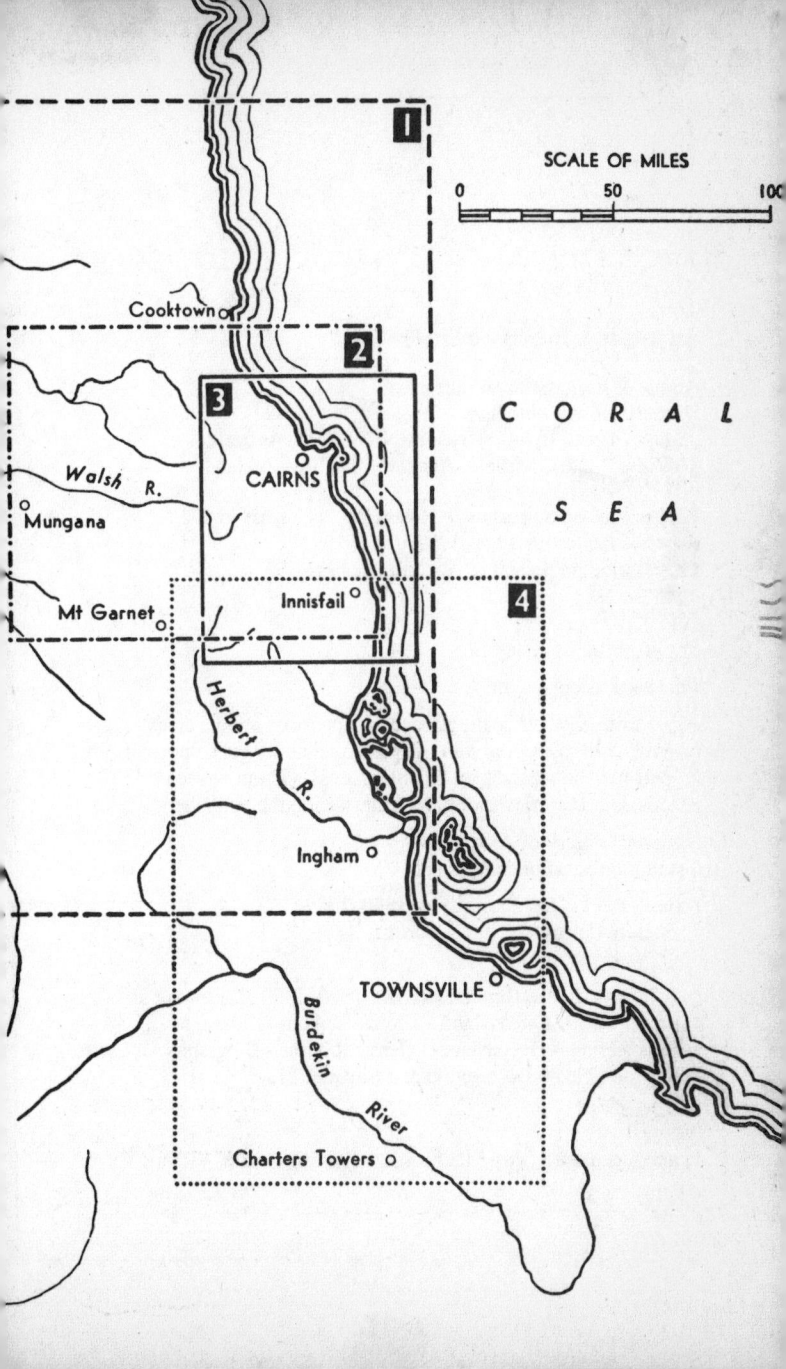

An Angus & Robertson Publication

Angus & Robertson, an imprint of
HarperCollins *Publishers*
25 Ryde Road, Pymble, Sydney NSW 2073, Australia
31 View Road, Glenfield, Auckland 10, New Zealand

First published by Angus & Robertson Publishers in 1958
Paperback editions 1979, 1981, 1988, 1991
This edition published in Australia in 1994

National Library of Australia
Cataloguing-in-Publication data:

Idriess, Ion L. (Ion Llewellyn), 1890–1979.
  Back o' Cairns.

  ISBN 0 207 18561 1.

  1. Idriess, Ion L. (Ion Llewellyn), 1890–1979. 2. Frontier and
  pioneer life—Queensland—Cairns Region—Biography. 3.
  Prospecting—Queensland—Cairns Region—Biography. 4. Cairns
  Region (Qld)—Description and travel. I. Title.
994.36

Printed in Australia by McPherson's Printing Group, Victoria
9 8 7 6 5 4 3 2 1
97 96 95 94

AUTHOR'S NOTE

WRITING this little book *Back o' Cairns* has indeed been a pleasure, memory refreshed from the faded notes of wandering years. But the writing has brought strongly home to me the fact that this book is but a page in the virile story of one of the greatest, and also most fascinating areas in our continent, with present and future possibilities unlimited.

Local historians, immeasurably better equipped than I am, will some day write the full history of "Back o' Cairns". Such a work could fill many volumes. But what a worthy subject! And brimful, too, of human interest. My best wishes to those writers who inevitably will tackle such a worth-while task.

For illustrations in this book, and also here and there for a little material such as extracts contained in the *Cairns Jubilee Production 1926*, I very sincerely thank folk in Cairns and the Cairns Hinterland. My thanks also go to my old friend Ern Mitchell of the Tableland in early days, now of Claremont, Western Australia.

To obtain illustrations for a factual book on life as lived in any part of Australia, excepting the cities, fifty years or so back is difficult indeed, impossible in numerous localities. Just on the off chance that the Cairns Chamber of Commerce might be able to help me I wrote to the Secretary. The response was wonderful—from officers of the Chamber who went to very considerable trouble in the friendliest manner, from press and radio and citizens throughout the entire hinterland. For this courtesy and friendly effort my publishers and I are grateful indeed.

I would very much like to say "thank you", particularly to Mr K. M. Kehoe, Mr W. M. Warner, and the officers of the Cairns Chamber of Commerce, to the officers of the Cairns School of Arts, to the Cairns press and radio, to the Atherton family, to Mr A. Garner of Innisfail, to Mr V. Tully of Atherton, to Mrs E. T. A. Cummings of Cairns, to Mrs A. Troppor of Lonox, via Edmonton, to Mr H. C. Eggers of Cairns Timber Limited, to Mr Geoff Hewitt of Tinaroo Falls, to Mr William Mildren of Mareeba, to Mrs S. F. O'Brien of Cairns, to Mr W. J. Hillyard of Chillagoe, to the Queensland Mining Department, to Mr Karl Luppi of Tinaroo Falls, to Mr James Rees of Cairns, and to that genial old battler whose address may be anywhere between the Antarctic and the Kimberleys, Captain Frank Hurley.

To the reader who may wonder at seeing me referred to as Jack within these pages (as in other books) the explanation is simple. In my school days there were few "Ions" in Australia; we were all "Bill" and "Joe", "Tom", "Eric", "Jack", "Harry", "Ted", "Ern"—my tough old dad from the wild Welsh hills little knew how heavily he was saddling his first born when he branded me "Ion". Mum, an enthusiastic Aussie girl, thought the name wonderful. I didn't. Just as soon as I reached school days those impish schoolmates of mine delighted in calling me anything but Ion, to mum's huge indignation when I'd come home with a "lovely stinker", a bonza black eye just because I'd vigorously protested at being called "Little Lord Fauntleroy"—and even worse indignities such as are only known, thank goodness, to the schoolboy world. Hence, when later I ran away to sea, I thankfully signed on, A.B. before the mast, as "Jack".

Life at sea in those days being anything but a bed of roses, I ran away again to the fastnesses of the good old bush with "Jack" still as a handle.

Which is why, even today, I hear of some disbelieving 'way-back bushman growling, "Jack Idriess! He didn't write them books! I knoo Jack Idriess well. He could no more write books than I can. *Ion* Idriess wrote them books—some city bloke!"

However, there are plenty of "Ions" and "Ians" throughout Australia today. But in my books I still am "Jack".

Cheerio!

Ion ("Jack") Idriess

CONTENTS

CONTENTS

CHAPTER I

NIGGER CREEK

IT WAS good to be alive. Sunlight sparkling on the Wild River, on white tent and cottages, too, over hills and flat. The quiet pools of Nigger Creek shaded by friendly trees offering home and life to bird, insect, and possum. Treasure within the earth. And youth, warmly spurred by hope, to dig it out.

Thus I felt, but I was in no hurry to climb down the shaft. A crimson parakeet screeched tauntingly by and I stood a moment with head peering above the windlass logs. Away down the slope stood the bold line of tough old trees caressing the Wild River singing over its rocky course. Gleaming ribbons of the brand-new railway line. The beckoning horizon of misty hills. And the wee village of Nigger Creek perched somewhat aloof from that bone of contention, the "Two Pubs". On the veranda of the New Pub the publican in shirt-sleeves stood frowning down the road at the Old Pub. The New Pub had been built to help assuage the thirst of the navvies building the line from the railhead at Herberton. But now the steel ribbons were laid past Nigger Creek and the hard-toiling, hard-drinking Knights of the Pick and Shovel were slaving a few miles farther on, their white tents and hessian huts stretching a mile through the green bush echoing to their toil as steadily they laid the rails mile after mile closer to those wind-blown Tumoulin and Evelyn scrubs. What wealth of timbers, maybe of minerals, too, certainly of rich soils, lay within those vast green depths no man yet knew.

Thus the turbulent gangs had toiled on, leaving Nigger Creek to dream in peace again. Gone was that hectic period, that sweat and toil, the growling of the gangers; some among those "slave-drivers", so truculent navvies swore, would have liked to swing the knotted whip as did the taskmasters of old. Vanished the sun-glint on the long line of shovel blades, the up-and-down of the picks, the shouts of the sleeper haulers, the creaking wheels of drays and wagons, clanging of hammers, mingled sweat of straining teams and gangs of men, the fire and song from the blacksmiths' and tool-sharpeners' anvils, the shrill ring of the drill, the thunderous *Boom! Boom! Boom!* from a rocky cutting. All this virile energy had whispered itself away towards the setting sun. Again there was the murmur of the bush, the trilling waters of the Wild River, the joyous song of birds far and wide over creeks and hilltops, spreading ever farther to peaks of forest and jungle. Calm and lovely were the nights now—strangely lonesome, though, for gone were those hundreds of campfires along the Wild River and tucked away in by Nigger Creek, with here and there some firelit group singing sentimental chorus to fiddle and concertina; gone the rhythmic step-dance on the pub verandas, the lively clicking of the bones. Strangely sweet, those rough voices in haunting refrain drifting from the listening night across the tinkling waters of the river. The river voice had the night to itself now, the trill of water, gloomy hoot of the mopoke, unabashed screech of some ambitious possum. But gone was the murmur of men's voices from many a campfire and hurricane-lamp-lit shed—gone, too, the uproar of those wild and woolly pay-nights.

But hark! Rollicking voices now came floating up from the Old Pub. Standing on the ladder in the shaft mouth, I listened a moment, gazing down the slope towards a pretty girl feeding ducks by the little cottage across the creek. Buck navvies', those voices were, celebrating. I could see their empty pump-car waiting on the line. On their way into Herberton for something or other, these Knights of the Banjo could not resist pulling up for one or two at "Mrs Reynolds's place". Just to renew old acquaintance, most likely, and crack a joke with the girls. Presently they would come stamping out over the ant-eaten veranda, mount the trolly, seize the handle-bars, then, with lusty farewell to Mrs Reynolds and the girls, start pumping and make the wheels fairly hum on the way to town—and the next pub.

Those navvies lived hard. Played hard, too.

Up at Grigg's store the storekeeper was hammering at a case. The girl across by the cottage was patting a fat, greedy duck. I half wished I were a duck. Life seems harsh at times, when you're a stranger, and lonely, and absurdly young—and imagine yourself hopelessly in love with someone far, far away. The young girl was doubtless smiling as she patted the duck. Dreamily I thought that if she clutched an axe in that caressing hand I would not then envy the duck.

Up over the hill loomed the grey dumps of the Deep Lead, until recent years one of the great alluvial tin-fields of Australia. A rumbling of thunder came from away back in the hills around Herberton where the reef miners were blasting the rock in their ceaseless search for tinstone. Enviously I wondered whether the shots were fired by the lucky Bimrose brothers, whether that murmurous thunder came from the Bradlaugh, the Lyee Moon, the Rainbow or Great Northern. Maybe the St Patrick or Black King —I'd hardly hear it from the Ironclad. Some of the big shows had struck rich patches of ore; how wonderful it must feel to be blasting out a rich crushing, with everyone in town wondering what percentage the stone would go! I could not then imagine anything more wonderful. Just what could that heavy, dull, greyish-black stone mean to a man!

It meant for the lucky ones the laughing heart. Fortunes lay hidden in these far-flung hills, somewhere, far and few between, deep down in the granite, deep under the basalt. Man the insect, sometimes on blind chance, was burrowing down foot by foot, inch by inch where the rock was particularly hard, sometimes slaving on bread and dripping, sustained by the heart of a lion and that grim determination that holds a man together until he drops. On many a mining field fortune has thus been won on bread and dripping. Or was it dogged determination? Yet no matter how I toiled—I sighed at the lovely morning.

The girl had finished with the ducks. Empty dish in hand, she paused by the cottage door, lightly touching at gaily coloured flowers adorning the creepers ever striving for entry into the very cottage. She stepped inside. To me, with my lonely heart, she seemed very cuddlesome. A parakeet sped past on his way to his mate anxiously waiting at the creek, the hurrying beauty fairly shied at my head above the windlass logs.

"Think you're a Scarlet Pimpernel!" I grumbled as the lovely bird flashed by. "Think Man is a silly insect for scratching his way into the bowels of the earth while you whistle in the sunlight sucking honey from gum-tree blossoms! I s'pose *you* wouldn't even *look* at a good fat duck!"

With a self-pitying sigh I climbed down the dark shaft to be an insect, yet eager now for work, though the sunlight was calling above. Crawled away into the cool, earthy drive, lit the candle, and peered at the face, which here was an old river-bed deep down under the basalt rock. Ages ago this now long-dry bed of water-worn stones and gravel and sand had been the bottom of a swiftly flowing river gleaming in the sunlight. Strange birds, some as tall as a man, had flown over it, goggle-eyed fishes and weird lizard things had swum its depths, rending one another with tooth and claw. Mighty animals had roamed its banks, eating and snorting and playing, loving and fighting their lives away, doubtless believing they were the lords of the earth. But a time of terror had come when the earth trembled and rocked in awful thunders, volcanoes burst up in fire, belching forth rivers of molten lava, one of which poured down into the water-river and buried it and its banks, even its very valley, buried its trees and rocks, its waterfalls and rapids and frantic living things, the fiery waves of molten rock surging, flowing on, burning, burying everything deep under their path, irresistible even to the might of this then mighty river. What chaotic sizzling, earth-shaking explosions, clouds of steam must have gone swirling and roaring to the heavens as the frothing river waters fought that relentless rush of red-hot lava!

And now, buried deep down under the solidified lava rock, right here in the darkness of the pit was a fragment of that old river-bed, uncovered after millions of years by the pick of a miner. I was the proud miner whose insect sweat had bored a hole down which the ever-living sun again dimly sought to kiss its long-dead river-bed. There in the damp gloom the candle flame lit up the water-worn wash-stones, the gravels and sands which millions of years before they had become a river-bed had been proud mountain-tops. Thus do even mountains live, and die. Ay, but to be born again.

Peering, I held the candle flame to the very bottom, where the larger layer of wash-stones was cemented into an inch-thick layer of heavy mineralized sand resting upon solid bottom—the clean bare bosom of Mother Rock. And here faintly showed a lament-ably thin black line that was made up of grains of alluvial tin. That line was barely visible, like black match-heads wedged in amongst the gravel. To think that of all the millions of tons of mountain slopes washed down here throughout millions of years all of value to the slaving miner was a few concentrated grains of black stream tin!

With a sigh I shoved the iron-pointed spider (candle-holder) into the wash-dirt at eye level and, squatting on crossed legs, picked up the pick. This wash-dirt was not payable, but the "thud, thud" of the pick kept steadily on, biting slowly deeper into the face, seeking a spot where the tin might "make". Should it sud-denly blossom out into a black patch, then a lonely lad would smile with glee, for it would mean that at least tucker money was assured. If not, I'd have to roll up the swag and trudge away out along the line and seek a job as an unwilling navvy until the tucker-bag was filled again. How we prospectors and "on our own" miners used to hate the very thought of being compelled to work for wages! Freedom is worth all the money in the world.

Quaint thoughts come at times to help pass the labour away, when a man is working alone underground. From whence do these thoughts come? Except for the steady, dull thud of the pick a deathly quietness, as if everything had stopped. It is lonesome down there.

Swing the pick—queer thought—some mighty Power made this tin, made *all* tin, during ages past when the earth was forming. Did that (*swing, swing*) Power purposely make tin so that (*swing*) in millions of years to come it (*swing*) would help Man to make a living? If not, what did it make tin for? What *is* tin, anyway? And how did the Power make it? Why can tin do what it *can* do? And how did it happen that Man was born with some power called reasoning that taught him how to make tin do what tin can do?

Only the thud of the pick gave answer. Quaint questions like these keep flowing through a man's mind as water dreamed over this river-bed long, long ago. Vanished water—that all the same must have shot up to the skies in hissing storms of steam—which of course would form real clouds—and fall again as rain—into some other river—and wear away other mountains on its never-ending journey to the sea—to rise in cloud again—and fall. . . . H'm! Then water, too, *never* dies—well, I'd better shovel this mullock back into the shaft!

Thus the Earth Gremlins whisper to a man when he is toiling alone deep under below.

This was very different mining work in every way to the opal-gouging at Lightning Ridge, that colourful New South Wales gem-field that I had said good-bye to only a few months before.* Nor was this a mining field under hundreds of tents, the noisy rhythm of a human ant-bed feverish with visions of quick fortune. Except for Herberton and Stannary Hills, Irvinebank, Chillagoe, Mount Molloy, Wolfram Camp, Bamford and a few other established timber, agricultural and mining townships, throughout the Tableland and its fringes there were only groups of little mining camps, and scattered bands of men throughout a hundred and more miles of ranges. Nigger Creek, with its little store and two pubs was a comparatively big place, also supporting one of the tiniest schools in Queensland. The schoolmaster, Garnet Aitchison, and I had chummed up—the bush lad of the pick and shovel, and the white-collar lad. Unlike slow, solemn me, he was ever ready with a smile, bustling with energy, eager with ambitions of what he was going to become—something big in the Queensland Education Department. A likable type of a lad, but an atrocious cook—or rather, mixer of fruits. For he couldn't cook an egg unless the hen laid it ready fried. He gloried in what

* Those joyous days were described in *Lightning Ridge*.

he called "fruit salad". He'd come hurrying over to my camp on red-letter nights loaded with a smile and bananas and papaws, sour-saps and five-fingers, and all manner of tropical fruit that the school kids had collected for their popular master throughout the week. We'd borrow a wash-basin from the New Pub, scrub it clean with sand at the creek, then squat down by candle-light and seriously peel the fruit. Garnet, sleeves rolled up, with studious mien would slice the delicacies in pieces not quite large enough to choke a hungry swallower, tip a couple of tins of condensed milk into it, and mix well and conscientiously, a drop or two of sweat from his forehead dripping down into it on hot nights.

"A little salt brings out the flavour, Jack," he would say cheerfully. "Sodium chloride is the salt of life and puts lead into your pen and ink."

"Yes, a sweetener. It's only salt water, anyway. Keep on stirring, it looks good."

With furrowed brow and energy he'd mix the whole sticky mess again with a spoon like a navvy's shovel—he used to borrow the iron ladle Mrs Reynolds at the Old Pub used for stirring the clothes in the copper on washing day. When the whole basin of tricks was trowelled into a sort of rocky cement we'd "get stuck into it". It used to take us a couple of hours to finish it off, sheer gluttony. When exhausted we'd lean back, grin at one another, lick our lips, declare how good it was, then stagger to a sitting position and "get stuck into it" again. It really was good, even granted we possessed the endurance and digestion of youth to guzzle it.

Garnet, of course, "boarded out". As schoolmaster, he stayed at one of the little cottages. Most nights, after the evening meal, he would come strolling along to my camp and, chatting over the events of the day, we would wend our way across the flat to Old Mick's camp down by Nigger Creek. Mick's camp was roomy and comfortable, as only a fastidious bushman can make a camp. And Jim Bell, Old Mick's mate, was a bushman through and through. Able to travel and live on the smell of an oiled rag if necessary, when in a "permanent camp" he could make it as neat, roomy, and comfortable as a real home. A fact quietly appreciated by Old Mick who, like me, would chuck down his swag and camp anywhere, too lazy, or too incapable of making ourselves comfortable even in a "permanent" camp—which generally meant one of but a few months' duration.

At Mick's campfire, under the moon with the possums screeching in the gums, we smoked the pipe of content and sat out many a yarn. Big Old Man Brookes would generally come lumbering along, bringing his quiet ways and goatee beard of iron grey. Little Tommy Turley, too, active as a wildcat though all bent up from years of excessive toil and hardship. Occasionally Long Stewart from Flaggy Creek would saunter along with his quiet, "Good night, boys"; and Matt Stillane might appear, or young Gallogoly, and now and again an old-timer from somewhere along the Deep Lead. All the old hands had loneliness in far-away places relieved by hectic periods in roaring mining camps to yarn about. Excepting Mick, who in his quiet old voice could yarn the night away with railway construction in the raw, though just occasionally with hauntingly elusive tales of some quite other life.

Old Mick was a hard-bitten railway ganger who recently had decided that tin-mining was a much happier life than toiling for "the Boss" in the construction camps. A grizzled old veteran of almost every railway line in Queensland, he looked as if he could chew nails without bothering to spit out the heads. Under bushy brows his twinkling eyes gave the only outside hint of a kindly heart and quaint philosophy. Though he was shaggy-faced, tough-looking as they make them, burnt nearly black by many and many a sun, there actually was nothing of the "gorilla" about him, as I gradually learnt. And in those days most gangers relied on toughness to handle the mixed boys of the construction camps who lived and toiled under conditions that we would call slavery today. Old Mick could not bend a crowbar with his teeth, though he looked it; he was just a wiry little ball of muscle and sinew with twinkling eyes, a deep, secret ambition, and a kindly heart in the right place.

To my boyish astonishment, as to Garnet's, we had now learnt that Mick was—a poet! A railway ganger from a tough North Queensland construction camp a poet! Ye gods!

I well remember our amazement.

"You cannot judge a book by its cover," declared Garnet wisely, "but who'd have thought it!"

Who indeed! Since he was a toddler Mick had seen and lived life in the raw indeed, had been hurt very often, I'm sure, and feel as certain that he never showed it, *dared* not show it. But hard times had only made him the more understanding. Even after these years memory brings back his ugly face, which was so kindly when you grew to know it, his friendly grin, his chuckle at a harsh word, his smile that so often turned away wrath. But only his mate Jim Bell and his closest friends knew that he loved the birds and the trees and the moonlight on the Wild River—and wrote "pomes" about them.

Something even more astonishing—he wrote "pomes" about Beautiful Women!

Women, in those days and environment, seemed as elusive as the angels.

Of course, Time teaches. Also, Time speeds up. As I write this, Sputnik I is tranquilly sailing far away out in space over Australia—over the world. Yet I can still see the muscled arms of navvies pushing heavy loaded wheelbarrows up a steep plank on the Tumoulin construction line at six bob a day, hear a lilt of girlish laughter coming up from the Old Pub down by the creek, feel myself bending over the windlass barrel laboriously hauling up a bucket of dirt from the shaft by Nigger Creek.

CHAPTER II

THE POET OF NIGGER CREEK

By the "Council Fire" one evening I remarked, "I never dreamt that railway gangers wrote poetry, Mick."

Warily he grinned. "There's more things in heaven and earth —but it comes natural, lad. You've seen the moon cactus, haven't you?"

"Yes."

"Well, you know what an ugly plant that cactus is, under what harsh conditions it grows, how drab and spiky and unlovely it is."

"Yes."

"Well, you know, too, its beautiful flower, the lovely vision that at rare intervals peeps coyly out from that ugliness to throw a kiss to the moon?"

"Well, yes, Mick, it *has* a wonderful flower."

"Well," said Mick, grinning, "my poetry is my moon-flower."

We laughed as much at Jim Bell's disgusted expression as at "our poet".

"Moon-flower! My sainted aunt!" Jim exploded. "You're the ugliest cactus on the range, I give you *that* in! But moon-flower— you smirking old cart-horse!"

"But what a delightful comparison," chuckled Garnet, "worthy of Nigger Creek. After all, beauty may be only skin deep, even upon a somewhat weather-beaten cart-horse. Yet look what our Michael has produced! Poetry, the very essence of words—just as the lowly cactus brings forth its lovely flower."

Mick grinned delightedly at this flowery praise from the school-master, he had had a win indeed. Jim Bell rolled a log on the fire in obvious disgust. Little Tommy Turley chuckled at the grizzled Mick.

"Oh, the moon cactus! Just what *would* his navvy mates say if they knew their buck-toothed ganger was the flower of the moon cactus!"

"They'd be struck speechless," declared Jim Bell, "for once!"

A big green centipede came wriggling up from a crack in the warming log, twitching legs outspread, writhing in hideous dismay at the choking smoke. Agitatedly it began to hurry along the top of the log to escape the now burning heat.

Sprawled comfortably there under the stars by that galley fire, a breath from the creek wafted me a vision of the moon cactus. To come on the big flower suddenly in the bush at night is an experience. Its flower seems of an unearthly whiteness as it unfolds to the moon, some effect of moonlight and ghostly petals and deathly quiet surroundings, I suppose. In some localities, generally if growing upon harsh ground, the flower almost seems to possess a delicate fluorescence. I've half wondered whether the plant might absorb mineral pigment from the soil and in some chemical way transfer it to further beautify the flower. In those days I was too bashful to ask the old hands lest they think "young Jack's got a rat"!

Jim Bell bent again to the logs and a bright flame illumined the rough-hewn, deep-lined face of Old Mick beneath those bushy eyebrows. Tommy Turley chuckled again, the shadow of his skinny, bony, hunched-up little body queerly reminiscent of a parched eaglehawk with drooping wings slumped upon a log. The hard toil of a struggling lifetime had played havoc with that frail body of Tommy's.

Jim Bell sniffed meaningly towards his grizzled mate.

"Ah well," sighed Mick, "I don't care if I'm no beauty. Adonis was not fated to be my name. But, alas, I'll never go down in history!"

"Only as the greatest liar unhung!" declared Jim Bell with conviction.

"Alas, how cruelly you flatter me," murmured Mick. "I could never hope to rival the unrivalled Baron Munchausen."

"What race is *he* in?" asked Jim suspiciously.

"What is your latest 'pome', Mick?" asked Garnet. "Or is it a love epistle this time? Come on, out with it to the Council!"

For, apart from his "pomes", Mick Moore, just like Mick Cullen at far away Lightning Ridge, was born possessed of an imp. And the imp of both Michaels ran to the female species. While Mick Cullen sought the company of women at every rare opportunity and delighted in all the trouble he could stir up with that impish tongue of his, Mick Moore was very shy of the female and did the damage at a distance with his "poetic" pen. Both men in their own way loved to torment the female sex, though Mick Moore did it "to be kind", Mick Cullen "for fun". Both methods had certainly proved effective.

Whereas at the Ridge it was the silver tongue of Mick Cullen that started the gossip and catty backchat, here it was the honeyed pen of Mick Moore that caused a lot of heart-burning. From Cairns to the Tumoulin he delighted to write love-letters to any girl and woman whom he met, or merely saw by the most casual chance, should she captivate his quaint fancy in some way or other. Those women must have been astounded. I don't know what they would have thought could they have seen Mick seated on a box by the campfire in bare feet—and *such* feet!—clad in toil-stained dungaree trousers, belt, and patched old grey working flannel, forehead all creased in wrinkles, tongue in cheek as he laboured over his "epistle", his tough, grinning old face lit up by the campfire.

"A labour of love!" he would murmur reverently.

"The only labour you *ever* do!" would growl Jim Bell.

At such times of deep inspiration we'd smoke and yarn and think out wise remarks. Jim Bell's would be sarcastic ones.

"Romeo to his Juliet by Nigger Creek!" Garnet would wink at me.

"Yeah," said Jim Bell, "and I wish that skirt in Cairns could see her stub-toed Romeo wolfing tinned peas with his knife!"

"Surely not!" Garnet laughed delightedly. "Surely such are not our Mick's table manners!"

"Table manners!" growled Jim. "He hasn't any. One day in

Townsville he nearly choked trying to swallow a hard-boiled egg in its shell."

"But why in its shell?"

"Because he was in a hurry—he reached over and pinched it from a late boarder's plate on the other table just as the waitress came in."

But Mick would complacently grin, and toil on.

"How's that?" he proudly asked one evening.

I took the letter, held it towards the firelight, and read:

> *Wondecla,*
> *North Queensland.*

Dearest,

    With a mind ever wandering to your lovely self I must reveal my passionate love for you. Even in my dreams you appear before me.

    Dearest, never before did poor deluded man struggle so hopelessly against the allure of your presence. The world seems a dreary place with you so far away. I cannot eat, the wind seems to howl in desolation. I retire to the paradise of imagination where you ever are, and then all the world is joy. Alas, could I but wield the magic wand that would make dreams come true! If only I could convey to you my heart's deepest yearnings! Alas, I can only pen these few poor words. They contain but the whisper of my soul's affections. And the forlorn hope that you will drop but one little line to make my wildest dreams come true.

> In humble waiting,
> Yours very truly,
> HAROLD HAWTHORNE.

How Garnet and I laughed! And Mick sat grinning there, grinning more the more we laughed.

"How do you think she'll respond?" he chuckled.

"By hurrying to the police station and certifying you a lunatic!" replied Jim Bell disgustedly.

"But you haven't signed your real name!" protested Garnet.

"He would have been shot years ago if he *had*," growled Jim.

"How many husbands and fathers and lovers, do you think, are looking for the idiot who writes those silly letters?"

Old Mick beamed from under beetling brows. I knew he had some wary private arrangement for the delivery of his surprisingly voluminous correspondence.

"You'll receive a reply by return mail," chuckled Garnet.

"Perhaps not so quick as that," said Mick, grinning confidently, "but I think she'll reply to the serpent."

"You ought to be pole-axed," growled Jim Bell. "Some of those women," he said to us, "actually think what he writes them is true! Or they want to find out, anyway." He turned to Mick with grim prophecy. "I only hope I'm here to see it. One of these days a fourteen-stone Amazon will come waddling along here and give you the hiding of your life!"

"I nearly got it one day." Mick grinned reminiscently.

"Tell us about it," I asked eagerly.

"Well," drawled Mick, "it was when we were building the Biboohra-Mareeba section. But my gang were on repair towards the head of the gorge, below the lip of the falls. I'd posted several epistles to ladies in Cairns and received satisfactory response. One reply was a flea in my ear, but another was sweet balm; this fairy had swallowed the bait, hook, line, and sinker. Feeling pleased, though smarting under the other letter, I sat down that night to spread myself in reply. And I flatter myself I made those humble pages fairly glow with passion. In due course a very pleasing reply came. I answered as a cavalier must, then started on another romance. Unfortunately, this promising affair happened to be addressed to a niece of the stricken one, though I didn't know it at the time. They swapped love experiences.

"Well, it was a warm afternoon some days later. I was bossing the gang in that deep cutting towards Fairy Falls. The supply train came grunting up the range, and groaned to a stop. From the driver's cab there stepped one of the most ponderous, the ugliest, the most athletic, the most determined-looking female that ever sent a shiver down my spine—if she didn't sprout hair upon her chest then I'm a Dutchman. A glint in her eye, too, looked like murder. The gang saw her, *heard* her coming, there was an uneasy, guilty movement here and there while I wondered what my beauties had been up to this time. I soon knew.

"She came lumbering along to the gang, her hoofs crunching on over the blue metal as if shod with iron. She carried a waistline like a female elephant, she fairly towered over the gang. She bent down and snatched up a pick-handle. Then she snarled at the nearest navvy, 'Where's Mick Moore the ganger?'

"He jerked his thumb towards me, the fool. I got one gleam from her eye and knew it was time to be moving—straight down the line for the tunnel, double quick—you should have heard the gang roar! She came within an ace of dashing my brains out, but I lost her in the tunnel. I knew my way about in there, of course. But I've never been so grateful for darkness before."

Mick's little story was quite true. There was no other hope of escape. To one side of the rails the cutting wall forms a cliff, impossible to climb up there. On the other side of the rails the sheer drop down into the Barron Gorge. And what a gorge! The one chance of escape was the tunnel and—keep going.

"You'll be cornered for sure one day!" prophesied Old Brookes.

"Never!" Mick grinned. "So long as I'm smart off the mark, never while I've breath in my body to run."

"You're a cruel old devil, Mick," I said reprovingly.

"A breaker of hearts," declared Garnet. "He ought to be hung!"

"No, lad," Mick answered quite seriously. "Like Santa Claus, I really bring a tiny gleam of happiness into the world—though it be but as a pearl lost in the ocean."

In the pause—I believe Mick paused on purpose—Jim Bell groaned.

"For the love of Mike, won't you *ever* come down to earth?"

"I was coming—"

"Well, hurry up, you silly ass!" snorted Jim. "And pass the damper."

"Go on, Mick," said Garnet, "tell us all about your 'pearls of happiness'. Take no notice of your mate—he's not a poet!"

"Poetry is a gift," said Mick, smiling, "given to but a few."

"Yeah!" declared Jim. "And *you* just can't give it away."

"Go on, Mick," urged Garnet. "Tell us about the happiness and the pearls."

"Well, lad," explained Mick solemnly, "women were made for pearls. And there's few indeed out in these parts. Life is pretty hard in this country, especially for women. Life is mainly toil, they haven't so very much to look forward to. So I do my best, in the humblest way, to strew their path with a wisp of happiness now and then. Lots of the women I've written to have only the vaguest idea, if any, who I am. And I take jolly fine care they don't learn just *where* I am. They know, or presume, I'm a man. And there might be romance in anything in pants."

"My God!" moaned Jim and leant forward with his head in his hands.

"These ladies' husbands," resumed Mick dreamily, "or fathers or brothers or sweethearts may, or may not, have had me pointed out to them in the distance by some kind friend of mine. Being of a shy, retiring disposition, I shun introductions. Hence when *she* receives the letter she wonders what it's all about. Then she reads it again, squinting out the corner of her cornflower-blue orb to make sure no one's looking. She develops a bit of a thrill now, she begins to wonder! And when she reads the letter a few times more she grows sure *someone* loves her! After all, it's nice to be loved, we *all* like it. Even Jim Bell—though you couldn't believe it. Why *shouldn't* someone love someone else, anyway? And being a secret makes it all the sweeter. So she hides the letter away, hugs it to her warm little bosom, and thinks over it all day, and reads it again at night—that witching night! Oh, what dreams come whispering in those loving arms of night!

"She might answer that beguiling epistle—or she might not. After all, it breaks the monotony of the long, hot months, and gives her a warm little glow. So there's no harm done."

"But what about the end of it?" I inquired. "Because you string them on, you answer those letters month after month."

"When the right time comes," said Mick, "I just fade away,

gracefully, like the Arab folding his tent. I write her one last heart-throb of farewell, something with the tang of despair in it. Something terrible, something tragically unforeseen has happened—I must away. So she never knows, and I leave her a memory."

"One of those husbands will be leaving *you* with more than a memory," prophesied Jim grimly, "and serve you right, too."

"One very nearly did one day."

"What saved you *this* time?" asked the interested Garnet.

"He tackled the wrong Mick Moore," replied Mick, grinning, "and this particular Mick could fight like a thrashing machine. When hubby came to there was a bit of explaining. But I'd rolled my swag—just in time."

CHAPTER III

BY THE COUNCIL FIRE

OLD MICK'S "Campfire Council" was an evening joy to Garnet and me, after sunset closed the day's work. We soon saw through Jim Bell, though. The morose Jim, with those piercing black eyes, scolded the old ganger but really thought the world of him. Two men seemingly entirely unsuited as mates, yet working so well together. The old ganger was really a dreamer, while the grim Jim Bell was a man of action. The navvy, free at last of a navvy's life, was happily content to let the world drift by, caring little what tucker he cooked and ate, satisfied if he could find a dry place to camp, happy to dream the day away by the banks of the Wild River, doing just a little tin-scratching when the mood urged. Now, however, he was taken in hand by the taskmaster, his mate Jim, a younger man, good either on the track or camp, a toiler handy with tools and horses, and determined to knock all the tin possible out of their claim. He made Mick toil, too.

"We may fool away our money when we make it," he would growl to the easy-going Mick. "We were born that way, I suppose. But we're going to keep the storekeeper's bills from worrying us."

And Mick would murmur agreement as they walked from camp to work, though with a sigh and lingering glance towards the inviting old trees shading the Wild River.

Jim was a man who could work on his own or with a mate, who could knock up a good feed out of nothing and a comfortable camp that would defy the heaviest wet season. His gear was always in tip-top order; he could pack up and be miles away on the track within hours, finding his own way to any point of the compass without a compass. A bushman-miner who never worked for a boss while he could pay his own storekeeper's bills, a quiet man of action now working mate of a delightful old navvy dreamer. Apart from what both men could teach us of their varied ways of life, they were a constant source of interest to young Garnet and me. And jolly good friends they were when once we began to understand the taciturn Jim, who could laugh when least expected.

He wore a heavy moustache, as so many men did then; his shrewd eyes were of a piercing black when he was angry or excited. Quick-handed, a dark-skinned little bushman, wiry as a brumby.

"And as big a fool as ever breathed," he growled bitterly one evening, frowning at the fire, his dark, heavily moustached face set in grim lines. "My mate and I had one of the richest claims in Wolfram Camp," he declared. "We should have cleaned up a fortune. But my mate was a great booze artist, and I was a fool that way, too. Worse, I got poking my nose into other people's business. A whisky still was hidden away out there in the ranges, in some gorge back of Mount Spurgeon. It brewed vile stuff— sent half a dozen fine young fellows into the horrors, then off their heads—ruined them. I threatened to tell the police, a thing I'd never do, of course. But the threat frightened the moonshiners. Father and son, two long streaks of vindictive malice with the manners of grizzly bears. They'd barely growl a word to one another even when absolutely necessary, let alone spare a greeting for anyone else. Which made them all the more dangerous— their tongues would never hang them! They used to come down out of the ranges at night, with the grog packed on horses near tough as themselves. They swore to get me, but never said a word to me—I understood when they sent a bullet whizzing past my ear. But the son was drowned crossing the Walsh in flood; he believed nothing could kill him, but his own horse rolled over in the stream and kicked him on the head and down he went. Pity the father didn't go with him." Reflectively Jim pulled at his pipe.

"But it wasn't the moonshiners who drove me from the field, it was two young fellows, and new-chums at that. They were stealing bismuth!" His dark face was scowling at the fire. "No, it wasn't the moonshiners, though when the son was drowned the father did his block, swore that one day he would catch me up a dry gully, strip me, carve me where the bull lost his pedigree, then peg me down on an ant-bed. And there are plenty of dry gullies around Wolfram Camp, lonelier hide-outs back in the ranges. When working on my own I got to be a hell of nerves, all eyes and ears and jumping around at sound of a wallaby or goanna scuttling in the grass; even the blasted crows had the daylights scared out of me. I knew just what would happen if that devil sneaked up on me and knocked me senseless, I knew what I'd wake up to!"

Jim paused, thoughtfully ramming tobacco into his pipe bowl with stubby finger, firelight on his grim face.

"For all that, it was not the moonshiners who hunted me from the field, it was my own stupid sense of justice. Those two young fellows were camping near me, such innocent young devils you'd think them, they were stealing bismuth from Moffat's mine. He was paying them good money, too. It was lovely stuff, they'd worked into a bunch of it down below, a clean bunch of oxides. They brought a specimen of it down to my claim, dollied it, washed a couple of pounds' weight of near pure bismuth out of it right before my eyes. They were all smiles, and know-all winks, thought they were great smarties, outsmarting the 'Father of the North'. I told them that as they were working for Moffat and being paid good money for labour it wasn't a square deal that they should steal his bismuth. They laughed and replied that Moffat was a millionaire and anyway wouldn't miss a few pounds' worth of bismuth. Neither he would either, maybe, but he's a good bloke, Moffat, and he's been hard up against it himself at times. Anyway, it was the principle of it worried me. Besides, those two young chaps had got a taste of easy money by stealing and it could spoil their lives. So I threatened to put the show away. They laughed like it was a kid's joke. Then I threatened them just like I'd threatened the moonshiners—threatened to tell the police! And just didn't *that* surprise them! But they still would not believe I meant it. But when they saw I was in earnest it scared them. The police out there are easy-going, but they'll stand no nonsense."

Jim paused, staring morosely into the fire, puffing his pipe as if smoking charcoal. The hectic life of the Wolfram Camp he missed was very different to the peace of Nigger Creek.

"What happened then?" asked Garnet.

Old Mick chuckled softly.

"Guess!" He smiled. "But don't interrupt the story."

"Well then, what *did* happen, you know-all old baboon?" snapped Jim.

"You made a deal with the two young coves," chuckled Mick, "bought their bismuth day by day on the halves, then struck a sweet little patch of bismuth in your *own* claim. And one fine day sold it all back to John Moffat."

We smiled at the impish grin on Mick's face, turned accusingly to the exasperated Jim.

"You ought to be a fowl," he snapped at his mate. "You can pick *up* things!"

"A little bird told me!" chuckled Mick.

"Must have been a lyre bird!" retorted Jim sourly.

"Well then, just what *did* happen," asked Garnet, "after you threatened the young fellows you'd tell the police?"

"I left Wolfram Camp—in a hurry." Jim frowned.

"Why?"

"Because the police came one morning and found a bag full of Moffat's bismuth—hidden in *my* claim."

"But who put it there?" asked Garnet innocently.

"*I* didn't!" replied Jim bitterly.

"Just imagine those naughty little new-chum boys," said Mick, "putting it all across the poor innocent bushman."

Wolfram Camp was a roaring camp out Chillagoe way from Herberton, a perfect Bret Harte mining camp, as was Mount Carbine, north along the Mount Spurgeon Range from Mount Molloy. In wild surroundings, with wild men, the camp "open" day and night—the greatest wolfram camp in Australia; there has not been one found like it since. The heavy, brownish rock—that which lay exposed on the surface looked like dull lumps of weather-tarnished coal—some years before had suddenly become of surprising value. That is what men then thought. Oversea financial interests must have milked Australia of millions of pounds in metal prices alone before we developed a little national sense. However, bush telegraph had spread the news and four or five years back men had begun to turn their thoughts and horses and roll their swags for that harsh, wild country vaguely known as the Wolfram Camp via Herberton, Chillagoe district. The increasing bands of dusty new-comers found, to their unbounded astonishment and delight, that there was "plenty for everybody"! How very different from the great majority of mineral fields where that elusive Lady Luck favours only the very few! Here, in the early years, you had but to trudge over the ground carrying a bag and knapping hammer and "pick the wolfram up" in reality. Perhaps in no other field in Australia has the wealth been lying there so widely exposed, every here and there among the tree roots and grasses, over so many square miles of country. Along the scantily timbered ridges, even along the flats, in the dry gullies and creeks, it was to be found in the form of reef cappings, leaders, floaters, and alluvial. Where the mineral-bearing reefs and leaders outcropped above the ground the cap was rich in mineral, tons of it in some cases broken away and lying sun-baked upon the earth, so rich that the specimens merely had to be picked up and thrown into bags, ready for sale without further treatment. Other tons were merely knocked from the reefs with the pick and hammer, the adhering quartz and stone knocked or dollied off, the specimen material thrown into bags. The gullies and creeks were rich in concentrated alluvial.

And, just to cap it all, to this Fairy Bush of a Miner's Dream obliging men with a strong foreign accent came plodding along, even to every miner's camp, eager to buy this "worthless iron-stony stuff" and pack it away on their very own horses. These fool foreigners would give £10 and more a ton for this stuff! Get busy while the going's good! That was some years ago.

Soon, over the ridges and gullies, men burnt brownish-black as the very ore they were picking up were toiling from dawn to sunset "while the going was good". But still those apparently sleepless, genial buyers came plodding along to buy this stuff and at slowly increasing prices.

And then French buyers appeared, offering a much better price!

And John Moffat came along! He seems to have been the first of our "business-men miners" who woke up.

Thus sprang up the truly roaring camp of Wolfram Camp, the shanties never closed either night or day. Out there in that sun-baked wilderness soon everyone had money in the days where nearly everywhere money was scarce. And there was nowhere to spend the money, and little to spend it on but grog. Only too often the grog was moonshine stuff.

Horse-teams labouring over long, hot tracks find difficulty in keeping big, lively camps supplied with bulk goods. Such goods are expensive also, whereas a moonshiner is on the spot, and "makes his own goods".

Here, as in other camps scattered over that huge area not yet developed into a settled district like Herberton, for instance, it was an object lesson in resource and sheer grit how the "thimble-ful" of police kept order, an elastic order that must not be stretched past certain bounds. The first of the police at Wolfram Camp were a raw-boned sergeant and a young constable—in a camp among hundreds, soon to be a thousand, of vigorous men isolated from any restraining influence, making more money than they'd ever known before, with always a few among them ready to go fighting crazy under the influence of moonshine.

But the sergeant would pull off his tunic at any time when challenged. And he could fight like the proverbial "thrashing machine". More dangerous still, he proved unbeatable, for he never knew when he *was* beaten. And the young constable beside him proved an able second, eager to "have a go", too.

Of course, as on any mining field I've ever been on anywhere throughout the continent, the big majority of the men were naturally quiet and law-abiding. Besides which, all had a deep sense of fair play. If a man chose fight instead of submitting to arrest then the crowd would see that it was a fair fight. If the man won, then the Law and he shook hands. If he were thrashed, then he was expected to go quietly when he came to. He could swear as much as he liked in mortification at his hiding, which he sometimes did —several badly battered hearties that I saw did so anyway, in intense disgust at themselves as they walked away to durance vile beside the triumphant but, on both these occasions, nearly as badly battered policeman. But if a man demanded a fight and he was beaten there was no chance of his mates rushing in and putting the boot in. The crowd would not stand for that.

It was picked men who were sent to these hectic camps that over a period of years sprang up like magic back o' Cairns across these wonderful hinterlands and beyond—timber camps, teamsters' camps, gold camps, tin camps, silver camps, copper camps, wolfram camps—the more lasting of which would develop into townships, whether pastoral or mineral. Men who not only could look after themselves, but possessed something deeper, a knowledge of human nature in the rough, reacting to the feverish making of good money within a frontier environment. Men who, practically single-handed, could control hundreds of others within reasonable bounds, men who would not seek unnecessary trouble, or try to put such wild and woolly places under excessive restraint, men with the understanding and self-control to assume and carry out an individual responsibility. The real law and order would come when, and if, such a camp developed into the dignity of a township.

An excellent training ground for such police had been along that wonderful engineering feat, the construction of the railway up along the Barron Gorge to Kuranda, thence by stages to Biboohra, Mareeba, Tolga, Atherton, to the railhead now at Herberton. And still the little lines were pushing farther out.

Old Mick at his Council Fire used to delight in telling us of brushes with the police as slowly, but surely, in periods of years, the big navvy camps built that remarkable line.

"At six, lastly eight, bob a day," reminisced Mick grimly, "take the job or starve. I've seen an ocean of water go pounding over those Barron Falls and the spray in it was the sweat from the navvy gangs."

"I'll swear not one drop of it was yours," murmured Jim Bell.

Always faithful to the gangs—and tough indeed were some—Mick could still chuckle in particular over the exploits of a Sergeant Bauldy Smith and a Sergeant Walsh. Old Mick's description of both these men was what Garnet described as "a cross between a gorilla and Old Nick". Anyway, to take a man out of any navvy camp, of course, meant fight. Either of these sergeants, when duty called, would stride into such a camp alone and call upon the man.

"Come and bloody-well take me—if you can!" would be the growling reply, no matter how big or small the delinquent.

Coolly the sergeant would strip to breeches and singlet. Both men would face up and hammer it out. If the evil-doer was no match for the sergeant in the first place the sergeant would simply flatten him with one merciful blow, then coolly await the inevitable. The "gorilla" of that man's gang would then stand up, exclaiming, "I object!"

The sergeant would nod. The gorilla would strip to his trousers, tighten his belt, stroll up to the sergeant. They would get into it, hammer and tongs, skin and hair flying in no time, in beefy grunts they would thump hell out of one another until sooner or later the sergeant "knocked" his man. Spitting the blood from his mouth, he would hitch up his strides and demand, "Anyone else here object?"

If any champ did so, then the sergeant would take him on. All in fair fight, the crowd looking quietly on.

When all was finished the sergeant would pull his tunic over his blood-stained torso, nod to his "arrest", and both would stroll from camp. On those occasions where the arrest had put up a savage fight and been badly knocked about his mates would carry him from the camp.

Mick would grudgingly but admiringly admit that he never knew either of these two sergeants to be beaten. And he described some awful fights, sheer butchery. For in those tough construction camps there were always a few iron-fisted men who stood out even above their truculent fellows as "butchers", who loved nothing better than the chance to batter a fellow fighter to "near the death".

CHAPTER IV

SOME MEN DO THINGS

BUT NOW, away across the hills at Wolfram Camp, wolfram had gone up from an original £10 to £70 a ton. Almost in a night, it seemed. The surprised miners had put it down to an influx of French buyers. Toiling to dig every pound possible from this "miracle" while it lasted, they were sinking shafts now and tunnelling on the reefs, working the gullies and the creeks. Fantastic returns for those days were being made as the price climbed to £100 a ton, then more.

John Moffat the enterprising had erected a battery to crush stone from his own mine and those of the miners, which helped all hands a lot. It was from one of Moffat's mines the new-chums had stolen bismuth and hidden it in Jim's own claim, then whispered to the police.

Soon the price of wolfram would soar to £170 a ton. A little school was built there now, the "baddies" were wagging it to scratch round the dumps and eagerly "louse" the big grey refuse heaps for small specks of wolfram for which they received a shilling a jam-tin full—what eyes those youngsters had for a speck of wolfram! Whispers of this widespread wealth occasionally drifting across to Nigger Creek fairly made our mouths water. We wondered, too, at the remarkable demand for this once despised mineral. Lads of Garnet's and my age, now making hay while the sun shone at Wolfram Camp would know in a few short years, when we shivered to hear those steel-hardened shells screaming in amongst us. That Australian wolfram, of course, would be used as tungsten for toughening the steel in guns and battleships in the coming Great War we were silly enough to believe was the "War to end Wars".

How the politicians have thrived on wars and rumours of wars ever since!

However, in those North Queensland days few people guessed at the actual wealth of the minerals pouring from the camps by rattling tramway, by mule, camel, and teams along rough bush tracks to some railhead, thence to Cairns or Townsville and overseas. Meanwhile we at Old Mick's campfire thought it quite a joke that from the hectic boisterousness of Wolfram Camp two "innocent" new-chums by subterfuge had driven Jim Bell to the now peaceful quietness of Wondecla, Meeting of the Waters—much less poetically called by white men Nigger Creek, "where it junctions with the Wild River a few miles outside of Herberton".

"Isn't it strange, Jack," said Old Mick dreamily, "that from primitive clay can spring the poetic essence of words?"

"What on earth are you talking about?"

"The Meeting of the Waters—which the white man calls Nigger Creek. Understandably so, of course. For the first white men to ride this way found this lovely spot swarming with natives who hotly disputed the right of way to this their choice tribal lands, their Wondecla, Meeting of the Waters. That poetic name was given by men whose language knows but a few hundred words. Men who, to us, are animal-like, caked with clay, daubed with snake-grease and ashes—worse at times, rancid human oil. Yet from such environment springs poetry."

"H'm," I said doubtfully.

" 'Tis true, Jack. There is much of poetry in them. I have treasured some of the names that came my way—the Valley of Lagoons, Lake of the Swans, Mountains of the Mist, the Happy Camp. In my wanderings I memorized many such gems of aboriginal poetry."

"H'm," I said. "You'll remember some poetic gems if Jim Bell catches you here."

But Mick was barely listening, hearing only the busy humming of insects, the cheeky call of birds, the gurgling poetry of the Wild River playfully caressing its rocks. Head cupped with hands resting upon a gnarled root, he was sprawled on his back drinking in the shaded sunlight, bent on dreaming the day away.

Squatting on my haunches beside him, I pulled out the pipe, thinking his face was lined and gnarled as the old oak root upon which his grizzled head rested. I just needn't have been there for all the old sinner cared.

"Just think, Jack—" and Mick gazed at me appealingly—"what joy must sing in the heart of a man if he could only write such lovely words."

"*What* lovely words?"

> "*I sometimes think that never blows so red*
> *The Rose as where some buried Caesar bled;*
> *That every Hyacinth the Garden wears*
> *Dropt in her Lap from some once lovely Head.*"

He was beyond me, I don't think he expected, or wanted, an answer anyway.

That particular morning had dawned most beautifully. Frying a chop or something or other for breakfast, I had felt vaguely discontented. Belting into that old river-bed down that black hole day after day, all for the sake of a few bob—the tin wasn't making, anyway. . . .

Instead of walking to the shaft and work my feet had taken me down the slope towards the Wild River. And somehow, on this glorious morning, on to a dry bank fair in the middle of that Wild River, sitting down with my back against the massive trunk of a great oak, with the old river gums and stringybarks and sword-grass all around me. And the birds were singing—what a paradise of hunting grounds was the Wild River for birds!

It was delightful. And then, of course, I had to think morosely, Somewhere far away there's a great world of civilization. It moves on, keeps moving on, and doesn't care a damn. Well, *I* don't care a damn either! What does it matter in another hundred years, anyway?

It was then I saw the Big Foot! Up in the air, parting the long grass before it flopped down—none but a tin-scratcher could grow such a hoof! And Old Mick the Ganger was away up there on top of that beetle-crusher gazing down at me in surprise.

"Hullo, Jack!" he said mildly.

"Hullo, Mick! What on earth are *you* doing here?"

"Jim has gone to town, on business. Maybe his sins are catching him up." He smiled.

"Don't try to crawl out of it," I sternly accused. "So soon as your mate's back is turned you sneak away here to loaf the day away!"

"I thought *you* were working down your shaft, Jack?" he queried impishly.

"I'm my own boss," I boasted, "or rather, the storekeeper is, I suppose. But *you'll* catch it when Jim returns to camp."

"I may think out some subterfuge of evasion," he replied as he settled himself comfortably. "However, don't let's spoil a lovely day by worrying over troubles that may be dodged. Time flies. Let us enjoy to the full this Meeting of the Waters."

And that was how the conversation had started.

We both enjoyed a perfect, stolen day.

Jim Bell's "Moffat the Millionaire" was no millionaire, though apparently again on the way to becoming one. The bottom falling out of the metal market, and other mining hazards, had ruined him before this. He had "squared up" every shilling, £50,000 worth, and had added interest, a truly vast sum in those days. The fact that he had been under no legal obligation to do so may have been one reason why Moffat's word was considered "solid as the Rock of Gibraltar" in the North. He was now building up again, misfortune seems but to steel such men to have another go. And he would have to do so yet again, destined to be on the eve of great things, putting behind him bitter disappointments to build up yet again throughout a long and useful life. Already he was becoming known as the "Father of the North". And no one would have begrudged his becoming a millionaire.

At this period many of the men who had "made" the North were alive and energetically working, their names household words along the east coast and up and over the Tableland and west even to the Gulf. The richly varied and wonderful jobs they had accomplished were taken as a matter of course, each more of a local favourite than a local hero. Now and again I met one of them attending stock sales in the little towns, or out in the timber country, or riding into town for supplies. A chat among the mines or yarns round the campfire about the doings of others always intrigued the young schoolmaster from Brisbane and me. Alas! Why had I not some intuition that one day I would become a writer of books? Ever I was looking for a mine, a rich mine. But what a priceless mine of hope and courage, of dogged will and almost superhuman perseverance, of unlucky failure and dazzling reward I missed. Around me men had been and still were reaching for the stars, while I was looking for a mine at my feet.

One evening at the Council Fire I asked Jim Bell in how many fields John Moffat had become interested.

"Oh, in a good many," he replied indifferently. "The prospectors found the fields. The miners opened them up. Then Moffat stepped in and helped develop them if machinery was needed. He brought transport to a few fields, too, now I remember, went away south and interested capital and built two or three big tramways through isolated country—made a flaming good job of them, too. As have other concerns also."

"Well, in how many fields has he had a finger in the pie?"

"Let me see now. Irvinebank, of course, seems to be his favourite, he is making a real town of that place. But when Jack and Newell first found Herberton and really started the Tableland he soon came to their aid with a battery—teams of horses, too! Then helped in development at Watsonville, Coolgarra, Mount Albion, California Creek, Kooboora, Wolfram Camp—stone the crows!" he exclaimed. "How has he done it all? I never thought of it before! He seems to have built batteries and smelters and dams and tramways and sawmills from one end of the country to the other!"

"He's built a battery away out at Northcote on the Hodgkinson, too," said Old Brookes quietly, "and another away south on the Theckla and McAuley mines at Kangaroo Hills. He's got men working in the timber out Ravenshoe way."

"Yes," said Jim, "and at Mount Carbine, too, and a smelters at Mount Molloy. Why, he's covered the Tableland from east to west, and south to north and beyond! Mount Garnet, Mount Elliott, Stannary Hills, Smith's Creek, Mount Mulligan, and now he's busy again with smelters and tramway at Chillagoe, O.K., Mungana! Phew! Now just how has he done it all?"

"By working while you were sleeping." Mick grinned.

"Talking in your sleep as usual," snapped Jim. "Why don't *you* wake up?"

"I was merely thinking of Rip Van Winkle," said Mick mildly.

"Oh, were you! And what race is *he* in?" demanded Jim suspiciously.

"Now then, you boys," said Garnet, "no pleasantries in the midst of a serious discussion. We've all got a touch of Rip Van Winkle in us, remember. By the way, Mick, what tomfoolery was that lanky navvy friend of yours indulging in this afternoon? I was looking down from the school veranda and saw the noble wight scratching gravel on all fours in the hotel back-yard. The silly ass was yelping like an excited pup. He appeared to be chasing the squawking fowls like a dog! The girls were sooling him on, laughing their heads off."

"He was only acting the fool," said Mick.

"Must have been mimicking you!" snapped Jim. "So *that's* what you were doing! While I was down below yelling myself hoarse for you to haul up the windlass bucket *you* were watching some other fool acting the sheep-dog in the pub yard with Mrs Reynolds's fowls!"

"He was only imitating Paddy the Ganger's cattle-dog," explained Mick bashfully. "That dog knew as much as I know," he added admiringly.

"Yeah!" said Jim. "That's why he caught his death of cold sleeping out in the wet!"

"I'm sorry I started you boys off." Garnet laughed. "I wouldn't have mentioned it had I known Mick was supposed to be manning the windlass. But that ass *did* look a fool. Would have felt one, too, if he had not leapt up on the fowlhouse roof when Mrs Reynolds sooled the dog at his heels."

"Did you hear what Mrs Reynolds called him," chuckled Mick,

"when she came out the kitchen to see what all the row was about?"

"No, I was too far away. What did she say?"

"That he had lost his brains where the doctored tom-cat lost his! That if he'd hurt any of her fowls she'd brain him! That he could perch up there on the fowlhouse roof and cackle his head off until he'd laid an egg! And that if he dared sneak down she'd sool *both* dogs on to him!"

"And she *would*, too!" Old Brookes smiled. "She's got a heart of gold, has Mrs Reynolds, but the devil of an Irish temper when her paddy is up!"

"And what has happened to the playful navvy?" chuckled Garnet. "Is he still up there trying to lay an egg?"

"He's long since back at camp," said Mick. "One of the girls coaxed mum back into the kitchen. Then, of course, the younger girl called off the dogs and held them while the joker scuttled down to the creek and away."

"Small things amuse small minds," declared Jim Bell.

"If a man *has* one," murmured Mick.

"Now, you boys," said Garnet sternly, "no more goat talk. Tell us about Mrs Reynolds and the roaring days when the line was being built past here—I just missed it, worse luck. How on earth did one lone woman, with two attractive daughters to care for, manage to run that pub successfully and still prevent it being wrecked by those boisterous he-men on those wild pay-nights?"

All hands present had stories of those hectic days. The lone woman and her two capable daughters had really done a big job. But then, Mrs Reynolds had quickly won both the respect and affection of those lively gangs. For she was not greedy, and would "doctor up" and do anything for a man who was sick, nothing was too much trouble for her then. But when needs must she certainly could look after herself, and the girls, too.

A hale and hearty woman of brawn and forceful character, she needed both at times. Handy behind the bar she kept "me trusty shillelagh", a murderous-looking ironwood nullah that had cracked even aboriginal heads. I've seen the little low bar packed with riotous navvies returning from a spree at Herberton, so overwhelmingly happy they just had to "up and break something". Right then the hostess took a hand, negotiating that bar with a flame in her eye more dangerous even than the nullah. But the laughing navvies never waited. They knew that nullah.

I only saw Mrs Reynolds lay out one man. He had given a power of cheek and threatened to "take over the place and boil his billy with the remains". But he was a trifle slow on the getaway. The motherly soul cried over "his pore cracked head", nursing it on her lap and bathing it with Condy's while the wan victim swigged the rum the girls poured down his neck. Perhaps it was just as well Mrs Reynolds did not catch his sly wink upward at the girls.

There was only one navvy I really believe had Mrs Reynolds bluffed, though she never let him know it; he would have chewed that nullah to splinters and spat it out into the beer had he been certain. This beauty was nicknamed "Murder" behind his back, and he looked it. Six feet four, with hands like shovels, his gorilla-like strength matched by his awful face—plain Murder. The first night he glared at me, a stranger, his bloodshot eyes like a raging bull's, I was nearly scared stiff.

"That's Murder!" whispered Mick in awe-struck tones. "He cursed a Tumoulin ganger yesterday and the ganger apologized!"

I quite believed it. When they sacked Murder they handed him his time on a long-handled shovel. I felt sure this brute had Mrs Reynolds bluffed, and she was a better man than I was, where Murder was concerned, anyway.

Long afterwards, when in the Far North, I heard that Murder had come to a nasty, sticky end. And I was quite pleased.

But now we only saw a tricycle-load or two of the navvies pumping their way back and forth occasionally to Herberton, though they still enlivened the place on a thirsty week-end.

CHAPTER V

HOW IT STARTED

KNOWING the busy, established port of Cairns—what a Bigger Cairns today!—and the little sugar townships now rapidly developing from south to north along that beautiful coast, I was surprised to learn at Old Mick's Council Fire and elsewhere that plenty of men still working throughout the Tableland had known Cairns when it was but a sandy beach hedged in by swamp and sea, walled to Trinity Inlet by that scrub-clad rampart looming ten miles inland. That once impenetrable barrier was now scaled by a railway that would seem to have been always there to the traveller admiring the gorgeous scenery in comfort. Difficult to realize that among the rising townships up on the Tableland men now farming had known each township when it was windswept forest or dense jungle. While to me, anyway, Herberton seemed one of those solid little old bush towns that had "always been there". True, it had been the first on the Tableland to develop into a town, even though the railway had arrived only a few months ago. And beyond was still a wilderness of scrub and forest.

With what speed were those forests now to fall into farmlands!

When I was a toddler coming into town with dad in the sulky, he would sometimes pull the pony up and point across the dusty street.

"There goes a man who has helped make this country, my boy. Take a good look at him! See how sturdily he walks! And he has a right to—he helped carve a town out of this wilderness so there could be homes and jobs for you and me."

That town in New South Wales was now the City of Lismore. How different this, too, to the dusty little township of my toddling days!

Dad had similarly pointed out to me pathfinders, timber-finders, land-finders, water-finders, mineral-finders, engineers—"men who have done things, my boy"—in Tenterfield, Tamworth, and Broken Hill. Probably that was why now I took keen interest in the pathfinders of this, to me, new country.

Jim Mulligan was the daddy of them all, certainly was thought so throughout this huge district and beyond, even though in his first great discovery, payable gold on the Palmer, he followed directions given by William Hann.

Hann's party, travelling from the south northward, had crossed these ranges well inland from the coast, and after a remarkable trip of exploration returned to civilization reporting the discovery of a vast area of new pastoral country, and of gold in a river Hann named the Palmer. About the land he was enthusiastic, but reluctant to declare the gold-bearing country payable. Understandably so, for he and his party were cattle-men, not familiar with gold values. A rush to that utterly isolated, unexplored wilderness would mean that many inexperienced men must perish, and others would be killed by the blacks and fever, should gold not be found in payable quantities as an inducement to teamsters and storekeepers to hurry there with supplies.

Hann, unfortunately, was drowned near the then little port of Townsville, a city now. At the time of our councils by Old Mick's campfire one of his mates, Tom Tate, was "going strong" and would continue to do so for another score years. Barring tragedy or typhoid, those old-timers were difficult to kill. Old Ned Troughton, one of the earliest of the Palmer carriers, was still working like a Trojan and enjoying it. And he had a good many years to go yet before crossing the Last Divide at Mareeba at the age of 104. Mulligan then had recently gone west at Mount Molloy.

Mulligan's second name was Venture—James Venture Mulligan. Some prophetic instinct must have inspired his parents, for his long lifetime was to be constant adventure. (He had spent some time in the Tenterfield district, by the way.) His name was fairly idolized on the Tableland, as the leader of that goodly company—John Atherton, Jack and Newell, Oswald Mazlin, Bill Smith, Douglas, Alf Hort, James Robson, Joss and Brandon, Sub-inspector Johnstone, Warner and Christy Palmerston—there were plenty of others, a little host of men who did a mighty job "back o' Cairns".

According to the many who knew him, James Mulligan was a very likable man who smiled easily, blessed with a quiet humour. A shrewd thinker, he could listen and weigh matters out and still not be unnecessarily abrupt with the inevitable "know-all". As a leader he was an excellent bushman, as all such adventurers must be, possessing a stubborn streak of persistence tempered by a quiet thoughtfulness which many a time helped him overcome seemingly insuperable obstacles. His mates would follow him anywhere without question, the best of bushmen would give anything to be chosen as a member of a "Mulligan party".

William Hann, before his discovery of the Palmer River, had proved himself as a responsible leader in this unexplored bush. He had found the way to a huge area of good pastoral country upon which stations were quickly being formed. He was of a more anxious type than the "take-it-easy-now" Mulligan, more inclined to be fiery. Little wonder, perhaps, for such men, in dangerous isolation, far from help, always dogged by hostile blacks, never knowing what lay before them, carried the fate of their entire party upon their shoulders.

Upon Hann's return south from the Peninsula Mulligan got together a party of prospectors from the Etheridge goldfield, then rode north in the direction told by Hann. In crossing these far-flung ranges, one sunset they had camped right here, or almost, somewhere very near the Herberton of today. In the morning, seeking gold, Mulligan tried a dish in the Wild River—and got tin. Wryly they joked about it. They might have found a tin-field, for all they knew. But what value to them? Here, in this tangle of ranges, with the howls of the blacks around them, distant from civilization, let alone from any hope of transport, of what value would be even the richest tin-field to them? They joked about the vagaries of Fate—"luck", they called it—over breakfast, with a wary eye to their horses, weapons ready beside them. They packed up, and rode on.

It was Mulligan's party that proved the Palmer payable, a river of gold, thus causing that mighty rush which within a few short months saw a fleet of ships within the mouth of a far northern river that had barely seen a ship since Captain Cook beached his stricken *Endeavour* there. Little did Captain James Cook dream, while under difficulties his pigtailed Jack Tars repaired the *Endeavour* with timber cut from these strange trees, that this wild,

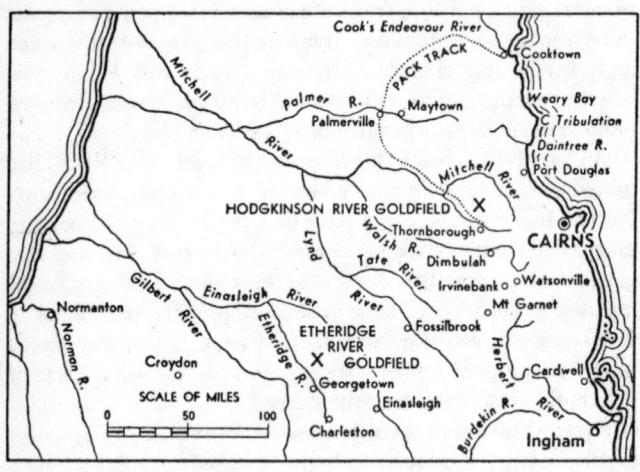

outlandish spot would one day be called Cooktown, the broad river mouth packed with vessels of all descriptions, from the new cities of the south and even from China, brought there by the most romantic gold rush in Australia's history.

There was no Cairns then, of course. The ships, packed with diggers, horses, and stores from Brisbane, Sydney, Melbourne, and New Zealand sailed past that far northern inlet vaguely known as Trinity Bay under the black shadows of the coastal mountain chain.

At the Endeavour River mouth, stores and horses and wagons were landed, and from there, men could trudge overland to the discovery.

As for Mulligan, he did not work long on the Palmer, he was satisfied just to have "seen it started". The Bush called again, and with his mates Warner and Abelsen he rode away from the River of Gold, seeking "another Palmer".

He found it three years later—the Hodgkinson. It was not as rich as the Palmer, but proved a valuable goldfield for all that.

And thus, actually, was born Cairns, and in great degree the eventual opening up of the country "back o' Cairns". But it was to be a long, heartbreaking struggle before Cairns would come into its own.

Men rushed the new find in droves from the Palmer, hurrying south, heedless that they were leaving gold behind them. Meanwhile, from the distant south, Etheridge men rode north, others trudging doggedly on foot carrying tools and guns and what tucker they could stagger under. And in those many dry gullies to cross some left their bones.

Right on the heels of the prospectors rode the pioneer cattlemen. John Fraser from down Ingham way brought a mob of cattle to find country and start a station on the Mitchell, for the miners would need beef. A few months later John Atherton, with all his family, was on the gold-diggers' tracks, to turn east and find good country, which would soon be called Mareeba.

To the miners came the ever serious question of transport. Gleefully Cooktown declared itself the one and only port of access. And it was so then, too.

Ships from two thousand miles away and more sailed for Cooktown loaded with stores for both goldfields. The dust of teams stretched for miles as heavy-laden animals trudged out from Cooktown towards the Palmer, carrying on from the Palmer south to the Hodgkinson. The way was long and rough through wild bush, the packers of necessity sleeping with rifles to hand. It takes rich goldfields indeed to pay for transport as slow and expensive as that.

Actually, after the Palmer, the Hodgkinson was the real spur which began the rapid opening-up of those fabulous lands from Cardwell north. A library of books could be written on the romances of that fascinating period of North Queensland history.

However, far south of Cooktown, two hundred miles inland from Cardwell, on the Etheridge, Jack Martin's teams, struggling to find their own track, headed north for the Hodgkinson in a bid to wrest a share of this trade southward, to make Cardwell the port for the fields. In such a simple way did men set out on high enterprise in those days.

But in this venture the difficulties proved, to Cooktown's northern delight, insuperable.

Then George Clarke took to the bush with a few natives from Cardwell, on the coast, blazed a trail north-west over the Seaview Range, followed up the Herbert River, then up and over the watershed to the Walsh and found his way to the Hodgkinson, one hundred and fifty miles across trackless, mountainous bush, nearly killing himself in the job but battling on in the belief that he was finding a way that wheeled traffic could negotiate. But when delighted miners followed back along the track they found water-swept gorges and valleys to cross, stiff peaks to climb, rivers that were raging torrents in the Wet, a thousand ravines to cross. No chance of having bridges built out there those days, of course.

All along the Hodgkinson from the rapidly increasing camps the miners gazed longingly towards the east where the heavy ranges, these very Tablelands, loomed between them and the sea. A track straight across the tops of those ranges, if one could only be found, would lead direct to the coast; maybe as the crow flies the sea lay barely a hundred miles away.

Jack Moran proved it. And when he started out he was not looking for the the sea, but for a strayed horse.

Moran was of Bill McLeod's party, who on the heels of Mulligan, had been roaming this maze of river heads for months past. The adventures of this daring party alone would fill a book. They were camped eastward of the now hectic gold camps, trying the headwaters of the Little Mitchell. Moran set off on the tracks of the wandering horse alone; the party for so long had been pushing their way through hostile tribal lands that each man had developed a cautious indifference to the blacks. They had to, like all the early prospecting parties, for again and again circumstances would demand that a man must tackle some particular job and see it through alone.

That venturesome horse, blissfully unaware that it was inviting a spear through its ribs at any moment, had wandered away straight towards the rising sun. Moran followed doggedly on, camping on the tracks. Eventually he caught up with the wanderer. And he still gazed eastward. Before him, as ever, was ridge after ridge, well grassed, forest timbers sweet with the lure of a beckoning breeze. Oh well, he was in for it now; he would either succeed in returning back to camp or be killed. But now he had the horse. What could a few more miles matter? What might lie beyond those ridges?

He now rode on. And on. And on. And at last pulled up on a grassy hill crest and gazed far away out to a sparkling sea.

A wild coast, and no sign of bay, or inlet, or sheltering place.

But—he was the first man to see the sea from those inland mining camps. He had proved the sea was there, barely a hundred miles or so as the crow would fly.

Cheerfully he turned back for the camps. The boys would be pleased indeed to hear the news.

They were.

But, even so, there was no known harbour. Could they find one? Find a track, and a harbour at the end of it, a harbour that would "lead ships" to the track?

Half a dozen parties tried, and failed. The blacks, sickness, and accident held some back, others were beaten by dense jungles.

And then Bill Smith, one of Mulligan's men, remembered that some years ago, while he was on a bêche-de-mer cruise northward to the Coral Sea, the cutter had sailed the coast and the crew one day saw what appeared to be the mouth of a large bay or inlet right under a wall of big black mountains, somewhere between

Cardwell and where Cooktown now was. He could not be sure, of course, from this camp here away back in the bush, but that inlet, if it really was one, might lie nearly east of this camp on the Hodgkinson River. His mates on the little fishing cutter had surmised that that hazy outline to landward might be the Trinity Bay of the early sea explorers. But of course everything was only the merest guess, looking at things from this unmapped spot away back in the bush.

CHAPTER VI

PATHFINDERS BY LAND AND SEA

MULLIGAN called a "roll-up" meeting, and five hundred men dropped their tools and came strolling along. The mining warden, whose name was St George, took "the chair" by climbing up on a pile of logs. His speech was short and to the point, and it went over well; he had a voice like a foghorn to help it. Enthusiastically all hands agreed to a pathfinding party, which Mulligan immediately organized. Other venturesome ones followed suit, saddled up, and rode east—Will Smith, Johnny Doyle, John Cardnow. They saddled up and rode away east, seeking this Trinity Inlet of Captain James Cook, from the miners' largest camp, now called Thornborough, rapidly growing into a lively township indeed.

Bill Smith was the man who had seen the inlet from a trepang boat at sea. John Cardnow was a seaman, now taken to the bush as sailors sometimes did. Johnny Doyle had been the leader of a number of prospecting parties, and was the bushman of the party.

Smith believed the inlet must lie south of where Jack Moran had reached the coast, so Doyle rode east while gradually veering southward. And this inevitably brought them into the Big Scrubs.

Slow work indeed, hacking their way through jungle, the horses presently shivering at the smell of wild blacks, instinct warning them of barbed spears ripping into quivering flanks. Well indeed the horses of those days knew the smell of the wild men.

Yes, a slow job, one man chopping a path ahead while the others stood by the terrified horses with guns ready, a nerve-racking job, hemmed in by dense vegetation and the unknown. Finally they were blocked within the heart of a big scrub when Cardnow went down with fever.

After enduring so much, John Doyle determined to make one last desperate effort to push through for at least a glimpse of the sea. They rigged this last camp for defence, then Doyle crept away alone. Expecting a spear in his back at any moment, he pushed cautiously on, praying for forest sunlight to break through the gloom of the scrub. Hours later he heard a humming noise, ominously growing. Setting his teeth, he still pushed on, certain that the sound was made by the bull-roarers of the natives in triumphant corroboree. But the humming steadily grew into a deep murmur; now and then as he paused he thought he caught a faint rumble of thunder seeping through the jungle.

The time came when he stepped out of the scrub into brilliant sunlight and the surprising sight of a swiftly flowing river almost at his feet. And there was no doubt now of a thunder. Walking quickly on, now in open forest country, straight into the risen sun in the heaven of delight to see all he could as quickly as he could. And presently he saw, and heard, plenty. The river swiftly surging by in its black, rocky bed, and ahead clouds of glistening spray rising, and from them came a thunderous roar. At last he stood by the edge of the great waterfall, staring in awe down along the gorge and away out beyond to sunlight sparkling on the distant waters of Trinity Inlet.

Thus as a greybeard John Doyle delighted to tell how he first saw the Barron hurtling over into the gorge where Kuranda now stands.

Other parties found that tangle of range and river heads hard going, and most were finally blocked by the great rain forests that were impenetrable to horses, and to all but a few of the best bushmen.

Bill Smith made several attempts, getting close enough to the edge of the range to recognize the distant waters of Trinity Inlet, which misty sight sent him into the seventh heaven of delight, for it proved he had not led the Hodgkinson men astray.

A miners' meeting sent him out again with men, horses, and axes to try to cut a dray road to at least within sight of the sea. The attempt failed. Other parties also were beaten back. Finally, the miners voted that Smith should take a party north overland to Cooktown, and from there tackle the job by sea. He was to sail south down the coast from Cooktown, to see if he could locate and poke his way into that elusive inlet; if so, to land and, if possible, climb the range from that seaward side and make his way back overland to the goldfield. So Smith rode away north on this tricky job, "round-the-circle" by land and sea.

Meanwhile party after party still doggedly tried to reach the coast overland from the Hodgkinson, and others from southward, from Townsville and Cardwell, came hurrying up in little vessels seeking an inlet from which they could make contact with that inland goldfield "away back over the mountains".

Meanwhile Smith came riding into Cooktown away to the north. With Brown, Lipton, Stewart, and McKay and several blackboys he sailed south seeking that inlet. He found it. Not only so, but in an open boat battled his way through that ten-mile maze of swamps and gloomy mangrove creeks in which then a man most easily could have become lost for ever, battled his way on to the very wall of the range. Nothing could beat him now. With Stewart and Lipton he struggled up the face of the range, then carried on by foot, his head his compass, through forest and scrub safely to the goldfield—and a rip-roaring reception.

From the sea itself a way had been found overland direct to the Hodgkinson.

Smith and another party had passed one another, totally un-aware of the fact. Sub-inspector Douglas, who had already made a name on the Palmer and was to make a much bigger name during the lively years now arriving, had ridden out a few days before Smith's triumphant arrival on a well-organized, determined attempt to reach the coast and the inlet. With him were the Warner brothers—one the quiet, tireless surveyor who had ridden with Mulligan's men—and Williams the prospector. And they managed it. And at the inlet they met Sub-inspector Johnstone, who had arrived by sea. Events were now moving fast.

The very next day after Bill Smith's men trudged elatedly into the goldfields camp nearly a hundred and fifty miners, with police, followed the three men back to cut the track to the inlet and the sea. They toiled with a will, over ridge and rocky spur, making many a gully crossing through forest and scrub. And at last it was done, right to the tip of the range.

A miner drew a long breath. Then solemnly declared to all and sundry, "Stone the crows! Our flamin' horses will have to sprout wings!"

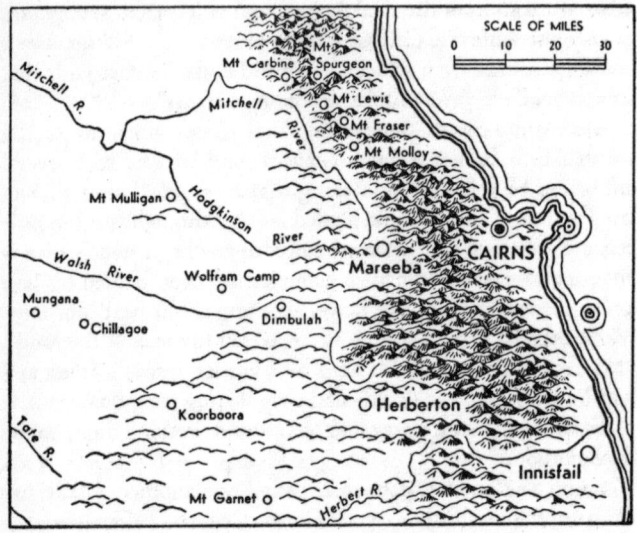

He was standing there gazing from the jungle edge, the black mouth of a leafy tunnel where they had cut the road through the jungle. Land and sea stretched out and away—a beautiful sight. But he saw the edge of a precipice that dropped almost sheer to the flat country a thousand feet and more below.

Two men stepped beside the flabbergasted one.

"Phew!" one exclaimed. "A mountain goat could hardly get down there, let alone a pack-horse!"

They managed it, by the skin of their teeth. But it was overwhelmingly obvious that no wheeled traffic would ever travel by this track, either up or down.

Nor by Sub-inspector Douglas's track either.

Meanwhile, during these hectic months considerable gold had been won along the Hodgkinson, three rough-and-ready mining townships—Thornborough, Kingsborough, and Northcote—had sprung up, with camps growing all along the river. It took an army of packhorses ceaselessly plodding the long Cooktown trail to keep these growing townships supplied.

While all this was going on inland behind the ranges there was feverish activity for the tiny Queensland population of those days, seeking along the coast from the south to find a port not only for that new inland northern goldfield but for whatever else of advantage might lie behind that sea of ranges. The Queenslanders from earliest times have doggedly, most energetically, kept pushing out from Brisbane north, north-west, west, year by year creeping yet farther out all over their vast, rich state, and still are doing so, as witness Mount Isa, the Mary Kathleen, the west coast of the Peninsula.

While Mulligan and his men were battling to reach the coast and locate an inlet from the Hodgkinson, the Government was sending expeditions north from Cardwell. Business-men from Townsville chartered the S.S. *Porpoise*, gallant little Tom Thumb. Cardwell men manned other vessels. Away north at Cooktown tiny vessels came sailing south in this race to seek a new port to tap inland wealth that as yet was not even proved, it was only believed in. But so much so that a man and his wife and baby, the Kauffmans, sailed in an open boat from Cooktown to grasp what the gods might provide. Happily, their Guardian Angel sailed with them, for the *Porpoise* by the merest chance picked them up at their last gasp near Cape Grafton. Strong parties of enterprising police sailed in the pilot boat from Cardwell, destined to do great work in exploring the new inlet between sea and range, and in helping to lay the camp which by now has grown into the City of Cairns. These and other parties, months before, had been stirred into a very fever of activity when news had drifted through that the first bushman from the goldfield had actually penetrated to the lip of the range, had seen a big inlet giving access by sea, and that several had actually scrambled down the face of the range.

Once the seaward parties had sailed into the mouth of Trinity Inlet, the ten-mile maze of swamps, mangrove creeks, and jungle still barred their way to the range, while they were continually dogged by wild blacks. Party after party tried, by foot and horse and boat, before men from inland and sea finally met and a track was cut right to the Barron Falls, just as Sub-inspectors Johnstone and Townshend found the outlet of the Barron, named it, and sailed up it to near the falls. From then on all was plain sailing so far as a water traffic was concerned; small vessels could sail up the Barron itself to near the foot of the range.

Within a week there was a settlement of miners at Smith's Landing below the falls, immediately named Smithfield, while another settlement of sunlit tents on the beach way back by Trinity Inlet marked the birth of Cairns, whose swaddling clothes would be calico, swiftly developing into bark and slab huts, rapidly "advancing" as ships came from the south with building materials. Many would be the trials and tribulations of this eager and energetic camp before it grew into an established port.

For, though by now men had scaled the heights, never would wheeled traffic ever come down either Smith's or Douglas's Track. Lightly laden packhorse and mule teams would struggle up and down, but that black wall looming behind the baby port would still hold back the secrets of the Tableland.

Twelve months later the rapidly growing Cairns fairly buzzed with excitement, tinged with dismay.

Christy Palmerston and his mate Layton had found a way from the Hodgkinson goldfield to the coast which they said could be made into a dray road! A strong party of miners had followed their tracks and were now camped on a beach at a place they'd named White Cliffs, some thirty miles north! But—they had failed to find a port there. And baby Cairns breathed again.

But little vessels sailed north from Cairns eagerly seeking an anchorage, for a wheeled track inland was big news indeed, bigger news even than the discovery of a new goldfield would be.

For what is the good of a goldfield if you cannot supply it with goods?

These vessels returned beaten and disappointed. They had seen that party of Hodgkinson miners camped hopefully on a hopeless beach, but still, even by sea, they had found no anchorage.

Then Captain Owen of the Cooktown passenger steamer *Corea* reported he had seen what appeared to be a possible anchorage about ten miles north of those White Cliffs. Cooktown enterprise chartered the *Corea* on a second voyage of discovery south. Captain Owen discovered anchorage at Island Point, which led to the formation of Port Douglas—and a rush to take up land there in building the "new port" that was very like a gold rush. From Cairns, Smithfield, and Cooktown they came in all manner of boats and commenced building even before the track inland was a proved fact.

But Inspector Shaw of Cobb and Co. rode over the blazed track and, returning, declared he could make a coach road out of it. A brave declaration, even for that remarkably enterprising Cobb and Co., considering that this mountainous land beyond the coast had never yet known a wheel. However, the range here was "easy", it was not that precipitous wall that stretches from, say, Mourilyan to Cairns.

Settler Mackay, with a dray and six horses, was the first man to drive up over the range behind the "new port". A month later six loaded horse-teams, to volleys of cheers, slowly creaked their way inland from Port Douglas bound for the Hodgkinson.

Ships, loaded with hope, have sailed out into uncharted seas seeking trade routes from long before the days of the Phoenicians. Here, from this lonely North Queensland coast, the creaking wagon-wheels, toiling so slowly out and over and around the northern flank of the hinterland, were the forerunners of a spider-web of roads that were to criss-cross the great Tablelands in a hundred routes as mineral field after field was discovered, and pastoral, agricultural, and timber lands opened up, bringing prosperity to the country, joy to many, heartburnings to others.

For Cairns and Smithfield rapidly declined, while Port Douglas went ahead at a great pace, its rapidly increasing citizens almost hilariously triumphant.

Towns and ports are mixed up in the emotions of those people who build them. Fiercely energetic had been Cardwell away in the south, and Cooktown in the north to seize and hold whatever treasure might lie within that huge mass of mountainous country that lay between them. And then an upstart named Cairns had appeared to win the race, though heckled by some bark-and-slab-and-log interloper called Smithfield. But now a new rival called Port Douglas had shot up like a triumphant comet. And without doubt it seemed to have won, to its energetic citizens' undisguised delight.

Had won—and all because of a wagon-wheel!

Civilizations have been built on the discovery of the wheel. But what a "modern" example in "progress" was the Port Douglas wheel!

Cairns languished. Smithfield, too, more than half its citizens abandoning it for Port Douglas before the Barron in majestic disdain wiped it out. Away up above there amongst the swirling mists came the roar as of a sea in wrath. In thunder that rocked the very gorge the flood surged in roaring might over the falls.

And Smithfield was gone.

CHAPTER VII

THE RAILWAY

WHAT helped the Cairns folk carry on was the hope that springs eternal, the fact that after all, they *did* have an inlet that could be developed into a real harbour, and now they were learning that between coast and range was a belt of wonderful land, and cedar in plenty! Pine and beech and walnut, too. For pathfinders by land and sea had been creeping up northward from Bowen and Cardwell, urged by hunger for new sugar lands and cedar. And now they were finding a wonderland all along that coastal strip between range and sea: along the Johnstone good land in plenty, and at Mourilyan sugar lands and timber, dense scrubs destined to rapidly grow into the famous sugar lands of Innisfail, along jungle rivers, the Russell and the Mulgrave, right north to Cairns Inlet, forests of magnificent timbers born of lands which surely would grow anything. Even north of that so cockily thriving Port Douglas a new river, named Mossman after one of the prospectors of Charters Towers, was found, also rich in timbers and lands. And now the Daintree, farther north still. There Mt Peter Botte and Alexander walled off all chance of penetrating farther north to the Cooktown side.

Cedars helped build Australian towns and cities. Far south in Brisbane, farther south in Sydney, was a hungry, ever-growing market. Grimly the citizens remaining in Cairns hung on. Their inlet, the one and only true inlet by sea, was in the very centre of this coastal land and also those lands up over the range. Surely a wheel-track would be found somewhere up over that barrier in time; surely this fine, strategic outlet to the sea and southern markets must make good!

And then—Jack and Newell found the Herberton field, on the Wild River near Nigger Creek. And a few months later they found the Great Northern. This actually was the dawn of three great mineral fields—Herberton, the Walsh, and Tinaroo.

When Mick and I occasionally strayed into Herberton we invariably made for Jack and Newell's store. Those two prospectors now turned business-men were very much alive indeed; it was difficult to realize that when they and Joss and Brandon first rode here the "blacks were bad", Cairns was but a collection of huts hanging on by the skin of its teeth to a swampy beach by the distant sea. Port Douglas northward was rapidly developing, all because a wheel-track connected its sea-way with the inland, that successful wagon-track to the Hodgkinson River goldfield.

One sunny day in Herberton we were lazing in Jack and Newell's hospitable store. "Only twenty years or so ago," said Mick, "and a spear whizzed past Newell's head right where he's weighing that tin now. Or very nearly so. And hark! Here comes the iron horse, puffing into this well-established town of Herberton. Believe me, I often puffed myself during those long, hot summer days when I was helping lay the ribbons upon which our little train comes puffing, over the ghostly trail of a thousand horse-teams. And bullocks. And mules. And donkeys. The donkeys were the ones who laid the rails. Fortunately, I was a driver. And it all happened before my whiskers blossomed into silver."

"Not too much silver at that," I said, grinning. "But your mate Jim declares it's not through age alone that your whiskers have become somewhat tarnished and moth-eaten."

"My mate Jim," said Mick soberly, "is one of the best in the world, even though his insinuations about my moral character are of the worst."

"I wish the schoolmaster could have heard that speech, Mick! He couldn't have bettered it himself."

"Ah!" said Mick eagerly. "And so I'm improving, lad. You think so?"

"Sure. Your next 'pome' should be beyond reproach."

"I'm working on it, working hard," he said earnestly, "when Jim isn't noticing. But the Muse is shy as a maid, elusive as a will-o'-the-wisp. Alas, the creative effort is difficult, very difficult!" He sighed.

"Shall we seek inspiration?" I suggested. "We can afford just one or two."

Rising from his jam-case seat with alacrity he quoted as we strolled out the store:

> *"Or leave a kiss but in the cup,*
> *And I'll not ask for wine."*

"Maybe." I grinned. "But you'd better not offer to pay for it with stamps!"

This witty remark was passed because of a somewhat unfavourably known character nicknamed "Billy the Hum". He had slunk bleary-eyed into the bar of Bradshaw's Hotel.

"I'm dying for a drink!" he croaked. "Will you give me a long beer for six stamps, Mr Bradshaw?"

"Oh all right," agreed the publican distastefully, "then clear out before someone sees you and feels ill."

He handed over the beer, which Billy quaffed as if badly needing it. Putting down the glass with a long-drawn sigh, he gaped at the expectant publican. Then he solemnly proceeded to stamp on the floor with his heel, calling "One! Two! Three! Four! Fi—" By then the publican was leaping over the bar, but Billy had already reached the door.

But such futilities inevitably happen in the wake of Big Things.

Jack and Newell's original discovery caused a rush to the Wild River, the remarkable tin returns of which made Herberton the first town on the Tableland. Immediately, of course, transport and a port became the burning question, and Cairns bucked up again, for this rich tin discovery was located really at her very back door. Yet again, over a length of thirty miles, men tackled that wall of the range. Stubbornly yet again it defied wheel transport down to the inlet, defied every effort of some good men indeed. Meanwhile, from up on the Tableland, pushing through jungle and forest southward John Atherton found the gorge of the Mulgrave River, and this gave James Robson a possible clue.

He cut his way down along the side of the gorge, eventually succeeded in blazing a pack track from Herberton, then came down along the Mulgrave to the flat coastal land. Then he turned north and blazed the track right to near the foot of the falls—to the delight of Cairns. Unfortunately, this, too, proved impossible for wheel traffic, though soon the Herberton packers had hacked a track up along the side of the gorge. It was so precipitous that it provided only one-way foothold, horses and mules struggling to retain a footing. In the most dangerous places again and again laden horses and mules were lost, one fatal slip and the frantic animal went hurtling to crash on the water-drenched rocks below.

It was on tracks such as this that the first children from Cairns climbed the range on their great adventure to the tin Eldorado at Herberton, securely packed in boxes, one to each side of the most sure-footed horses and mules. Clinging to their swaying boxes, the moan of the windswept gorge falling breathlessly away to one side, to the other the tendrils of that wall of jungle brushing their excited cheeks—how the heart of each mother must have been in her mouth many a time during that struggling climb! Yet other parents put their babies and trust in the baskets of sure-footed old John Chinaman. A youngster in each basket, the baskets suspended from the ends of the pole which John balanced and gripped so securely over his shoulders.

And then Christy Palmerston walked out north-eastward from the prospering tin-field and found a somewhat roundabout track which with McLean and Mullins, he connected to that busy wagon road from Port Douglas to the Hodgkinson goldfield. And thus the longed-for wheel traffic could come to Herberton, not from Cairns, but from that lucky Port Douglas again.

The track edged round the flank of that mountain wall, bringing to Port Douglas greatly increased trade, and disappointment indeed to struggling Cairns.

The much shorter, dangerously rough tracks still continued to be used by the pack teams, but of course it was the wheel (and Port Douglas) that got the trade. Which is a simple illustration of what the humble, so soon forgotten pathfinder by foot or horse has meant to many an Australian town and port. Indeed, but for the pathfinder in the first place no towns would have been possible.

By now, prospecting parties had scattered far and wide over plateau and ranges, finding their own way west, north, and south-west, keen to find another Palmer, another Hodgkinson, another Herberton. Still other parties were seeking new timber lands, sugar lands, cattle lands, pastoral lands. Nothing could now stop the wonders of the hinterland becoming known and used for the advancement of man.

Meanwhile those hardy ones from Cardwell way, creeping up along the coast and poking into every gloomy inlet or beautiful river mouth, now found gold deep within the jungle wilderness of the Russell River. The Jordan, too, the Mulgrave, Johnstone, Tully, Towalla. Not big fields like the Palmer and Hodgkinson, but payable gold for all that—though incomparably more difficult to win than from the open forest country of those two big fields.

These coastal rivers come pouring out of that mountain wall which faces the Pacific, towering up there clothed in its virgin forests and jungles, cleft by gorges and precipitous spurs and deep ravines defying further penetration for years yet. Deep within this overwhelming greenery torrential rains began anew the cease-less battle of Man against Nature.

And cunning, adaptable Man here would presently learn to use the might of Nature against Nature herself. For he would turn her own waters against her and wash away her very own mountains that held the golden grains so deeply hidden, wash away her broad terraces from her own mountain-sides, guarded by mazes of almost impenetrable jungle though they were.

By the simplest of all power—hydraulic sluicing by gravitation. When last I saw the Russell, miners must have cut a hundred miles of water-races along those mountain-sides.

Mighty Nature with her raging torrents cuts her own channels and washes away mountains, too. Strange to think that insect Man can take her own forces from her, harness them, and do the same job ever so much more quickly.

Nature can take two thousand years to grow a tree. Alas, that destructive little devil Man can chop it down within hours. However, Man cannot make a seed, nor one drop of rain.

For these coastal adventurers seeking gold or timber or new sugar lands the only communication with the south was by the occasional cutter or lugger creeping up the coast and poking in anywhere, seeking both adventure and loading wherever it might offer.

Thus, while away "up on top", west of the sea, men sought other Herbertons, those down on the coast cut and hacked and crawled and climbed up and down into that seemingly impenetrable jungle of wild cliffs, rock-bound gorges and icy streams, battling on their own initiative on a scanty bag or two of flour and whatever the gods would provide. In these days we would first raise impressive capital and fit out a big expedition with all modern conveniences.

Meanwhile, away back up on the plateau, Bob Watson, Connelly, and Dougherty rode out from Herberton and almost immediately found rich mineral which quickly developed into the lively township of Watsonville. Jim Mulligan found Queensland's first silver mine deep in the scrub-clad depths of Silver Valley, then Mount Albion was found and the silver town of Montalbion sprang up like magic, fed by rich silver from the mountain-side. Alas, a short life though a merry one. Away south-east, among a sea of sun-baked hills, the Stannary Hills field was found; its name means "Hills of Tin". This led on to further discovery and the brave little township of Irvinebank, and the Vulcan Mine, which for long years to come would support numerous families. In no small measure this was due to the tireless energy and far-seeing enterprise of a certain John Moffat.

And a place now called Innisfail, carved from scrub and forest near lovely little Mourilyan Harbour, was busily advancing on a career which was to launch it into one of the most prosperous sugar-cane districts in the world.

And still Cairns was seeking a track—a wheel-track.

Port Douglas was thriving mightily, gaining wealth and constantly increasing population, all because of the wheel.

In desperation, Cairns eventually demanded a railway!

Where they had been unable to get even one dray-wheel up the range—a railway!

It was going to be a long and bitter fight. But, once having given voice to the idea, those citizens of Cairns kept on and kept on keeping on. They *had* to. For loud indeed in the land became the cry, "a railway!"

Three lusty young voices—Cairns, Port Douglas, Mourilyan.

For immediately, Port Douglas formed a committee to insist that *they* had the one and only practical route. But so did the Mourilyan Harbour people, energetically pressing their claims from south down the coast.

Vigorously each little settlement declared that only through *its* back country could a railway be built, emphasizing also that it possessed the one and only port capable of tapping the wealth of that hinterland. Cairns fought stubbornly, almost bitterly, against this embarrassing, very energetic competition. This obviously was to be the last fight for a real port, no holds barred.

It seemed but a dream, an engineering fantasy, to get a railway up that mountain wall. Mind you, in those days—'twas but yesterday—they only had brains and enterprise and brawn, dogged persistence, horse and tip-dray, picks and shovels and wheelbarrow, spawlding hammer, hammer and drill, gunpowder, and a very carefully shepherded supply of gelignite to work with. Motorized mechanics, let alone bulldozers and suchlike gadgets, were as yet not even a dream in men's minds.

For forty miles along the face of the range men, and good men too, searched in vain for a shorter, more suitable route than the Port Douglas wagon-track. In vain. That barrier behind Cairns beat even Christy Palmerston, in so far as finding a track for wheels was concerned. He suggested, though, that it might be just possible to hew a railway line up along the side of the Barron Gorge. There would be many difficulties, numerous tunnels must be blasted through rocky spurs, but he believed it might be done.

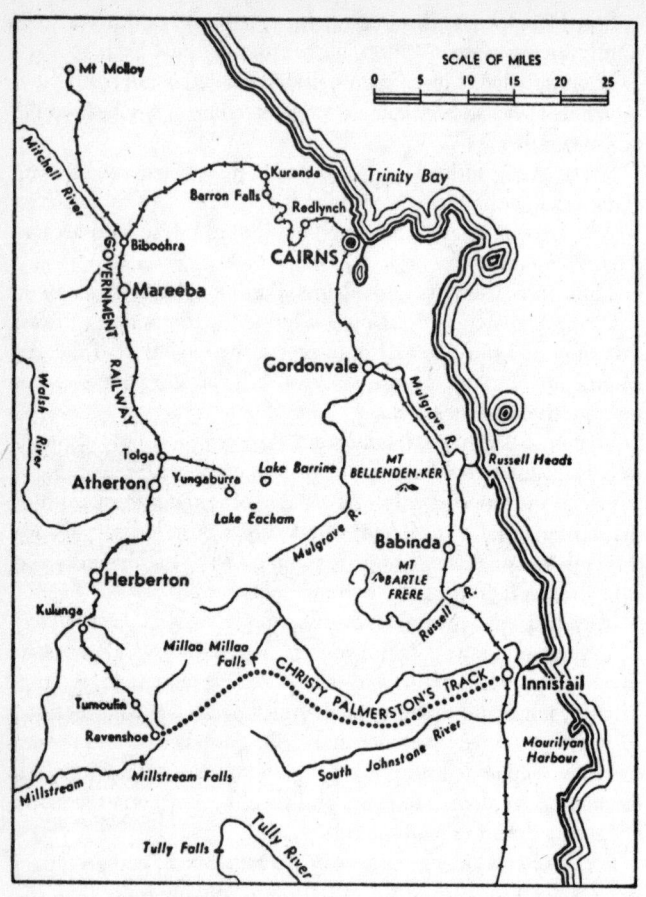

Finally the Railways Department appointed Surveyor Monk to try to find a suitable site. After more than twelve months' constant travelling along the range between Mourilyan, Cairns, and Port Douglas to Herberton, he finally made the fateful decision —"The Barron Valley Route".

There was an immediate and fierce outcry from north and

south of Cairns against this decision. Naturally so, for the prize was great. Men of Cardwell and Mourilyan, of Port Douglas and Cairns, fully realized now that whichever gained the railway must grow into a city. That iron horse would mean the rise or fall in the fortunes of many men.

The railway authorities decided to build the line—the Barron Valley Line!

An awe-inspiring job, especially for those days. It took five years to lay the first twenty-five miles to Myola, easily the worst sections. In the gorge section of fifteen miles, a bridge under difficulties had to be built over every creek and ravine, some built over hundreds of feet of space; ninety-eight curves had to be blasted round the gorge side, fifteen tunnels blasted, huge escarpments cut from the mountain-sides. Fatalities were inseparable from such a hazardous job, illness and floods and landslides. But the line went through.

"And I was nearly through, too, many a time," Old Mick used to say grimly by the Council Fire, "hanging to the side of that gorge by the skin of my teeth with the wind blowing up my pants until my teeth rattled."

"Where were your bowyangs?" inquired Jim Bell.

"The gangers along my section did not wear them," said Mick, with a smirk.

"Oh!" Jim shrugged. "All hoity-toity, eh? Don't dine with the men like!"

That railway, gradually pushing on in sections through the years, had an enormous effect in the opening up of the Tableland. Not only did it mean that countless shiploads of valuable timbers were soon being railed down to Cairns, thus also opening up rich lands for rapid agricultural development, but it meant that towns could now be built and supplied, while mining companies could get trainloads of urgently needed machinery, tools and stores and iron for building materials, explosives, many miles of pipe-lines for water-carrying, the heavy materials for building their own railway lines.

Thus, as stage by stage the line crept on, so supplies came

rumbling up to the Tableland. Increasingly then the fruits of production began pouring down in trainloads to rapidly growing Cairns, thus vindicating the faith of her early citizens, mirrored in their ever-growing port.

Alas, Port Douglas just as quickly began to languish. The horse- and bullock-team cannot compete against a railway, the wooden wheel against the iron.

CHAPTER VIII

BILLY THE GOAT

WHICH brings us right back to where we started from, as it were —on a roundabout track like Bill Smith starting out from the Hodgkinson in his circle by land and sea to find the inlet and back overland to the Hodgkinson. So we are back to Nigger Creek by Herberton, where I now played an atrocious joke on poor Old Mick, my friend Old Mick the ganger. How funny it seemed, how the laughter spread from camp to camp, carried too by riotous navvies pumping their way back to the construction camps on the railway tricycles! And Old Mick forgave me, with that quaint old smile of his.

"Boys will be boys," he sighed. "Oh, for my lost youth!"

"*You'll* never grow old, Mick."

"Never in my heart lad, I believe you. But this old carcass is growing a bit rickety. The angle irons are not so staunch, the fish-plates are working loose, I feel a bolt or two a bit rusted here and there. While the bellows, like the old grey mare, definitely ain't what she used ter be!"

Poring over these old notes, I feel ashamed now; youth can be thoughtlessly cruel. I am seeking excuses. I believe I can find it in these notes, let's blame it on to youth and environment.

We'd recently enjoyed a laugh at the expense of the Herberton police, though the little township thought quite a lot of them. Away out on the construction camps, as with every line, there was often trouble from moonshine whisky. Here and there was a secret still in the hills that supplied the shady retailers thereof. To track a cunning moonshiner to his hidden still in those labyrinths was difficult indeed. Besides, his "cockatoos" always seemed to keep him just one jump ahead.

However, up along our line, early one sultry afternoon, a crowd of navvies, doubtless fed up with toil, were enthusiastically sampling a newly arrived supply of moonshine at a camp shanty. Of course, the stuff was poison. Within an hour a lusty uproar was bellowing out from the secluded shanty.

Deep within the timber along a bush track, just at hearing distance, a heavily loaded buggy was waiting, men listening, even the powerful horses prick-eared, expert driver at the ribbons.

An order and—the driver's foot was off the brakes as the horses plunged forward to "Gee-up!" and the "Crack! Crack! Crack!" of the whiplash. A dust cloud swirling out behind them, they came at a mad gallop as if certain to crash straight in through the flimsy shanty. With a screech of brakes and horses straining back on haunches they slewed at the shanty door, men leaping down from the buggy with the brakes still screeching, and as one solid body hurling themselves straight at the door. In that rip-roaring crash, that instant of stunned silence, the shanty-keeper found himself in the hands of the police.

The sergeant was justly pleased. It had been a craftily planned, well-carried-out little raid. And there was still ample evidence left in the shape of unopened bottles to convict a cunning, notorious shanty-keeper.

The sergeant dispatched the Evidence, in the buggy, in charge of two policemen, to Herberton. He saw them safely start out, then briskly set about his duties in "cleaning up" with his remaining police.

Well, that long, dusty road leading towards Herberton! It was oppressively hot, and the fine dust *does* penetrate down into a man's throat. The two constables wiped moist brows as the sweat-caked horses jogged along, now and then vigorously blowing the dust from reddened nostrils.

In sympathy, the police coughed, too, rubbing sweaty brow with limp hand.

Of course, it was the subdued clink-clink-clinking of that Evidence that really worked the trick, a suggestive imp in every tinkle. It really *was* hot, each long mile growing hotter, dustier, yet more thirsty to the tinkling of those bottles.

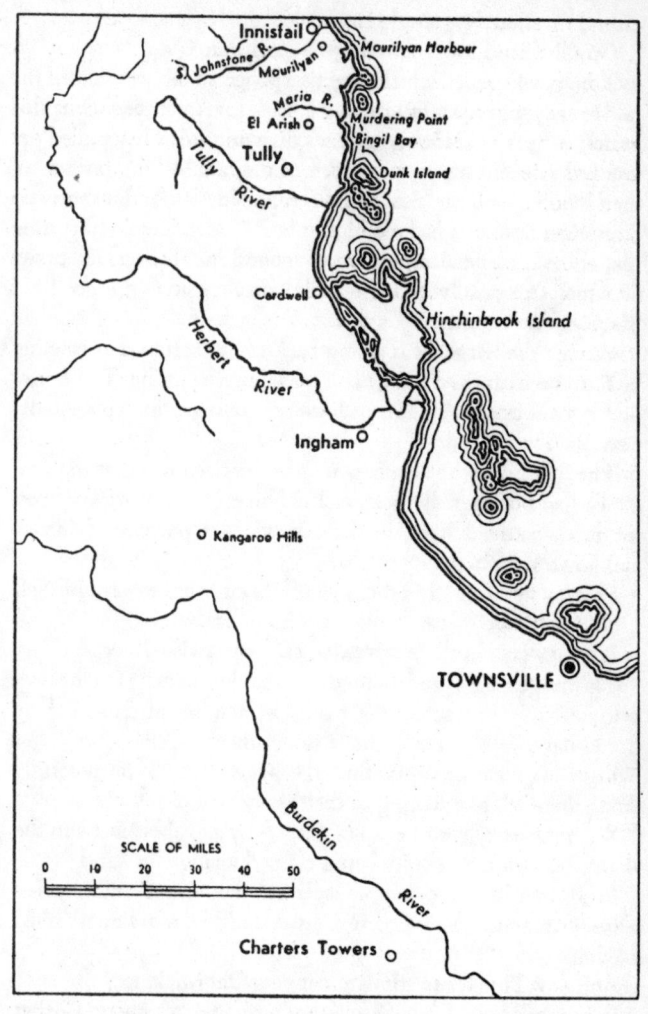

Innisfail
Mourilyan Harbour
S. Johnstone R.
Mourilyan
Maria R.
El Arish
Murdering Point
Bingil Bay
Tully
Dunk Island
Tully River
Cardwell
Hinchinbrook Island
Herbert River
Ingham
Kangaroo Hills
TOWNSVILLE
Burdekin River
SCALE OF MILES
0   10   20   30   40   50
Charters Towers

Just *one* little drink wouldn't do any harm. Wouldn't be missed either, for there was ample Evidence.

One little nip led to another—of moonshine!

Tongues loosened a little, the two police amiably discussed the raid as they jogged along, grew enthusiastic at its success, chuckled at that cunning old shanty-keeper's discomfiture. They pulled up, enjoyed a decent nip to the success of the raid. A little farther on, they shouted a nip to "the Sarge!—tough old bloke, a bit snorty on discipline, but not a bad old bird at heart". Completely forgetting that these occasional nips were of moonshine, the vicious brews of which are deadly as nightshade, they toasted "the good old Sarge" in yet another nip.

When "the Sarge" was riding back to Herberton that evening he found the capsized buggy half-way down a cutting. The horses had broken loose, but, still in harness, were grazing contentedly near by.

The first thing the agonized sergeant noticed was that the Evidence had not been as lucky as the horses. Bottles strewn across the road, bottles broken in the capsize, that precious Evidence had flown back to thirsty earth.

Praying he would find them with broken necks to save himself a job, "the Sarge" glared around for his police.

But they lay not there, sprawled out with twisted necks.

The sergeant's gaze alighted on the blackness of a heavily branched tree just across the road. On a sultry afternoon there would have been enticing shade under there.

Knowing what he would find, the sergeant strode purposefully across the road, foot itching in that heavy boot of his.

Yes, there they were, snoring peacefully as babes. Dead to the world, each with an empty bottle clasped lovingly in hand.

Well, that little incident appealed to the miners' and navvies' sense of humour. Appealed to Garnet and me, too, I'm ashamed to admit.

And now I'll have to admit about poor Old Mick, too.

It happened one lively Saturday. During the afternoon Garnet and I watched an impromptu shooting match out the back of the

New Pub, under the trees. Things would not get really willing until later on at night. Just now, the boys were only playing. Several were holding up matchboxes between their fingers while riflemen at thirty paces were knocking the boxes away. There wasn't one miss, otherwise there would have been a finger or hand blown off. In a few hours' time neither the trigger fingers nor the hands would be so steady.

And it was this day, or rather night, that I played *my* joke. Of course, it was sight of that old devil of a billygoat that did it, just as it was the tinkle of the bottles that had brought dire disgrace to the constables in charge of the Sarge's Evidence.

That dilapidated old goat now clung determinedly by the heels of the marksmen, effortlessly dodging irritated attempts to boot him in the ribs. A wicked glint in his shifty eye plainly told he knew he had only to hang on and play his own game to get what he thirstily desired. Which was beer, and more beer.

While the line was building along to and past the pubs the old goat had lived in a near-chronic state of glassy-eyed inebriation. In the crowded bar the navvies would ignore him, until menacingly he would lower those dreadful-looking horns, his dirty, scraggly old beard fairly shivering with nastiness.

"Give the old battering-ram a stiffener," someone would growl, "before he clears the bar."

No sooner said than done. A few pots of beer heavily laced with rum and Old Billy, glazy of eye and loose of lip, would stagger through the pub, fall down the back veranda steps, and lurch out the back seeking a shady tree under which to sleep it off.

But now that the line was pushing on past Nigger Creek drinks for Billy came only when a tricycle-load of navvies happened to pull up before the pub, or on a Saturday such as this.

And now it was quite obvious that Billy smelt tonight would be the night.

Mick Moore was coming across to the New Pub this evening, his navvy friends had promised to haul him out of camp and chuck him in the creek if he didn't.

"When we come a-visiting," they had declared, "we'll stand no airs from a haughty old splay-toed ganger just because he's now an aristocratic tin-scratcher." They had threatened Mick with much more dire penalties should he not turn up to join in their hospitality. And Mick knew full well that when they "had a few aboard" they would delight to keep their promise.

Mick seldom indulged. "The trouble is lad, I don't know when to stop," he would say with a smile. "When I'm in the arms of Bacchus, my brains fly out the window."

"You've got none to fly with," Jim Bell had said disgustedly.

I seldom had the wherewithal for more than a couple of mugs of beer, whereas Garnet was minus the inclination. We two were no good at all to either pub.

A peculiarity of Old Mick's was that when he did have an evening with his friends he did it in style—"booked a room" at the pub.

"Just as well he imagines he's the Dook of Timbuctoo," growled Jim Bell, "otherwise he'd end up in the creek in the middle of the night. And poison all the fish within miles."

A "room", of course, was just a bare cubicle of sorts with a bed, the door opening on the back veranda, as in most wood and iron pubs in those hot places.

Of course, I knew where Mick's room was.

A fair crowd turned up that evening, the "dead" pub was soon bedlam. From the outskirts I kept an eye on Billy the Goat. To Garnet's lasting sorrow he missed this joke, he had slipped away to visit schoolteacher friends in Herberton.

From the night outside the lively bar I watched the succeeding phases of alcoholism of Billy the Goat. From thirsty greed, to aggressive demand, to fighting mad, to wobbly-kneed collapse.

Of course, they plied him with drink after drink. Then some wag yelled out to stage a bull-fight, with Billy as the bull. In a moment bar cloths were snatched up by eager bull-fighters, pocket knives opened, a sharp stick was a sword, and in a moment the amazed Billy found himself advanced upon by yelling matadors banging him with beery cloths, prancing round him to hurl the darts—which were playful stabs with stiff thumbs in the flanks.

Billy, shaking his head, retreated stupidly until a prod where it hurt most pulled him up right smart. With a hoarse grunt of protest, with fire in his eye, drawing himself up into a real he-goat again, he lowered his horns and charged—to bring up against the bar with a crash that brought a yell of protest from the publican. But the scattered matadors drew together with delighted cries—"Bravo!" "Hoop-la!" "El Spaniardo!" "To the ring again, La Senorita Bull-Bull!"—prancing round Billy, flapping his nose with cloths and hats, stabbing him with "darts", with the "swordsman" protesting, "Stand aside! Lay off the bull, you galoots, while I have a fair go for the kill!" Billy charged again, bringing up against the bar wall, this time with a resounding bang. The wonder is he did not go right through the flimsy partition; he had horns and forehead like a real young bull.

I watched until the exhausted and snorting Billy, sadly drunk, quite demoralized and with his faith in human nature badly shaken, lurched his dazed way through the pub hall. I ran round and met him on the quiet back veranda and there waylaid the panting old terror, quiet as a baby lamb now. With a loaf of bread thickly covered with jam that I'd purloined from the kitchen held to his bleary nostrils, he followed me meekly into Mick's room. I had the blankets pulled down all ready, but had to lift the smellful old carcass up into the bed. He settled down gratefully, thank you, his head comfortably upon the pillow, tongue weakly licking at the jam on the loaf that I left beside his nose. I pulled him as far to one side of the bed as possible so as to leave room for Mick. I could do nothing with those outrageous horns, though, they were terrific. At last I just pulled the blanket over him best I could, and silently stole away.

I was delighted; I had not foreseen that a goat that had imbibed so amply and so indiscriminately would sleep the sleep of Bacchus, just as a two-legged goat would. Billy the Goat certainly would not wake up until—

About midnight I heard Mick come singing some poetry or other through the pub from the bar. Easy to tell that Mick had "had it", too. Instinctively he made for his room. Found it. I heard him sprawl on the bed. Sundry grunts, then "thump, thump" as he threw his boots on the floor. He wore boots on such particular occasions as he visited the pub, lest he get his horny feet trodden upon.

A thump and creak as he rolled back on the bed, a burst of verse, something fierce about "And brave Horatius *shall* hold the bridge with *me!*"

"Once more unto the breach, dear friends, once more, and close the wall up with our English dead! Advance thee, Halbadiers! In the merry month of May we'll play upon the hay—"

A cavernous yawn, a sort of a shuffle, protesting groans, and—snores! Mick was sound asleep in the arms of Bacchus.

The joke seemed to have misfired. Regretfully I stole away to camp, wondering if maybe Mick would smother the goat, or the goat smother Mick!

In the haze of the awakening, so far as I could ever make out, what happened next morning was this. Mick awoke to find two big green eyes staring lovingly down into his, a long scraggly, hairy beard tickling his chin and lips, and crowning all a tremendous pair of curved, crinkled, scaly, weatherbeaten horns—with a smell of fowlyard and cowyard all mixed up together.

Mick's ghastly yell startled Billy, who jabbed him under the chin with a horn while struggling on his belly to get a foothold away from all that all-enveloping blanket. To Mick's roars Billy struggled yet more frantically and both went rolling to the floor from opposite sides of the bed. With the blanket entangled over his horns Billy charged straight into the wall with a crash that spilled the publican from his bed and brought all other sleepers bolt upright from sleep. Mick leapt up, yelling blue murder, as the goat bolted through the door to tumble headlong down the back steps. When the crowd came hurrying along Mick was yelling like a demented one, prancing round with waving arms and howling to fight any man who said he had not been wrestling with the Devil.

CHAPTER IX

THE AFFAIRS OF ANTS AND MEN

STILL being doctored by a grim Jim Bell, it was a wan and sorry navvy ganger who several mornings later greeted me with a watery smile. Somewhat remorsefully I'd strolled down to the Council Camp to inquire about the patient's "recovery".

Willingly he forgave me, but seeing I was quite relieved the cunning old dodger immediately added a proviso: "But you must write a 'pome', Jack. Don't look so flabbergasted, I know you've got it in you—and it's got to come out! Until it does I'll still remember that stinking old he-goat with his whiskers massaging my face and knees in my stomach—it's still horrid sore! I won't forget those horns! They felt like the hammers of Thor when they butted my poor sore head! I won't forget the smell of that awful joke until you read out your 'pome' by the Council Fire."

Neither amusement nor laughter nor the most earnest assurance that I had no more poetry in me than the Man in the Moon would pacify Old Mick. He was surprisingly serious.

At last I promised, thinking he'd eventually get over it. Not he.

So daily now, feeling like a silly ass, I climbed down the shaft to work—to do penance, to try my hand most unwillingly as a rival poet to Old Mick Moore the ganger. At each smoke-oh I'd plug the candle into the face, pull out a grubby piece of paper and stub of pencil, and in the deathly quietness below by the old river-bed proceed to make myself feel a perfect ass.

Thinking Garnet would help me out, I let him into the secret. Of course, he laughed as at a great joke; he was all for it, he *would* be.

"*Two* poets in Nigger Creek!" he declared enthusiastically. "The Muse of the navvy, the Muse of the tin-scratcher! Wondecla, the Meeting of the Waters, will become famous!"

"Do you take me for a loon?" I asked.

"No," he grinned, "Shakespeare!"

And he refused point-blank to scribble out a scrap of doggerel for me to read at the Council Fire.

"Dare try to bribe me again to such black treachery," he declared virtuously, "and I'll tell Old Mick! And every soul in Nigger Creek as well!"

That awful night came when I had to face the Council, and they'd made sure it was a full Council, too. Hardly daring to smirk at the expectant faces grinning round that bright fire, I mumbled through my first "pome". I've got it beside me on the table in the old notes, but daren't insert it here.

Instead of a tirade of disdain the audience broke into congratulations, of course they would. Old Mick's grizzled face was all wrinkled up in delight.

"Bravo! Bravo! You must send that to the 'Bullerteen' lad! You *must*!"

Like hell I will! I thought.

"We never dreamt you had it in you, Jack." Garnet winked. "Two poets in Nigger Creek! Well, well. You can never judge a book by its cover. How true!"

Old Brookes and little Turley congratulated me warmly. Uneasily I glanced at the amused Jim Bell.

"Two *poets* in Nigger Creek!" he declared. "Three goats! And the one with the horns the most human of the lot!"

Of course, Jim was howled down, but I certainly *felt* he was right. Old Mick had made a goat of me for sure. Served me right.

Mick was very fond of birds and in consequence the knowing little squabblers fairly took possession of his camp at times. He encouraged wild animals, too, to Jim Bell's lurid exasperation when he found the possums had ripped open the flour-bag or sugar-bag and scattered the contents all over the place. Mick could always see the wonder and beauty in wildflowers, too. So one day I called him down my shaft.

"I'll show you two flowers you've never seen before, you old sinner."

"It will be a pleasure, Jack."

I held the light to a prop that was helping support the roof. That timber had been cut from a tree months ago. Just where it supported the roof leaked a steady drip of water. And the prop had begun to sprout; ghostly white shoots were piercing out from all over it, away down there in the darkness deep within the earth.

"There you are, Mick. A stick of timber chopped down months ago. It has neither head, root, nor branches. It has not seen the sunlight which gives trees life, since it was brought down here, a mutilated stick of timber. It should have been dead months ago. And yet it is bursting with life."

"It's a miracle, Jack." Mick smiled. "A miracle proving how everything clings to life—but after all, what is anything *without* life? I've seen the same thing in the timbers upon the very rock in railway tunnels."

"I might have known I couldn't surprise *you*. Well, you haven't seen this, anyway." And I held the candle to a log in the face.

Deep set in among the gravels of the old river-bed, it was a petrified log that had been born and grown into strength and beauty under heaven's sunlight ages ago. Torn down by some prehistoric storm, it had been finally washed down into these once raging waters, had become waterlogged and sunk, to be buried in the river bottom. And then the river itself had been drowned under red-hot lava, which had solidified into solid rock fifty feet thick, compressing the very river-bed.

It took us all morning to dig out that log. It was now black stone, perfectly marked. By the candlelight we examined it.

"It is no tree that I know," said Mick, squinting. "Probably the species died out when the world was in convulsions. Do you know, Jack, strange birds have roosted on this prehistoric tree, quaint animals eaten its fruits and nuts and leaves, queer insects burrowed into its overcoat of bark. I'd give a lot for one glimpse of the world as this old tree must have seen it!"

"If you'd lived in those days, Mick, you might now be petrified like this tree."

"I'd be my own monument then," grinned Mick, "whereas now I'll merely blow away in dust."

"What odds!"

"None at all. Death is but a pause in Life. My innards assure me it is dinner-time, Jack. Come along to our camp and I'll put the billy on. Then I'll show *you* something."

Mick showed me a wonderful little lizard. An ugly, ordinary, somewhat disdainful, sleepy lizard. But Mick lifted the lizard and placed it on a red cloth. Before our eyes the lizard began to change slowly to a soft pink colour, that gradually spread into red. Then Mick took it outside onto the grass. Slowly the lizard changed to green.

"No matter where you put it," said Mick enthusiastically, "it changes to just the colour of the material on which it is placed. Humans cannot do that. If only we could we wouldn't have to buy new suits of clothes. Just think of the saving in dresses to our lovely ladies. However, place our little 'change-me-coat' upon flowers and he takes the colour of the flowers, really seems to absorb the colour. If upon a piece of bark, then he becomes a piece of bark. He looks very ferocious, but he can't fight—which doesn't matter, for his enemies can't see him to gobble him up."

"H'm! It certainly is more curious than my dead timber and petrified log."

"Yes." Mick grinned. "How have the mighty fallen! Size is not everything. In fact, sometimes I wonder if the littlest things prove to be the greatest after all. But this little lizard, by being alive, has its problems."

"How?"

"The problem of how to keep alive. In this case the worry is mine, I've been trying to feed him this week past and only three days ago learnt he lives on ants. Have you ever tried to catch ants, Jack? Sufficient ants to feed a lizard with the appetite of a fat old pig?"

"Of course I haven't."

"Well, I've been trying to satisfy this little tinker for three days past. Seemed it would be easier to catch a tiger than catch ants. But I've solved the problem." And Mick looked really proud.

"How?"

Grinning, Mick picked up the lizard and gently put it in a kerosene tin. He fastened down the lid. Hundreds of small holes were punched in the tin. Over these, Mick smeared jam.

"Now," he said, "billy's boiled. We'll have *our* feed, then come out and watch our little pet enjoy *his* feed."

After lunch, we strolled outside the galley. The kerosene tin was black with ants. From inside, out through the holes, was shooting a tiny tongue. The ants were disappearing nearly fast as they came.

"I was getting real worried," said Mick. "The little fellow was starving to death in the midst of plenty. But now he'll grow fat and I'll have a new mate."

I laughed. "And what does Jim think of his rival?"

"Oh, Jim just thinks I've got lizards in the belfry, as well as bats."

"Oh, you're not *too* bad, Mick, I've known worse. But look here, there's something *you* haven't thought about."

"What's that?"

"Well, are you going to keep your new mate boxed up all his life—a bachelor prisoner, pining his little heart away?"

Thoughtfully Mick scratched his grizzled chin.

"H'm! No. I hadn't thought of *that!*" A quaint grin spread over his weatherbeaten face. "I'll have to do something about it; I'm responsible. Yes, I think I see daylight, and—" he chuckled enthusiastically—"I believe I can become godfather and all. Won't it be delightful to welcome the firstborn, the son and heir! But," he mused seriously, "it's going to take a powerful lot of ants!"

When each of us few alluvial tin-scratchers, after weeks or months of toil, had dug and hauled to the surface a few loads of precious wash-dirt, we'd combine in a community clean-up. We'd hire a horse and dray, and cart each man's wash-dirt down to a community sluice-box by the creek. Here, we would "put through" the dirt, run it through the sluice-box and separate the tin from the wash-dirt, the bottom gravels of the old river-bed. We would simply do what Nature, on a gigantic scale, had done in the first place. Nature had taken millions of years to wash this tin down into the river-bed, concentrating it in patches here and there. We would concentrate *our* tin in two days' work, a few hours. Ah, but Nature had washed away not only mountains, but mountain ranges to gather her treasure deep within her bosom, while we would put through the same process but a few dray-loads of wash-dirt.

One man would cart the dirt from the shafts down to the creek, another man shovel the dirt into the sluice-box, with its rushing water, forking out the wash-stones and concentrating the material as the water swept the refuse away. Another would stream (clean) the tin free of the concentrates, that residue of heavy sands. Thus, with each one of us in team-work concentrating on his job, we overcame labour, expense, transport, and other difficulties. It is wonderful what a few men can do when they work together with a common object. Our object was to make as good an independent living as possible, and not work for a boss.

We had no man-power except our own. To get a living we had to produce more than our own labour was capable of doing, so we made water work for us. We harnessed running water into a long, narrow sluice-box that was set with a fall, that is, with a certain slope. The confined water rushed down that box, and that rush of water was power. We shovelled the wash-dirt into the head of the box and the water rushed the useless material away, the heavier grains of tin gradually sinking as the water carried it more slowly down along the box. Long Stewart was the best box-man and streamer in the district; it was a pleasure to watch his expert work. Jim Bell was our boxman, though, and a good one, too. His was the job of working against the water while allowing the water to do *its* work, his the job of throwing the tin concentrates back with a long-handled shovel to the head of the box, keeping the tin there while allowing the useless and lighter gravel to rush down out of the box tail. With practised skill a good box-man can hold almost every ounce of tin to the head of the box, while as the day wears on tons of useless gravel are washed away out of the tail of the box. It means skill and ceaseless hard work, in combination with the accurately adjusted set of the box and the accurately measured consequent force of water. I believe that water, properly harnessed, is the greatest and cheapest labour servant of man. Even in our own tiny way we could make water in one day put through all the wash-dirt that it had taken us a month to dig with pick and shovel.

As we came and went on our separate jobs on that so important clean-up day we constantly cast an eye towards the head of the box—and smiled thankfully if we saw the black streaks quickly gathering there. For this would be the first sign of the stream tin. Well before midday the head of the box would be black with the concentrated tin grains. And Jim Bell, ceaselessly working in the box, kept every grain back to the box head as the eager water rushed the sands away.

The concentrated tin, exactly like heavy black sand, would be shovelled into dishes. Finally, in a smaller box with a special shovel, it was streamed, the last grains of sand were washed from it. Swift, skilful, very heavy work this, working the heavy tin swiftly and ceaselessly against the water to clean it of every grain of heavy iron sands. It was then spread out on a tent-fly on the ground to dry. Then we bagged it, in little canvas tin-bags. Each bag held a hundredweight, and each hundredweight was then worth £7. That meant £140 a ton, thought to be a very good price then. When I think of that toil, with the knowledge that in coming years tin would rise to £200, £300, £400, £500, £700 a ton!

Happy were we when we cleaned up a few bags. For the money meant we were independent men, still our own masters.

We would cart the bags of tin concentrates along the pretty road to Herberton for sale. And life was good.

CHAPTER X

BLACK SANDS

Lɪᴛᴛʟᴇ Herberton appeared to be built higgledy-piggledy upon seven hills within the encircling Herberton Range. Grey and brown roads ambled through the town to meander unconcernedly up and down the hills. Out into the sunlight rose the roar of the stampers as the battery crushed tin ore, right now a rich crushing from the Rainbow. This new show was bringing a fortune to its finders—lucky devils! Each wet season that roar was drowned by the Wild River as it foamed over its rocky bed round the town. In the dry season the river is pretty and deceptively peaceful, but its rushing waters are true to name when the mountain gullies tumble their brown floods down into its surging bed. Again and again would come rolling thunder from away back in the ranges, an extra big one seemed to come rumbling in from the newly found Froghole Extended.

Toilers out there were blasting a way through solid rock in their restless search for tinstone. For Herberton itself was mainly a reef-mining field, whereas Nigger Creek and the Deep Lead were alluvial. Reef tin, unlike the loose grains of stream tin in the gravels of old river-beds, is part of the rock of the reef itself which in turn is encased within the solid granite of hill and mountain. Hence, to break away the tinstone-bearing reef from the mother granite means "shooting work", hammer and drill and explosives to tear the rocks apart. Then the broken reef-rock is carted down to a steam power battery where the battering rams of falling iron-stampers crush it into fine sands. The tin is then separated from the worthless sands over inclined tables, really a sluice-box over which water runs, just as we separated our stream tin from the old river gravels. The battery, of course, had its noisy "steam arms" to help whereas we had but our humble man-power. So whether in river-bed, or in solid rock, Man had to unravel the work of Nature, to break free her tight clutch and rob her of her precious tin, which in the first place she had hidden so well. Too dashed well for me and many others!

Poked away in almost inaccessible places over that sea of valleys and ranges, over eighty thousand square miles of wild country, were the numerous mining camps. Long before you came to one such, either gold or tin or wolfram, you could tell if it were a reefing field. For, floating with the wind over valley or hilltop, would come the murmur, then the harsh roar of a stamper battery, echoing dully away to come again with a roar on a gust of wind. Whereas an alluvial camp would be quiet.

Herberton was put on the map by the prospectors Jack and Newell and their party, but the tin in the river was actually first seen by Jim Mulligan and soon afterwards by a cattleman, that "wonder man" of the Tableland, John Atherton. If any man in the Far North was as good a bushman, pathfinder, and discoverer as Christy Palmerston he certainly was John Atherton. As full of initiative, as cautious, as dogged, and as fearless. And, in my humble opinion, more far-seeing, a man of broader national vision. Christy was a "primitive" man, a wizard with tough local problems, whereas John Atherton was more of the map-maker. And he certainly put the Atherton Tableland, originally discovered by Mulligan, on the map.

A large family of "early day" Armidale people, the Athertons trekked north into Queensland where the baby brothers were to grow up and each make a name for himself, backed up to the hilt by their women-folk. Australian pioneers did a mighty work and have received at least some recognition. But seldom a word is said about their women-folk, who stuck to them through thick and thin.

After the finding of the Palmer by Hann and Mulligan it was John Fraser, followed by Atherton, who pushed up into and among and over those untrodden ranges with the first mob of cattle for the then starving miners, a wonderful feat repeated when Mulligan found the Hodgkinson. Apart from the bush,

Atherton's passion was cattle and cattle country, he was ever seeking new cattle country. He found it away up in the Tableland in wild bush which here would be called Mareeba, making his way through open forest country round the magnificent jungle-scrubs discovered by Mulligan; one such scrub in a few years' time would be called Atherton. Thus, the Atherton Tableland. What vast wealth of timber and produce of rich agricultural lands have since come from there—will *always* come from there, so far as we can tell.

In his restless wanderings ever seeking the wealth of cattle country, again and again Atherton rode over a wealth of mineral. Camped by a mountain stream he wondered at the conspicuous black sands here and there piled against rocky bars, and later told others what he had seen.

But ever he rode on, seeking pastoral country. On one return to the nearest civilization, which was in the vicinity of the newly discovered Hodgkinson goldfield, he rode upon two prospectors working in that same creek, which they had called Tinaroo Creek. The horseman reined up, noting with curiosity the two strangers so busily shovelling up those queer black sands. Willingly they straightened up to greet the horseman; visitors were rare indeed. They explained that this "black sand" was really stream tin, and valuable. Then they laughed at the realization that this big bearded fellow in corduroys and red shirt, smilingly toying with his horse's mane, was none other than that wandering cattle-man who had first brought news of tin in this very creek.

Atherton told them that "back over those ranges", down past some big patches of scrub country, in a wild-looking river tumbling along between the mountain-tops, there was plenty of that black sand. "Piled up all over the place where there's been a bit of a backwash from a flood. There's black sand in other creeks, too, but in that wild river it's so thick that you can just shovel it up and bag it if you want to."

Eagerly, but doubtfully they questioned him; it seemed altogether too rich. Carefully they explained that there are a number of kinds of black sands—black iron, for instance, magnetic iron sands, too, tourmalin also—it all looks just the same black sand if you don't know it.

The bushman dismounted and slowly ran the streamed tin from their box through his fingers in handfuls.

"No," he finally declared, "it's the same black sand. I've handled it at times out of curiosity when I've gone to the creek to fill the billy. It's heavy like this; it is exactly like this. I see those little crystal shapes you show me, and these water-worn grains, and this pinky colour on some of it, too. No, there's no doubt about it— the black sand in that wild river is exactly the same as *this* black sand."

John Newell organized a strong party of seven. Atherton was invited to share in any discovery, but resolutely declined. Good luck to them, but he was interested in cattle, and cattle country only. That quest took up all his time and interest. But he would guide them part of the way if they liked.

The party set out to cross over into the ranges from Tinaroo. The country, but above all the natives, finally beat them. The nearer they pushed their way through to the locality where they thought that wild river must lie the more numerous and menacing became the aboriginal inhabitants. And again and again the party had to slow down, when to advance farther meant to fight. The last thing Newell wanted to do was to antagonize the natives. Against such odds they probably would never have got back again, anyway.

Day and night constantly they had to guard their horses; again and again they were forced to make long, rough detours to get round threatening tribes. They did reach the river, but the amount of tin they found was meagre.

Several years later Newell, Jack, Brandon, Brown, and several others in a party tried again. And this time found their way down into that valley of the Wild River. And one morning John Newell gazed down into a gully black with tin sands.

And something at which they stared amazed, not believing their eyes, not believing the weight of stone in their hands. Weight! Why, some of those dull-looking slabs they could not even move, loose though many were. Then from a solid reef in the solid rock they saw more—tin! Solid tinstone!

It was the first tin lode yet discovered in Australia. Hitherto prospectors had sought and worked tin as grains of black sands in a mountain stream. But here it poked up out of the earth as solid rock within solid rock. No wonder they could not believe it; they broke it and crushed it and panned it off and weighed it and examined it for wondering hours. And still they could not be convinced.

There was only one way to prove it. Smelt some!

How, in wildest bush, when all they had with them was their ordinary rough camp gear?

They hollowed out a stump as chimney of a forge and furnace, lined it with clay, and burnt good "charcoal" wood for charcoal. Then they powdered a sample, mixed it with powdered charcoal as a flux, fashioned their own crucible, and made a bellows with the aid of a tomahawk, bark, a few sticks, and an old felt hat.

Then, working up a roaring fire in the "furnace", they actually smelted that sample, and poured it into a mould cut in the clay. When it was cold, they broke away the slag. And there was a shiny, silvery button of tin!

But think of the ingenuity necessary to cause and control the heat necessary to melt tinstone ore!

In wild excitement John Newell saddled up and all alone rode night and day through hostile native country to Thornborough on the Hodgkinson. There he reported a find as exciting as a gold discovery to Warden Mowbray and applied for the Reward Claim.

One of the richest tin discoveries in all Australia—right here near the Great Northern, whose battery was thundering out across the river as Mick and Jim and I brought our humble quota of tin into the sunlit township.

It was warm now, but it would be pleasantly cool tonight—a climate that made us feel good to be alive, three thousand feet up. Even then, the main street of the town was up and down a hill.

As we strolled down the street in our "town" shirts and strides —with boots on, too—it was with a wave and grin here and there to brown-armed men, alert horsemen born to the saddle, townsfolk in shirt-sleeves cheery of greeting, casually smoking blokes with not a worry in the world. For at this period the price of tin was up, rich crushings were coming from the lucky reefs, while new shows were being discovered, out at Watsonville, too. That was in the days before we'd seen a motor-car, the aeroplane, and high explosive bombs and super taxes. The youngsters all had rosy cheeks, the climate was vibrating with health. When you saw a dog-fight in Herberton it was a real fight.

"A dog bred in this district," declared Mick, "is a coward if he won't tackle a tiger."

"Keep your eyes off that young woman!" Jim scowled. "You've already used your allowance of postage stamps this month."

"Love will find a way," said Mick, grinning. "Did you notice her red hair? That coppery shade tinged with fire always urges me to burst into rhyme."

"You'll burst into—" began Jim and stopped, staring. We glanced across at the pub. Leaning up against a post with hands deep in pockets drooped a long, grizzled old man, hundred crows-feet round his eyes. Even from that distance we could tell they were "snarly" eyes, shadowed though they were under the rim of a battered old hat. He was staring expressionless towards us.

"Now how in the name of the Mighty Khan did he trail me *here*?" murmured Jim Bell.

"Who is he?" asked Mick as we strolled into Jack and Newell's store.

"The moonshiner," answered Jim, "the old man. It was them took a pot shot at me out Wolfram Camp way before the son was drowned. Looks like the old man is going to carry on the vendetta."

"Seems there's more dangerous pastimes than writing poetry to the Gentle Sex," said Mick. "You'd better buy a few postage stamps—they're safer than buying bismuth."

"Buying, hell!" snapped Jim. "Those new-chums planted the bismuth in my claim, like I told you—you grinning old hyena! This is the moonshiner. May he drink his own poison, the swine!"

"A spice of danger," chuckled Mick, "to relieve the peaceful monotony of Nigger Creek! Your friend holding up the post across the road there certainly doesn't look any lotus lily. Why not stroll across and oil his palms? He might shout you the Beer of Peace then."

"I'll have a piece of *you* in a moment, you splay-footed old skirt-chaser!" said Jim furiously.

But Mick was obviously enjoying himself. "Now don't lose your head," he chuckled. "I see you've got one. Anyway, I thought you were bushman enough to have lost your charming friend."

"I felt sure I had." Jim frowned. "I thought I lost him when I side-tracked from wolfram-chasing to railway navvying away across here, then slid aside into a backwash tin-scratching and let the line go on."

"You know what *thought* did?" mused Mick.

"Yes!" snapped Jim. "And *you're* the result!"

"Anyway, your snaky-eyed friend doesn't know where you're camped," said Mick unsympathetically, "so why worry, Jimmy boy? You might be poked away in any camp within a hundred miles of here for all *he* knows. Besides, you're in the depths of civilization now. Look! There's the sergeant with a wary eye on us across there at the police station. Maybe the moonshiner isn't the only one on your track!"

But Jim only frowned sourly.

CHAPTER XI

THE TALE-TELLERS

WE SOLD our tin. Anxiously we looked on, Jim Bell watching the buyer like a hawk, for this was a matter of professional pride with Jim. Had his swift, expert, unremitting toil eliminated the very last ounce of worthless, but so heavy mineralized iron sands? Washed the refuse clean out of each bag of one hundredweight? For the more valueless sands left in, the less the percentage, the less the money!

However, Jim had done his usual expert job. The verdict was seventy-three per cent tin concentrates, and that result is excellent.

Jim's strained expression relaxed, honour was satisfied. Casually he pulled out his tobacco pouch to roll a cigarette, basking in our silent approval.

You see, there is more than pick-and-shovel work in "tin-scratching". Much more.

Our few humble bags were weighed inside a big shed at the back of a store, alongside tons of bags of streamed concentrates neatly stacked on the wooden floor built on piles a few feet above the ground. In that long, gloomy-looking shed our few precious bags appeared humble indeed beside such an impressive stack.

"Reminds me of a youngster's battered little money-box leaning beside a bank," said Old Mick, smiling.

Ours were five bags, worth then £35. The stack was worth some thousands.

"And we worked like navvies to get that thirty-five quid!" muttered Jim Bell, with longing eyes on the big fat stack.

"Well—not quite," murmured Old Mick.

"Nuts to you and your navvies!" said Jim scornfully. "There's more sweat gone into the winning of all that tin than into the whole of the Cairns railway line!"

"Those would be fighting words," I said, "if any of the navvies were here."

"No need for the navvies," chuckled Mick. "One whiskery old moonshiner would do."

The business-like tin-buyer smartly opened each bag and thrust a long, narrow, grooved iron sampler right down through the contents. Deftly, with a twisting motion, withdrawing this tubular arrangement, he emptied the tin pellets it contained into a saucer and swirled it round, gazing with critical eye. Thus he assayed each bag. It takes practice, but a good man can assay tin thus, estimates the few grains of sandy impurities amongst the tin grains. Thus he values the contents of the whole bag. As a rule, the result is anything from sixty-eight per cent tin to seventy-three per cent tin, though "phenomenally pure" can go as high as seventy-five per cent. Generally it goes between seventy per cent and seventy-three per cent. A good streamer always tries, that is expertly slaves, to work his tin up to seventy-three per cent clean.

Time was to come when a tin-buyer on any mining field would sample the tin much more cautiously. For railway lines somehow bring in "civilization". In time coming shrewdies would doctor their tin-bags by filling the centre with a core of high-value stream tin, then packing heavy, black, worthless iron sands tightly round it. Other brainy coves shoved lumps of scrap iron within the concentrates, to make up weight. Thus they broke up the comradely trust between buyer and seller, making things difficult for everyone.

But there was no such trouble at this time. However, it was already brewing. As the buyer weighed our bags we yarned with Scrag Watson, who with his mate worked a few miles out in a rock-bound gully towards the Dry River. He was a scraggy looking little chap, frowning at the fat tin-bags stacked on the wooden floor.

"How's the luck?" asked Mick.

"No good," growled Scrag. "There's our two bags *there*. A month's solid yakker for two men for fourteen quid. Not blanky wages."

"You'll strike it rich sometime," reassured Mick. "We all have our ups and downs."

"We've had more flamin' downs than ups in all the gullies between here and Cairns." Scrag frowned. "We're just about fed up—right to the eye teeth and back again!"

We received our cheque and all hands strolled across to the pub to cash it. I noticed Jim Bell glancing sharply round, but there was no sign of the old moonshiner.

What happened later, so far as it could ever be reconstructed, was this.

Next day Scrag mooched away back to his claim in the hills, a weighty load of rations upon his bowed shoulders. He was frowning thoughtfully at the dusty road, puckering forehead and eyebrows against the drops of sweat that slowly rolled down his dusty nose. On those hot days, when trudging along under a load of rations, a man is soon sweating like a cab-horse. I know, for at times I've been a pack-mule myself. But I wish I could manage the same job today.

Now, the floor of that particular tin-buyer's shed was of wooden planks, built up on piles as the usual safeguard against the white-ant pest. And, as it turned out later, it was of this "underground" lay-out of the bottom of the shed that Scrag was thinking. A tiny puff of dust rose from his iron-shod boots as he trudged along. What does an ant think when it sees such a boot descending upon it?

A few nights later, when the little township upon the hills was fast asleep, two dark forms crawled underneath that floor. And one grasped a long auger and he sweated in earnest as with unseemly haste he bored a hole upward through the boards.

"Ugh!" he grunted. "She's through! Ah! I can feel a bag," he whispered excitedly. "Now she's through into it! I feel the auger grating in the tin—ready?"

"Yes," came the hoarse whisper.

As he withdrew the auger his mate held an open bag under the hole. A dribble of tin grains came rustling down into the bag. Both conspirators chuckled hugely. Then one thrust a length of fencing wire up through the hole and twisted it round. A spurt of stream tin came flowing down the hole into the bag.

"Good!" he hissed. "Bore into another bag, quick. I'll soon have this half filled, which is about all we'll get out of a bag."

All night long those crouching shadows, in a lather of sweat, toiled feverishly in their cramped position, boring hole after hole up through the floor into those fat tin-bags, then carrying away their heavy, ill-gotten gains and hiding them before dawn. Also hiding themselves.

Not until next night, of course, would they dare carry those heavy bags through the sleeping township to a hide-out on the outskirts, bag after bag, trip after trip. They would hide again before dawn, lie low throughout the day, then carry those weighty bags a further stage into the bush.

Each bag weighed one hundredweight; two bags is a load for a pack-horse. They had to carry those bags along a rough bush track for ten miles to their camp by a creek.

It was some little time later that two hard-working tin-scratchers found a nice little patch of tin. They dug it out of their claim out in the hills, in the bed of their creek. As men will when lucky enough to find a patch, in delight they downed tools, hurried into town to spread the news and order a packload or two of stores, good solid tucker. They had been living and working on damper, dripping, and roast wallaby for weeks past. Folk congratulated them, as all hands did those lucky ones who every now and again struck a patch. Our two hearties hurried back to their claim, toiled like galley slaves, cleaned up their little patch in double quick time and, of course, now could afford real pack-horses to carry the heavy bags into Herberton for sale. They enjoyed a bit of a beano, of course, then boarded the train for Cairns, looking forward to a well-deserved spell.

"We'll light out south somewhere or other," they merrily told friends, "maybe right away south to Brisbane. Enjoy the bright lights, and work this wallaby and damper out of the system before we come back to look for another patch. And we'll find another for sure, now our luck's in."

And all done up in the first new clothes they'd adorned for years, away they went for Cairns and the "Highlights".

Soon afterwards the date became due for a certain tin-buyer to train his accumulation of tin to Cairns for shipment south. Layer after layer of the big stack of bags was trucked away, tons of stream tin, until the stack was down to the two last layers.

The tin-buyer stared in amazement at the deflated, droopy, woebegone bags—especially at the flattened bottom layer. He stared unbelievingly when he found all those holes bored up through the floor into the nearly empty bags.

Little wonder at his concern, for he had paid out £7 for the contents of each bag.

Which is why he, and other buyers in other districts, glumly and angrily laid down sheets of heavy iron over the floor of their tin-stacking shed.

Maybe those floors are concrete now. For in the years since, tin, so they tell me, soared up to as much as £1000 a ton! At such a price, each bag would be worth £50!!! Oh, shades of all the old tin-scratchers past and gone and the still living "museum pieces" of my own day! Oh, Old Mick Moore and Jim Bell, Old Brookes and Tommy Turley and Long Stewart, Tim and Monty and the Baird Brothers, the Shiptons and "Bow-Wow" and Lennie Lawson and—I could easily remember two hundred others of us Knights of the Fork and Banjo! If in those days, when toiling from dawn to dark, we were happily on Easy Street if making a bag a week—oh, what if that bag had been worth fifty pounds—and that before the days of dynamite taxation!

Ah, away from such dreams of Paradise! Let's flop back to earth.

An occasional visitor to the Council Fire was Old Clarey, a grizzled relic of prehistoric days who delighted in yarns of the Baron Munchausen type. On this particular evening Mick and Jim had been yarning of champion "mean" men they'd met in their variegated lives, while Old Clarey sat puffing at his pipe awaiting his chance. And seized it.

"Yes, them blokes were mean. But I knoo a publican out Cunnamulla way," he began reminiscently, "he was so mean he'd skin a louse for its hide an' sell the salt. Skin it clean as he used ter skin the shearers of their cheques. He used ter brew his own fire-water, no fear of him buyin' real grog. And that gut-burner was real poison, not lolly water like weak stryckinen. One day he carelessly left a bucket of this same home-brewed whisky in the back-yard, he'd been flavourin' it with tobacco juice down at the cow shed. The old roan horse strolled up and sniffed it, snorted a bit, the fumes near choked him, but he guzzled it—I suppose it was the only thing he'd ever got from that publican except hard yakker, fer nothin'. Anyway, he croaked. He was only dead drunk but you couldn't tell the difference, it was that sort of brew, he seemed dead as a doornail. The publican was mad at killing a horse that still had a few months' work left in him, but determined to get all he could out of the old carcass. So he skinned him, thinking he might get a few bob for the hide. Six hours later the old horse woke up and tried to stagger up; he did, too, he was a determined old horse, one of them cantankerous sort. He tried to walk a bit, he seemed a bit wobbly in the shanks. Hoping to save him and keep the hide, too, the publican killed six sheep and grafted the hides onto the horse's ribs. He had the sheep carcasses for the pub table, he had the old nag's hide to sell, he still had the sheepskins on the horse, and had the horse too now, if he lived. He did, an' more, too, that fire-water musta done somethin' to him, for he began to pick up an' grow fat. An' that skinflint publican made even a better bargain than he thought. For he both worked and shore his faithful quadruped for many seasons after that and made a mint of money out of the wool."

This story quite fascinated young Garnet the schoolmaster, such yarns being new to him.

"Now, young fellow Brookes," he encouraged, "I can see by your face that you can beat *that* one. Out with it."

"No," said Old Brookes, smiling, "I'm no good at that sort of yarn at all. But a few years back I met an old sinner who was. I was escort for a young lady visitor arriving per Cobb and Co. from the city. I had to meet her and drive her out to the homestead of an outback station. A settler's wife waved us in for a cup of tea.

We were both glad; it was a dusty road, a long hot drive, and the horses were only half broken in. Besides, I wasn't much good as company, and she was chattering like a magpie all the way. We were glad to sit down in the coolness of the selector's home while the kindly wife busied herself boiling the kettle. The old man, a well-known old character, Old Henry is his name, was of course lolling at his ease in a home-made chair, pipe hanging loosely in his mouth, one shoulder hunched higher than the other as usual, rubbing tobacco between the palms of corduroy hands. If a steam-roller had gone over those hands it would only have given them a gentle massage. He's got bushy eyebrows that an eaglehawk could build its nest in. From under those eyebrows the old devil was quizzing the girl. She was a good looker, too, all eager with curiosity at the strangeness of her first visit to the real outside bush. She'd expected blackfellows to jump out at us from every tree along the road. I had a feeling she was a bit disappointed.

" 'Oh, what great big horns!' she said, gazing up at a tremendous pair of horns nailed to the wall.

" 'If you care to hear it,' growled old Henry, 'I'll tell you a yarn about them horns.'

" 'Oh, do!' chirruped the girl. All eager for the yarn, she listened to the old reprobate with parted lips, her big blue eyes wide open. I don't believe that gnarled old greybeard had ever had such a pretty, innocent listener at his mercy. I could have choked the old devil, he was enjoying himself so much.

" 'Them horns,' he growled, 'belonged to Browny, one of the best bullicks I ever owned. A bobby-dazzler of a leader, too. He had brains, had Browny, and they weren't in his tail neither. Well, one mornin' I went to yoke up the team, and found Browny missin'.

" 'So German Harry, me offsider, he says, "I'll go off and look for Browny acrost the other side of the river! Maybe I pick up der tracks!" So he saddles the roan and rode acrost the river while I saddles the mare an' rides down the other bank. My mare knows well as I do we're lookin' for Browny and hopes we'll never find him—unless dead. You see, one day she'd stopped a poke of his horn in her belly, Browny, not being partial to horses, perticulary flighty mares. Anyways, I carried a noo Mexican axe slung acrost me shoulder, I'd honed that axe-blade sharp as a razor; you never know when you want a sharp axe in the bush.

" 'Well, I'd been ridin' along fer erbout an' hour when suddenly I pulls in me mare an' looks acrost at the opposite bank. Lying poking up out of the scrub I sees somethin'. "Them's Browny's horns!" I says to the mare. "An' I'm glad ter see them. Come along, an' don't think you're goin' to throw me inter ther river!" So I spurs her where she feels it most an' we plunges into the river an' swims acrost. I ties the mare to a sapling, 'cause she's made up her mind she's not goin' near them horns. Mares has good memories, an' don't like being horned in the short ribs. Well, them things lying there sure enough was Browny's horns poking up, or rather they was pokin' *out*! But where was Browny?

" 'He was down in the belly of the biggest alligator I ever seen! That mighty lizard had swallered Browny right up to the horns! But them great big spreadin' horns was stickin' straight out one each side of his jaw. I could hear a smothered rumblin' now from somewhere down below, like thunder way down the river. It was Browny down in ther alligator's stummick gaspin' in air, an' the alligator tryin' to gasp in air an' Browny, an' Browny's horns, too! That great big scaly body, just like a whale all swollen out with the bullick inside, was quiverin' up an' down like a boat on rough water.

" 'Well, I got me Mexican axe, the one with that sharp blade, an' I draws that blade from the alligator's jaw right down his belly to near his tail. That alligator was fairly bustin' with the size and weight of the bullick an' the way poor ole Browny was plungin' and kickin' to git out. That gash with the Mexican axe did it! That alligator gives a long, shudderin' gasp as Browny comes snortin' an' coughin' an' tumblin' outer his belly. Then that mighty lizard gives a feeble kick an' thankfully passes out. I s'pose it musta bin a bit of relief, you know.

" 'Well, out jumps Browny an' runs like blue blazes down the scrub, I could hardly see him travellin', you'd think Old Nick was chasin' him with a red-hot pitchfork. Of course, I don't s'pose Browny had been feelin' too comfortable neither.

"'Well, it took German Harry an' me three whole days to corner Browny an' yard him in. He was always scared of alligators after that, though it had took the biggest one in all the river to swaller him. Well, I worked old Browny another three years in the team before the ticks killed him. Them's little things, them ticks. But they're deadly. Them horns up there saved Browny from the alligator, but he couldn't horn the ticks.'"

CHAPTER XII

GOUGER OF THE "BULLERTEEN"

OLD MICK MOORE had composed a new "pome", and was dying to read it by the critical campfire. By the way, any man with crowsfeet crinkling his eyes or with bristles of iron-grey in moustache or beard was "old" to Garnet and me. Quaint! I remember the shock I had a while back when I was strap-hanging in a city tram and a young fellow squeezed up from his seat and said, "Hey, pop, here's a seat." I gaped blankly. But he'd really said that—to *me*!

Oh well, any chap who looked a bit scrawny around the gills was an "old bloke" to the young "half-axes" of my day. So that "Old" Mick Moore was fidgeting to recite his latest masterpiece. Old Brookes would be there, little Old Tommy Turley, Long Stewart probably, hard-bitten Jim Bell who was solemnly middle-aged according to our standards, young Garnet and I and the old Bitzer dog. A Bitzer, because his pedigree was "bits of everything"—even to a touch of donkey, according to Jim Bell, who knew Mick was fond of the cunning old dog. So round the campfire that evening with pipes alight we comfortably sprawled, awaiting the treat.

"Oh, spit it out!" ordered Jim. "Just look at him, squatting there on a jam-box like an overfed Primer Donner smirking over-time for an oncore!"

Thus encouraged, with a bashful grin Mick pulled a neatly kept notebook from his hip pocket, opened it across his knees, peered at the pages from under bushy eyebrows, frowned, coughed, then in solemn tones read aloud by light of moon and campfire the following masterpiece:

I sat by the campfire musing,
On the dead, departed Past,
While spectral thoughts on memory's wings
Came crowding round me fast.

And golden scenes were rising,
Through the magic-tinted air,
When Earth seemed mostly Dreamland,
And life surpassing fair.

And I was thinking, musing,
If life was made in vain.
I've had my share of pleasure,
I've had my share of pain.

On fleeting wings of happiness
Those brilliant years did fly;
In robes of sweetness glowing,
Each golden month sped by.

Then, life was a sparkling Eden,
Where every dream proved true,
While Youth remained my bounty,
And Hope my pleadings knew.

My musing now is changing
To a misty, fog-bound land.
And I was gently veering
To Tassy's rugged strand.

I thought old friends were round me,
And old, familiar scenes.
And I forgot the bitterness
That follows after dreams.

My musing now was drifting
To that distant Mulga Land,
Where the lonely traveller's walking
Through a treeless waste of sand.

Where lies the gold alluring,
So many have led astray.
Where Hope is so assuring
That Fate might her obey.

The fire burns low—the moon has gone,
The sky is sullen black.
With never a thought like a silver star
To shine through the future track.

The Past has gone, the Future's near—
A vista of dragging fears.
No wonder that many a man goes mad
At the phantom of coming years.

Mick's quiet old voice trailed into silence, as with a doubtful grin he awaited the verdict.

"Eureka!" yelled Garnet delightedly and jumped up with waving arms. "Eureka! Eureka! You've got it! The laurel wreath upon the brow of Michael Moore, Poet of Nigger Creek!"

His poetry to be acclaimed by the schoolmaster! Mick undisguisedly beamed at the disapproving visage of Jim Bell.

When I joined in with congratulations Old Mick was sublimely content. For—I haven't told you before—I was "Gouger of the Bullerteen"!

Old Brookes leisurely filled his pipe, smiling all through his beard.

"No one would ever guess you had such learning, Mick," he said.

"Not until he wakes up!" growled Jim. "What did you want to

pull his leg for?" he demanded of Garnet. "He'll be useless for a week now, mooning about the place like a stuck-up milking cow."

"Cows produce milk," said Mick mildly.

"Which is more than *you* do!" snapped Jim.

But little Turley chirped into the congratulations, and there was a quiet compliment from young Gallogoly, Garnet's scholar. And Mick's cup was filled to the brim—so much so that I couldn't help saying that I'd be blessed if I didn't try to compose another "pome" myself and see if I could do anything near as good.

"Do so, lad, do try!" exclaimed Mick excitedly and I wondered what my stupid tongue had let me in for.

"Serves you right!" declared Jim Bell in a satisfied tone. "You'll never get a moment's peace now! Encouraging him in all that nonsense—talk about trying to make a silk purse out of a sow's ear!"

"Oh, I say, Jim!" laughed Garnet. "Don't nip the Muse in the bud."

"In the bud!" snapped Jim. "I'd nip—"

"Jim is handicapped," broke in Old Mick smilingly. "He hasn't got my bump of knowledge."

"Of all the swelled heads!" exclaimed Jim. "It's in hospital *you* oughter be—in a *woman's* hospital!"

"I was born there," chuckled Mick.

"The matron must have died of fright, then," declared Jim, "otherwise she'd have smothered you."

"And a poet would have been lost to the world," declared Garnet. "I say, Mick, yours is a very sentimental nature, you know. Why did you never get married?"

"Ah!" sighed Mick. "Those lost opportunities! When in the bloom of youth I could have married any fairy I pleased."

"There's your answer!" snapped Jim Bell. "Fancy a baboon like that pleasing *anybody*, let alone a woman! Not unless he was the last man in the world—and even then, she'd shut her eyes."

Certainly in the firelight a stranger would have thought the old ganger anything but handsome. But then a stranger would not have known the kindliness behind that granitic old face.

"Take no notice of Jim, he's jealous," soothed Garnet. "Go on, Mick," he encouraged. "Tell us all about *her*—about *all* of them!"

"She was a smart business-woman," began Mick dreamily, "interested in *everybody's* business. At that time I fancied myself a salesman. So I tried to sell her myself."

"No wonder she went broke!" Jim smirked.

"No," sighed Mick, "it was *me* who went broke. She told me she didn't like handsome men, they were too conceited. She gazed up at me with those dreamy eyes and whispered that *I* was not conceited."

"She must have been dumb from the neck up," declared Jim emphatically.

"I carried my swag away from that town," resumed Mick sadly, "wondering how I'd lost my charm. 'There was something about you I used to like,' she sighed at parting, 'but you've lost it now.' It was only when I trudged footsore into the Mareeba store to fill the tucker-bag that I found my pockets were empty."

Garnet laughed delightedly, he always seemed to see the fun in a tale of woe.

"Now, Mick," he challenged, "there must have been a woman —or women—that you truly loved. Tell us about *her*!"

"One comes sweetly on the wings of memory," mused Mick.

"Well, then?"

"She was very pretty," drawled Mick, "her cheeks a rose in the dewy dawn. So very nice, sweetly shy, real uneasy lest everything be not good and proper. One evening I was cuddling her under the porch when she whispered, 'Oh, Mick, are we not romancing here too long? How long do you really, *truly* think a man ought to keep his arm around a girl?'

" 'Until breakfast time, my dear,' I assured her." Mick sighed deeply at the fire.

"And how did you come to leave her?" inquired Garnet.

"In a hurry," sighed Mick, "through the window."

Lots of nights, long after the mopoke called we walked away laughing to our separate camps from Mick and Jim's cheery campfire. I'd say good night to Garnet, stroll up the slope to the tent, light the candle, shoo away the cheeky possum that was sure to be coiled up on the bunk, pull off the strides, roll into the blankets, blow out the candle, and drift into the Loneliness, that other world of Night.

I was "Gouger of the Bullerteen" because I wrote paragraphs for the Sydney *Bulletin*, and occasionally (after many heart-burnings) had one or two accepted. I had tried, and kept on trying, mostly out of sheer cussedness, some two or three years back on the opal-fields. But that has been told in *Lightning Ridge*. By now I was a full-blown "Aboriginalities" man. Which merely meant, to that distant, aggressive Sydney weekly that some bush wan-derer signing himself "Gouger", "Up North", or something of that kind, occasionally sent in batches of bush paragraphs, some-times scribbled on rags of paper, even on jam-tin labels, of suffi-cient interest to win acceptance of a dozen or so a month. But in the country or bush, where the *Bulletin* then was known far and wide as the "Bushman's Bible", to be a writer for the keenly dis-cussed "Aboriginalities" page was fame indeed. Should the news leak out, which it invariably did from the bush post office, the local interest was astonishing. To me, naturally lazy, the need to be ever alert for material for an interesting paragraph and the forced labour in writing it down in such concentrated form, were more or less drudgery. But every few months I'd send down for the cheque, and when it did arrive at some bush post-office-store just weren't those few pounds welcome! For until the final years I was never very lucky at either prospecting or mining; I always seemed to make just enough to pay the storekeeper and keep on wandering.

There was never any thought of writing a book during those years, of course, such a dream would have seemed a sacrilege. But if it had not been for all that travelling and forced observation and drudgery of writing things down I would not be sitting here tonight with the table littered with piles of faded papers scribbled on in faded ink and yet more faded pencil, with battered old schoolchildren's exercise-books closely packed with notes on Nigger Creek and Herberton and many a name of the hinterland, would not be sitting here grinning over the "poetry" of good old Mick Moore exactly as I'd copied it down years ago, reading again the down-to-earth yarns of Jim Bell, even gazing interestedly at the faded sketches I'd made of him and Mick and others of the boys. Wouldn't be reading, with a sort of comical disbelief, that I believed myself "in love, lonely, and far away".

Ye gods, how funny we can be! And yet, reading on through these faded old notes, it begins to come back to me how awfully serious it seemed then! I wonder if, as we grow older, we grow farther and farther away from youth until we become incapable of appreciating the problems of the young, those problems and troubles that seem so absurd to us, yet mean so much to them!

Was I really forlorn and alone and in a hopeless love those days, when sometimes to be happy I had to be beautifully miserable? With a silly sort of grin I hurriedly turn over these tell-tale pages.

It was when Old Mick the ganger had heard a whisper I was "Gouger of the Bullerteen" that eagerly he had taken me to his heart. He, a disguised poet, was delighted to find, away out here at Nigger Creek, a schoolteacher and "Gouger of the Bullerteen" his friends.

But for that leakage of vital information we might never have known that Mick Moore was a poet. And now that he had "retired" from railway work and the secret was out to us only, we never betrayed it. We, the privileged few, kept that dreadful secret inviolate. How his navvy friends would have roared had they known!

Garnet, or rather Mr Garnet Aitchison, the schoolmaster, had suddenly become very important, too. By Headquarters at Herberton he had been entrusted with the training of a future schoolmaster, young Gallogoly. A quiet, shy lad, the son of one of the local miners, he had distinguished himself at the Herberton school, and Garnet had been entrusted with the job of training him for his schoolmaster's exam. Since Garnet was taking his responsibility very seriously we did not see so much of him now.

Eventually young Gallogoly would pass his exam with flying colours, to Garnet's enthusiastic delight.

Interesting indeed can be the future. We little dreamt in those cheery days at Nigger Creek that Garnet, the young schoolmaster, was destined to train many thousands of Queensland children, to realize even more than his ambition could have been, that he was to become one of the real "Big Men" in the go-ahead Queensland Education Department.

CHAPTER XIII

MULLIGAN'S MONUMENT

JIM BELL's "End of the World" country was aptly named, even though it was the noisy, sometimes dusty, smoky, occasionally unpleasantly fume-tainted scene of very energetic enterprise. That harsh country during a dry summer looked and felt a sun-baked, barren wilderness, very different to the Tableland. This was a big district north-west of Herberton, south-west of the Hodgkinson, the Chillagoe-Mungana-O.K. district, rich in copper and other minerals also. Its exploitation was possible only when the Chillagoe Company had built its own hundred miles of miniature railway to connect with the Government Railway at Mareeba. Amongst the widespread limestones there are striking, weird-looking patches of country creepily suggestive of "left-overs" from the age of the giant animals. There are frowning tors of rock such as those upon which Darius of Persia cut his imperishable record of bloody victories, rape of cities, of civilizations vanished under fire and sword. Here, too, are great caves, some beautiful, some gloomy caverns deep and weird and dark. I doubt if even today all the caves in that far-flung district have been discovered.

A few years before the time of which I am writing, as the little railway-tramway crept nearer to this township at the "End of the World", Chillagoe was very much a law unto itself. The company had now pushed the tramway a further ten miles out to Mungana, where the Lady Jane and Girofla were booming. So was Einasleigh, a hundred miles to the south, while fifty miles farther out in the wastes from the "End of the World" O.K., but very recently discovered, was now very much "on the boom". This latter little human ant-bed was the "Green Mountain" of the aborigines, too isolated from civilization to be of more than passing interest to the few wandering whites of earlier years. Though several cattle-men had heard of it from the aborigines, prospector Paddy Boyle was the first white man to find it in all its green loneliness when the only things of value to him were his health, horses, water, rifle, tucker, and that ever elusive gold. A mountain of copper ore was useless. Years later, only recently, during a copper boom Jack Munro rediscovered it, said, "O.K., this will do *me*!" and brought the news with specimens back into civilization. John Newell at Herberton and several Cairns and Chillagoe men—Draper, Munro, Torpy and railway contractor Overend—got to-gether, formed a company, and had already, even under the appar-ently impossible conditions out in those wastes, begun to pay dividends when Old Mick the ganger was spouting poetry by the Council Fire. Only the very richest of the ore, "near pure copper", could at present be worked, of course.

But there was no place away out there in all that district for a prospector lad who did not have a ten-pound note to bless himself with, let alone the little fortune needed to buy the absolutely necessary horses or camels, gear and stores. The long strings of heavily laden camels swaying out into the heat-haze towards O.K., Klondyke, and Cardross in charge of the wide-awake Abdul Wade upon his "flying camel" were reminiscent of the camel-teams leaving Broken Hill for the sunburnt western plains. But here it was the weird limestone country, where poison bush had played havoc with the camel-teams. And it really takes a lot to kill a camel. The extension of the mining company's tramway from Chillagoe to Mungana and the tractors were no help to the labouring teams, either. In fact, the tractors were to prove the end.

Mungana was a lively, rough-and-ready place then, money, fights, two-up, and grog with a kick in it like a mad camel. But you had to work wages or contract to get that money; there was none of the "one-man production" possible with easily sold minerals like gold, tin, or wolfram. It was not the sort of mineral country where you could dig in on your own with just enough in your pocket to pay for a month's tucker, for copper-mining needs big capital, even though a few copper-gougers can work their own show for a time, providing it is very rich and handy to smelters or railway. Much of the work on the copper fields was not too healthy, either; at times fumes from roasting ores and fumes from the now busy smelters seemed to hover all over the place. Underground work in bad ground could be particularly unpleasant, too, the heat and air action liberating sulphur from the sulphides where conditions were suitable. A man's lungs could feel it at times, while sores and cuts, if not carefully tended, were liable to "turn nasty".

But that was generally so in all the big copper camps, which then did not possess the modern equipment and scientific treatment processes of today. If such fields could now be discovered, with modern mining machinery and metallurgical treatment processes, and with metals at their present price, what fabulous returns they would bring in!

Somehow I always felt vaguely sorry for the few women in those sun-scorched places; the men, tough as ironwood, could look after themselves. They did, too, so far as was possible. Looming beside the never sleeping township is the huge bluff pock-marked by the mouths of the great Mungana Caves. And in the cool mouths of these many of the miners would sleep while on night shift, whereas night and day the women must swelter in the iron and slab shacks. However, the money was good. And that fact in those times was recompense indeed.

A noisy place, with the arrival of coaches, the little Chillagoe trains coming and going with supplies and machinery and long lines of clanking trucks loaded with coke and limestone and ores for the smelters, while, setting out for O.K., some fifty miles north through the hot and barren bush with its scraggy timber and fantastic limestone bluffs, were numerous teams and those noisy but so handy traction engines pulling "road trains", blowing and puffing and clanking their way through bush as they hauled their heavy loads of supplies and ores and coke. A tough job in those days, the transport of all supplies and upkeep in the building of another new town away out in the barren bush. I suppose in these modern days we never give such a matter a thought. However, the boys simply tackled the job, as they tackled many similar "back-o'-Cairns" jobs with whatever "tools" were to hand. Neither the rock-strewn Walsh nor the bridgeless Mitchell stopped these teams and tractors, they simply "bullocked" their way across—and carried on beyond. Some of the noisier tractors were given good-humoured nicknames. I remember one Goliath nicknamed "Jumbo"; you could hear Jumbo roaring and snorting and clanking miles away through the bush, a terrifying sound and sight with its belching sparks and smoke to nervous horses, even more frightening perhaps than camels. Great work these noisy monsters were doing, and kept on doing for years; I don't know of their having been used so extensively elsewhere on the continent.

How different the huge motor-truck of today, speeding so swiftly interstate, to the smoking traction engine coming thumping and snorting and clanking through the bush! And yet it was only yesterday.

By the way, the "Big Six" lorded it at Chillagoe. Comparatively few people in all Australia even knew that those sun-scorched, do-or-die little communities even existed. But they would come to know of the Bix Six, though not as the Big Six. They eventually "came big" in another way, big in Australian politics. E. G. ("Ted") Theodore would become Premier of Queensland and later Federal Treasurer, "Big" Bill McCormack Chief Secretary, T. J. Ryan Premier, and Alf Jones Minister for Mines, while Darby Riordan would presently be looming big indeed in the political life of Queensland.

Throughout the Chillagoe district, as elsewhere, the names of James Mulligan, John Newell, and John Moffat were household words, as were a surprising number of others, for in this "hard" district pastoral and mining activities were extending not only over the Walsh and Mitchell but west and south-west towards the Gulf, too.

It was the women of those days throughout all the North who felt quietly thankful to such men. Their own men-folk, and also the little army of single men, could and did admire those men who went out and did things. But for mothers with children to consider their deeds had a deeper significance, a human interest, too, though subtly different.

When the price of metals went down, when the single men had all they could do to scratch out enough for tucker or were forced to roll up the swag and trudge away, or at those times when cattle prices were almost non-existent, when the farmers to be were struggling to the limit to clear their land and get a start—when minerals, timber, farm and pastoral produce were "low", then the storekeepers soon were struggling, too, and "the companies" tried desperately just to keep going until the price of minerals should rise again. That was the time the mothers feared, clinging to their hard-won little homes. Should the mines close down, should the price of minerals fall so low that even the men working on their own could no longer knock out a crust, should the storekeepers fail. . . .

That was the time when the work of such men as Moffat, Newell, and Mulligan really was felt, when "the jobs" held against the strain, for those jobs were the result of the often hard-won development of discoveries those men had made, whether of mineral or pastoral or agricultural or timber lands. So many a worried mother during those recurring periods of troublous times thought deeply of those men who had done and actively now were "doing things". And in little Tableland homes, kneeling beside the children at bed time listened to them whisper, "and God bless John Moffat".

Yes, John Moffat was not the only shining light by any means in the mineral development of the hinterland, but he is the only one, so far as I know, for whom the children of the district asked a blessing in their prayers.

Farther out in those Chillagoe lands an outstanding landmark on the Hodgkinson is a massive wall of rock overlooking "Mulligan's goldfield". A meeting-place of the aborigines from time immemorial, it had seen the passing of a thousand tribes. The first miners called this frowning escarpment "Mulligan's Monument" as a tribute to their prospector hero. In later years, to the surprise of the gold-miners, coal would be found beneath this massive rock and become the Mount Mulligan Coal-mine.*

Alas, coming years were to bring a day when the mountain would shudder with a terrifying thunder-clap. In that underground explosion in 1921 every man in the mine was killed. And thus Mulligan's Monument now broods over the resting place of many of his old mates of the golden Hodgkinson days.

* This new coalfield would not begin production for some years yet, not until that fatal year 1914.

CHAPTER XIV

OLD MICK THE GANGER LORDS IT

OCCASIONALLY our little group would take a day off, jump on the navvies' pump-car, and merrily pump our way out along the newly laid line to railhead. Here the busy gangs were working through the open forest country towards the big Tumoulin and Evelyn scrubs. I felt sorry for those lovely trees soon to feel the bite of the axe and come crashing to earth. There they would be sawn into gigantic logs and chained to railway trucks, the new railway would carry them back over the range down to the coast at Cairns, and steamers would carry them away to build houses and bridges in southern centres. Towns were being built from the Atherton and Tolga timbers, too.

They were great days, though, swinging to the pump-handle as the wheels went round in steely music while we hummed through blood-red cuttings newly hewn, between grey rock walls newly blasted. Then the open forest again and the new steel ribbons glistening ahead leading to the great scrubs.

For miles the sun-browned gangs were active, the toilers going all out on contract work and wages, too.

"Bend to it, you sons of devils, bend to it!" And the sun would gleam on sweating backs, gleam on shovel-blades as the earth shot up driven by muscles paid at so much a yard, or at eight bob a day. Tough-looking men among all these gangs, laughing-faced boys, too, with muscles already of steel. Above or among each gang a grizzled ganger walked with eyes at every strained back, at every clod of dirt, seeming never satisfied unless those clods were flying up to the embankment or into the dray; here and there a ganger seemed disgruntled even then.

"Bend to it, you——! Bend to it!"

And all would bend, those on wages at eight bob a day, too, and no mistake about it. The bucko mates of the old sailing-ship

111

days had a world-wide reputation for slave-driving, as man-killers in an all-in fight. They had nothing on some of the more notorious gangers of the old-time railway construction camps. I've seen murder on faces at times as such a sadistic ganger "roared" down into a cutting, the suffocating sunlight within the enclosed rock walls gleaming on the bending, rising, bending backs a-lather with sweat as the "slaves" toiled at pick and shovel, hammer and drill.

In those times jobs often were scarce indeed to come by, hard to hold. Men have ground their teeth in brutish rage as they stabbed their shovels into heavy, often sodden earth, back-breaking clay or broken rock, their straining bodies panting to leap up and swing the shovel and whizz down the gleaming blade and cleave some hated ganger from head to belt.

The cynical ganger on top would calmly see and know, knowing also that fear of the sack, or at the worst, fear of the hangman's rope, would save him.

As for any poor persecuted wretch who could stand it no longer —well, he could throw down his shovel, roll his swag, and go. To trudge along some lonely bush track with empty tucker-bags, with the "cark" of the crows for company.

Little wonder that occasionally, along some railway line or other, some particularly nasty "accident" would happen to a notorious ganger.

With contract work, though, the toilers made slaves of themselves and their mates, too, for they were paid by results.

I know. I have been a "slave" myself in cane-cutting gangs. Man's inhumanity to man. . . .

We'd stroll along an embankment and Mick would have a word or two with each ganger, while the men below would glance up and grin and yell, "Here comes the gentleman tin-scratcher! Just look, boys, what the breeze has blown along." "Whacko, boys! Take a bo-peep at comrade Michael Moore! The capitalistic old rort, he don't work for wages no more!"

"He's thrown away his bowyangs!" would come a yell from down the line. "He don't get the navvy's dust up his panties no more."

"He dusts his tender skin with powder instead!" a bearded navvy would roar. "That nasty navvy dust chafes his tender undies."

"Uses his sweat-rag for a hanky now," someone else would be sure to add. "Don't blow his nose with his fingers no more."

And Mick would grin down and yell ferociously, "Bend to it, you sons of mules! Bend to it!"

And some clay-daubed toiler would shout, "Ho, boys! He don't swing the whip no more! Look at his lily-white hands! Twirls beeswax on his moustache instead of axle-grease!"

"Sniff the scent on his whiskers—all lavender an' roses fresh from me lady's boo-de-wah!"

"Takes his feeds like a gentleman! Lolls in his bunk till midday —his vally brings me lord his shavin' water!"

At which Jim Bell would scowl darkly while Mick smiled tolerantly as we strolled along the line to a running fire of comments.

"Here comes Gentleman Mick the ganger, and he don't wear bowyangs no more, no more, no more!"

"Wears them noo-fangled gentleman pyjamas now! Silky fluffies with lace down the middle!"

But Mick disdained these insults. He was enjoying himself. He was obviously popular with the gangs, his quaint old nature could not have made him otherwise. But I began to realize how relieved he would feel if only he could be sure of making a living by independent tin-scratching, to be free of all this.

As we were walking along the edge of one cutting a navvy was toiling below in the broiling sun without his hat.

"Put on your hat," yelled down the ganger, "before the sun spoils your brains!"

"I ain't got none!" snarled up the man. "Or I wouldn't bloody well be slavin' down here." But he put on his hat, and bent to it.

At a mullock-shifting job a young new-chum had just been put on. He stood among the busy gang gazing round in a dazed sort of way.

"Here, you!" roared the ganger as he pointed to a wheelbarrow. "Fetch that locomotive along here!" The emigrant gazed helplessly round and saw a haulage engine puffing down the line.

"But I ain't never been used to drivin' one of them!" he replied plaintively. To the roar of laughter we walked along towards the next gang. Life often seemed hard to new-chums before they were broken in.

That evening, when we were comfortable round the Council Fire, Jim Bell grinned.

"That new-chum who mistook the engine for the wheelbarrow reminds me of a new-chum in Chillagoe," he said. "Only this bloke was an Australian who'd drifted out to the 'End of the World' from the cities, he'd never done anything but push a pen in his life before.

" 'Ever done any mining?' asked the manager.

" 'Yes.'

" 'Very well then. Go down with the afternoon shift.' So the hard-up stepped into the cage and went below—he nearly lost his insides when the cage dropped down. He stepped out on to the platt.

" 'Got your spider?' asked the shift boss.

"The new-chum stared at the drive, looking for a spider's web. The boys saw he'd never been down a mine before. The shift boss took pity on him, gave him a spider with a lighted candle in it, and pointed. 'Step out,' he ordered, 'and just follow the light until you come to those trucks of ore ahead. Then wheel the trucks back along the line, and tip them down the chute.'

"The new-chum didn't understand how to tip, of course. The first truckload he shoved along went crashing down the chute, ore and truck and all. The rattled new-chum at last found the shift boss and reported: 'The box has gone down the hole. I'm going up. I cannot manage this work.'

" 'No you're not,' said the boss encouragingly. 'Go down and get that truck. You'll soon get used to the work.'

"The new-chum groped his way back to the chute, stared down, and at last came back to the boss.

" 'I can't find the box,' he said miserably.

"The boss went back with him and there was the truck lying upside down in the bottom of the chute.

" 'There it is!' said the boss a bit snakily. 'Can't you see? Go down and get it!'

" 'No it's not!' insisted the new-chum. 'My box has got wheels on the bottom—but this one has wheels on the top!' "

"They do make stupid mistakes at times." Old Brookes smiled. "Though it's quite understandable, the conditions and work being so strange to them. Like a new-chum in the Girofla put on to hammer and drill work. Of course, he swore he knew all about it. He sat down all right and held the drill in the bore hole. The hammer-man struck smartly several times and then again, puzzled that his new mate never turned the drill.

" 'Turn the drill!' he said irritably.

"The new hand lifted the drill out of the hole and turned it upside down, then waited for the hammer-man to strike."

"I'll tell you one about a hammer-man," chuckled Tommy Turley, "only he wasn't a new-chum, he was the best hammer-man we had in the Ironclad. And the new hand who had been put on to handle the drill wasn't a new-chum either, it turned out he was an expert. The misunderstanding was his, though. You see, our hammer-man was cross-eyed. As he swung up the hammer the new hand called out. 'Hold hard! Are you going to strike where you are looking?'

" 'Yes.'

" 'Well, I'm not going to hold this drill then!' "

By quaint coincidence, in the near future I was to see the very same misunderstanding happen in Rossville away north on the Cooktown side.

"The new-chum soon makes good," said Mick indulgently, "but he's got a hard row to hoe at times. I've gone out of my way to help him."

"The blind leading the blind," murmured Jim Bell.

"Maybe so," Mick replied good-naturedly, "but I think it was that fellow feeling that makes us wondrous kind. I was a new-chum once, a new-chum to life. And to cure my mistakes my old man belted what he called sense into me at a very tender age."

"Pity he didn't start sooner," mused Jim.

"Your old man must have been pretty hard, Mick," suggested Garnet.

"He was. As tough as the mulga. But then he had to be. And he treated us all alike. Those were hard times. Mum and he had to slave to give us youngsters a crust. And my younger brother could eat a crust and a half, believe me. He was always hungry. He used to eat his dinner early, then cadge some of mine. I could near do a man's work when I was twelve, brother had to turn to when he was ten, for there always seemed to be other little brothers and sisters coming along to be fed. And they all seemed to be hungry, we were a hungry family, as poor mum knew too well. That young brother and me had to go out with the old man and horse and dray to give a hand with his wood-carting. The old man got fed up with the young brother cadging half my dinner from me so one day he ordered brother put his dinner up a tree and leave it there until dinner-time.

" 'I'll skin your hide if you don't!' dad promised, and we knew the old man would go darn near to keeping his word.

"Well, young brother turned up at the dray at dinner-time with a very long face. I was boiling the billy.

" 'Well,' demanded dad, 'and what have you done with your dinner?'

"The kid looked miserably anxious—he had cause to. 'I *did* climb a tree and put the dinner in a branch, dad. But when I wasn't looking a big black crow came an' gobbled it.'

" 'Ah!' said dad and started to unbuckle his belt, changed his mind, took a horse-sized chew of damper and cold mutton and declared, 'Ah well, a crow that can beat a bush boy for his dinner is a better crow than the boy. Now the only way you are going to get your dinner is to catch that crow and eat it!' And he wouldn't let me sneak the kid even a damper crust."

"A rough life, Mick, from the little you've let us know from time to time," said Garnet, "and it's to your credit, young fellow my lad, that you haven't allowed it to blunt your generous impulses or dull that poetical nature of yours. By the way, Mick, I've noticed that when you feel safe from discovery and pursuit you occasionally head your 'passion' letters 'Wondecla'. It is only poetic justice that you should explain the reason why to the Council."

"Fancy writing a love-letter from Nigger Creek!" Mick grinned. "Why, a man wouldn't possess a soul who'd do it! Not when he can pen the epistle from Wondecla, tree-lined Meeting of the Waters."

"Nigger Creek is a good enough name for *you*, suits you down to the ground," said Jim Bell sarcastically, "seeing as you're as ugly as an armful of monkeys."

"Beauty is but skin deep," murmured Mick.

"Then *your* hide must be thicker than an elephant's," replied Jim. "Why, you've got a face on you like the hind part of a monkey that a camel has trodden on. You and your Wondecla! That flowery lingo of yours will bring you your Waterloo some day," he prophesied darkly.

Mick's reply was his usual amiable grin.

"Been writing poetry again, Mick?" asked Garnet curiously.

"Well—yes and no," answered Mick guardedly.

"A love-letter?"

"Well—yes and no."

"Come now, you old rogue, out with it!"

"Yes," admitted Mick.

"Why are you so sentimental, Mick?" asked Garnet curiously.

"Because all lovers are happy," answered Mick quietly, "and I am a lover of lovers."

Jim Bell's scathing remark was drowned in a roar of voices, a thunderous stamping of feet from the flat down by the river.

When the natives gathered for corroboree they made the welkin ring of nights; their black bodies looked like devils dancing amongst the flames. They never stayed long, soon drifting back to the silent, gloomy scrubs. Alas, I suppose rapidly advancing civilization has quite wiped them out by now. What interested me most was their huge wooden swords. Some were almost the length of a man with blades six and seven inches wide. These giant swords were of hardwood, a terrible weapon should their descending weight catch a man fair and square. The warrior, of course, had to swing the weapon with both hands. He'd dance himself fighting mad then rush his opponent like a demon. Some of the swords were much smaller, and were used with a painted shield. Even so the sword was so weighty that the warrior would rest its point upon the ground while he howled defiance at his antagonist. Then he'd whip up sword and shield and they'd rush one another with a thump and thud of weapons while the women shrieked like mad things.

In half a lifetime's wanderings all over the continent I've never seen any other aboriginal tribes use swords—only those few in the depths of the big scrubs back of Cairns.

"Now that we can hear ourselves speak," coaxed Garnet when the stamping of the corroboree died down a bit, "tell us about your very latest epistolary effort, Mick."

"Stone the crows!" exclaimed Jim. "What race is *that* in?"

"The Nigger Creek Cup," laughed Garnet. "But come on, Mick, out with it!"

But Old Mick quite cunningly shelved the issue. Maybe my gloomy prophecy had made him cautious. For his last epistle had been addressed to the comely young wife of a policeman in Cairns. I knew, for in secrecy, with no little pride, he had shown the letter to me. If that pugnacious young husband ever got hold of that heart-throbber he'd take a blue fit.

"Be careful, Mick, whatever you do," I had warned. "That young policeman has got the name of being pretty smart. And he's so jealous he treads on his own shadow. You'll be getting an awful hiding one of these days!"

"Have no fear, lad," he said, grinning. "If they can catch Mick Moore red-handed doing his good deed then they can drown me in Nigger Creek."

"Which someone assuredly will one of these days," I declared. "There's a deep waterhole so handy to your camp."

"But what a lovely spot for a ghost to walk at midnight! Have you ever noticed the beauty in those tree-lined pools in the light of the full moon?"

CHAPTER XV

THE POETS OF NIGGER CREEK

THE irrepressible Garnet, in his clean white shirt, ironed pants and tidy boots, strolling across to camp each evening after imbuing the happy-go-lucky though scanty youth of Nigger Creek with their daily dose of knowledge, kept egging me on to write another "pome".

"Just to keep the flame of the Muse alive in the Council, Jack," he coaxed. "You know, it's great fun."

"For you, yes," I replied. "I do the braying, you do the laughing. No thanks—never again!"

Cunning Old Mick, of course, backed up Garnet.

"You can go and jump in your own Nigger Creek," I told him. "You made a goat of me once! Never again!"

But a paragraph in a southern newspaper, tickling my silly fancy, actually produced the "pome".

The moon on the great night showed a considerably enlarged audience; these mildewed old notes make mention of two swaggies, a wandering Indian hawker, and two stray, expectant-visaged dogs. But I smirked at the firelit faces, absurdly pleased with my silly little effort.

"On your own heads be it," I explained generously. "You've asked for it. You know I'm not a *real* poet like Mick. This verse only came to me when reading this newspaper paragraph—which reads: 'At a recent Medical Congress, a woman doctor gave her opinion that the increasing troubles of women-folk are due to the fact that the human organs are reverting back to the animal form from which Man evolved.' And this medical wisdom suggested I write this 'pome', entitled 'When Girlie Goes Looking for Nuts'."
I cleared my throat and read:

119

"The doctors tell us that our bones
   To them a tale unfold,
   Of how we're degenerating
   From the usual human mould.

"For we are slipping back, they say,
   To what we were before,
   And by our tails will swing from trees
   In a thousand years or more.

"But this to me seems passing strange,
   'Tis laughable if true,
   I pray my ghost will live to see
   The troubles it will brew.

"How will a politician look
   If monkey he must be?
   Will he harangue the crowd for votes
   While sitting on a tree?

"And will he promise them the nuts
   Of others that he'll scatter,
   And waste the precious fleeing hours
   On things that do not matter?

"What tickles me, though, most of all
   Is how will Girlie take it—
   Will she quite spring up from her tail
   Should a male monk strive to shake it?

"And will she comb her pretty fur
   Then gaze upon a pool?
   And will she fold her furry tail
   When sitting on a stool?

> "Or will she pass her time of day
>   In looking out for nuts,
>   Or coyly wander through the bush
>   A shyly meeting knuts?
>
> "Or maybe she will climb a tree
>   And crack upon her knees,
>   The really choice collection
>   Of her daily catch of fleas.
>
> "Oh joy 'twill be if I am there
>   To watch the pretty dears,
>   To watch their little antics
>   In another thousand years!"

The response was all that any poet could aspire to though one of the stray mongrels, not to be outdone, began energetically scratching an ear.

"Get to blazes out of it, you flea-bitten mongrel!" ordered Old Brookes. "Spraying your fleas all over us!"

"No wonder," said Jim Bell, "after what he's just had to listen to!"

"Now, Jack, that really *is* poetry!" declared Mick enthusiastically. "You just *must* send that to the Bullerteen!" and his grizzled old face was all lit up.

"Bravo! Bravo!" Garnet clapped. "Milton and *Paradise Lost* have nothing on the poets of Nigger Creek!"

"Except fleas!" said Jim Bell.

"Shut up, you goats!" I protested.

"But it's real good, Jack," declared Old Brookes solemnly, "and so true to life!"

"I'll say it is!" chirped little Tommy Turley. "So true to life— I've met a few women in *my* time!"

I grinned across at the chuckling Jim Bell and half-heartedly challenged him. "Out with it!"

"I've heard worse," he declared, "from Mick—and once from a navvy in the horrors!"

But he was talked down from all sides.

"Jim just hasn't got a soul!" declared Mick. "Take no notice of him, Jack."

"The only sole I've got is where it counts," snapped Jim, "as you found out yesterday when you trod on that rusty nail! And it wasn't poetry you spouted when you hopped around, either."

"Quite true," replied Mick placatingly, "but then, no man can be prepared for every emergency, accidents happen him from the cradle to the grave. But that 'pome'!" and he smiled towards me. "Real true to life it could be. Why, I remember right now when I was an innocent lad, active as a monkey, dad chased me up a sapling—he meant to chastise my rear with a belt. I grinned down defiance from high in that safe refuge, thereby finding out I little knew the deep cunning of my parent. Keeping a baleful eye upon me, he retired to the woodheap, but right smartly returned with the axe. And I felt the ring of doom as the axe bit into that quivering tree. It began to sway most sickeningly, with me clinging like a frightened monkey up in the breezy void. It leant slowly over, toppled, crashed down with a *whoosh*!—but I had jumped clear as it hit the ground and was racing for the mulga while my respected parent raced to loose the dogs and sool them onto me. And I had barely dived into that sheltering scrub, had not quite reached a friendly tree before my distant parent stood transfixed with pleasure at the music of my agonized howls."

We applauded this youthful reminiscence while Mick grinned ruefully.

"You coves have never experienced the fangs of an ambitious dog tearing into the seat of your pants while you are in a hurry to climb a tree. I can assure you you *cannot* climb that tree—I can feel those fangs in my vitals now! To return from a painful subject, I learnt a moral from that story—be wary of monkey tricks. Moreover, when the old man means business, be certain that your tree is too big to be cut through in a day. Moreover again, be certain its branches are too high for him to reach you with a rock!"

"Too right!" laughed Jim Bell. "My old man has caught me bending, too, more than once! And I hope you've also learnt the moral that next time you tread on a nail be sure you have your boots on."

"We live and learn," said Mick.

"If you've got anything to learn *with*!" said Jim pointedly.

"Now, you boys," Garnet broke in, "ease off the back-chat. *You* tell us a yarn now, Jim."

"Silence is golden," replied Jim.

"That's why we haven't a feather to fly with," said Mick mildly.

"You smirking old baboon," declared Jim wrathfully, "if you'd do a bit of toil instead of scribbling poetry we *might* knock out enough coin for the storekeeper."

"But you've been doing a lot better lately," said Garnet encouragingly to Jim. "Your ground is making richer all the time."

"No," replied Jim despondently, "we're too unlucky. If it rained tin it would be sure to fall down on the other fellow's claim."

"And rain does fall that way, too," said Mick brightly. "Why, the selection next to ours always had more rain than we did."

"Why?" asked Jim suspiciously.

"Because they had more land," chuckled Mick.

"Pity it didn't drown you, you moth-eaten old relic," replied Jim disgustedly.

"Come on, Mick," said Garnet, "tell us some more about your boyhood days."

"Those boyhood days!" sighed Mick. "Oh, why does man grow old?"

"Because he's got time," growled Jim.

Garnet refused to be put off. "Now, Mick, you must have had a boyhood of sorts. Tell us about the times when your mother was wondering, 'Where is my wandering boy tonight?' "

"Ah!" sighed Mick. "Times have changed. In my young days, poor mother used to wonder where her wandering boy might be. But now the lads spend half their time wondering where mother is."

"You old reprobate!" Garnet laughed. "Why, you're much more sentimental than I am. Tell us about your first love-story then."

"Lost in the mists of antiquity," sighed Mick. "Vanished with the wraiths of romance. But," he added modestly, "I'm sure *she* made the first advances."

"Stone the crows!" exclaimed Jim Bell helplessly.

"Just the facts of life," went on Mick evenly. "Experience has proved to me it's really the female of the species who is the hunter."

"Go on Mick," Garnet urged. "Let's hear that love-story."

"I've lost track of the one I was going to tell," answered Mick mildly, "but she was lovely as a rose in the moonlight."

Jim Bell clutched his chest, breathing heavily.

"But which one?" demanded Garnet.

"Oh," said Mick, "the one I told she was the prettiest girl in the world. She whispered I was a handsome boy."

"She was blind," declared Jim decisively, "and dumb as a fried egg. If she'd put a hand over *your* face she'd have thought she was stroking a gorilla!"

Mick sat smiling at the fire. "She used to kiss me lingeringly. I was flattered until I tumbled to it that she was just smelling me for some other cat's scent." He sighed, then, "Ah, but her every sniff was a thrill to me! No lovesick girl ever waited so longingly for her mail as I waited to meet the postman's daughter. Ah!" He sighed again. "I loved that girl. But the local butcher put it all over me."

"But, Mick," protested Garnet, "I could never believe a poet would let a butcher beat him for the postman's daughter!"

"Ah!" sighed Mick. "Her father only owed me a tenner. But he owed the butcher fifty quid!"

CHAPTER XVI

JIM BELL'S PASSING WORRIES

MEANWHILE I had chummed up with my "Jungle Mate", as half laughingly I came to call him. Eventually I came to realize it was *he* who had chummed up with me—and then only for a short trip at a time when his irresistible "walkabout itch" came. For this man was essentially a "silent" prospector. He wanted no mate, he worked, and travelled, entirely on his own. Lived on his own, too. Not until some years later, when I had learnt through experiences in the Peninsula farther north, did I gradually realize why the Jungle Man had partially chummed up with me. It was because at times he became desperately lonely. He loved loneliness, loved all the lonely places and the beauty that so often broods there, but at times loneliness "got him". And something else that is born deep in human nature. *He had no one to tell his secrets to!*

Secrets of nature that he hugged to his heart, secrets of the wild bush that he had learnt in loneliness and I don't know what years of constant wanderings, seemed to well up within him now and then. Secrets of humankind, too. And far deeper, hauntingly elusive secrets that puzzled me uneasily on occasions.

How he intuitively realized I was so anxious to learn and would be sympathetic, I don't know. It was not until years later I realized how much I could have learnt from that strange man.

We had met casually in Herberton. To the few who took any notice, he was known as a very quiet chap. Came into Herberton occasionally for stores. Had a claim somewhere out on the Dry River. Was vaguely known as a wanderer. And that was all.

While Mick and Jim strolled across to the post office on our little business the stranger and I had yarned away in the sunshine sitting on our haunches outside Jack and Newell's store. He seemed a youngish man, only a few years older than myself—though I realized later that he could not be as young as he seemed

—but I soon found out that he was immeasurably older in bush experience. Eagerly I asked questions about the Dry River and the country around. He answered in a soft voice with a slight drawl that brought a chain of pictures to the mind's eye. Soon I was merely listening.

The Dry River, he explained, joins the Wild River near Herberton. Jim Mulligan himself had a claim there a few years back. The Dry River heads back south from Herberton into very rough country. From near Mount Misery Woolooman Creek runs into it, through country a goat could hardly scramble over. Good tin there, too. The Dry River heads in gullies like the wrinkles round a very old blackfellow's eyes, up by the Main Divide. Cross over the Divide and you drop down into Irvinebank.

"Maybe we'll take a trip across there some time, if you're interested?"

I nodded. "Any time will do me," I said eagerly.

"The Wild River watershed," he drawled, "is a maze of mountain-tops and spurs and ravines gone wild. You barely see the outline, down here by the river—it must have been a hell on earth in the days of the big volcanoes. The river valley is only a miniature now, compared to the valley of those times. Just across there—" he pointed—"is Chinaman's Hill, where Macdonald the prospector sank a shaft and found the first sign of the Deep Lead. The same that you're working on at Nigger Creek. Shafts running for miles, and tunnels have now proved that the Lead is really some old-time valley of a vast river system, long since filled up with lava. The Lead runs around the town roughly parallel with the present river right to Nigger Creek, where it junctions with another buried old river coming from under Bradlaugh's Gully. So right where your camp is now was once a sea of molten lava boiling on for miles over Flaggy Creek, we don't know for what distance. You know that the main river *did* carry on past Flaggy, for tunnels there have now proved to be half a mile wide—the Big Tunnel is driven in right through the old bed for three thousand feet and more—some tunnel that! Mazlin's Tunnel goes in over a thousand feet—a great job that, for working miners on their own resources in that dangerously unsafe ground. We don't know *how* big and deep and wide that old river was. You see how 'narrow' the Wild River is just across there? Well, imagine a river away below it half a mile wide and think how differently this country must have looked then! The mountains must have been much higher, too; if Herberton had been built those days we would have been perched thousands of feet higher up."

"Up amongst the smoke!" I grinned.

"How true!" He nodded grimly. "And hurtling rocks white-hot, the sky a dense blackness of fumes shot through with flame—as you'd realize if you knew of the old volcano craters stretching all the way throughout these ranges. Many of them have not been seen by white men yet. Jack and Newell's store would be made of white-hot pumice stone and we'd be queer-looking things with snouts breathing sulphur fumes instead of air. Where a man sat down to cool off he'd have to be made of asbestos, otherwise he'd burn his trousers! I've often thought of it when camped alone up on the old mountain-tops, gazing down here through the star-light." He smiled fleetingly. I was to learn he seldom smiled.

"Maybe there's asbestos men up in the stars," I suggested.

"I've wondered that way, too," he replied seriously. "Why not? Anyway, how differently the country must have looked then! The old bed carries on miles farther than Flaggy, of course, we don't know the end of it. Nor the beginning. Nor how many other ancient rivers lie buried under the basalt. By the way," he added, "have you seen the Old Crater yet?"

"No," I replied with interest, "but I've vaguely heard about it."

"Overshadows the town," he said, "so far as a crater is concerned. It must have rained hell and fury across here many a time, for a hundred miles and more. Much more. This particular crater is not so very far from your camp. Just a bit of a climb."

"I'd very much like to see it."

"Very well, I'll pick you up at your camp one of these days. Have you seen the Crater Lakes?"

"No," I replied eagerly. "I've heard about them and that's all. They seem to be very mysterious, and beautiful."

"They're both. They're down Yungaburra way. We may have a look at them, too. Easy to get at—only take a few days. But here come your mates. And I must get back up to camp. So long." Casually he stood up, with a nod to Mick and Jim, and strode quietly away.

Thereafter, before we took that "stroll", that "just a bit of a climb" to see the Old Crater, he appeared at Mick's camp twice. Just walked quietly in from the night into the firelight, nodded a greeting and accepted Mick's welcome to "a seat in the Council". He listened quietly throughout each evening, never speaking unless spoken to. And at the break-up each evening, with a "Good night, all", he strode away into the darkness, having quietly declined a camp with Mick or me. And yet his camp was miles away up along the Dry River. Whether he walked along on that rough climb where another man would break his neck, or just lay down and camped when he felt like it until sunrise, I don't know. He was always like that. But I was to learn he had owl's eyes, and was tireless.

"Quaint bird!" mused Mick.

"A lone wolf," declared Jim Bell. "I've met just one or two like him before—they're scarce, but they exist. Sort of bloke who would murder you nice and quietly, all very methodical like, as a matter of course. And not a soul ever know a thing about it."

"Oh, come now, Jim!" Garnet laughed. "He's a listener and exceptionally quiet, but I took a vague fancy to him." Which soothed my somewhat startled thoughts, for we all were familiar with true stories of murdered prospectors who had "dug their own graves", but never knew it.

The first evening that he came Mick was due to deliver himself of another "pome".

"It's a real masterpiece, Jack," chuckled Garnet when he had called for me that evening. "Mick is all het up and mysterious about it, fairly breaking his neck for you to come across and hear it. Come along, or Old Shakespeare will go into a decline with suspense."

It was when we were just nicely settled down that the tall

figure had stepped into the firelit circle. I thanked my lucky stars I wasn't the one who had to deliver a "pome". But he sat there and absorbed it all, making no comment even in the inevitable chit-chat at the finish.

And here is "Mick's Masterpiece":

THE BELLE OF NIGGER CREEK

Some say it's dark-eyed Polly,
More say it's Rose or Nell,
But I think it's only folly
To try and pick the belle.

There's lovely maids in Nigger Creek
Both white and black and brown;
And I think it's height of insolence
To look for girls in town.

For here you'll find the prettiest maids
That any could wish to see,
And some their colour never fades
Through dye of ancestry.

We'll toast them all in sparkling wine,
The dark ones and the fair,
And when we find that precious tin
We'll have a grand time there.

In an expectant silence Mick modestly closed his manuscript book. Then—"Well, of all the awful tripe!" burst out Jim Bell. "Is *that* the muck you've been chewing your pencil over for a week? He strains his tripe out and brings forth a gnat! Thank Heaven there's no more of it!"

Garnet tried to protest, but was gurgling with laughter, so the rest of us hastened to congratulate Mick.

"The best pome ever written in Nigger Creek," we assured him, "or ever likely to be!"

And Old Mick's grizzled face broke into a smile.

"To think that for a solid week," spluttered Jim, "I've been toiling down that shaft while this idiot—"

"I've been pulling up the buckets," protested Mick.

"Pulling my Aunt—"

"Now, Jim," broke in Garnet, "you've been toiling like a galley slave, we know. But then, you do not understand the throes of composing poetry!"

"Throws my fat aunt!" snapped Jim. "He'll have me throwing a seven one of these fine days. And *you* blokes will be to blame."

Old Brookes poured oil on the ruffled waters by declaring that while Jim was a good worker, Mick was a good poet. "The boot-maker to his last!" he declared.

"I don't know how long *I'm* going to last," said Jim morosely, "with a lunatic like *that* for a mate!"

"But then, Jim," chuckled Garnet, "the dividing line between genius and imbecility is known to be very fine indeed."

"Then he's gone over the line!" declared Jim. "Gone over by a mile!"

This, of course, set us all championing Mick.

"What if *you* take the floor tonight, Jim?" chuckled Garnet. "Come on, be a sport! You've often promised to tell us some of your reminiscences."

"It was on the tip of my tongue," said Mick.

"Then hang on to it," advised Jim disgustedly, "and you might get tongue-tied for once."

"Do you remember," asked Mick, grinning across at his mate, "that sourpuss of a waitress down in the pub we stayed at in Cairns? You remember, the one you complained to because there were flies in the soup?"

" 'An' what do you want for a zack?' she snapped.

" 'Civility!' you growled.

" 'Then take your money's worth!' she yapped, and slapped your face."

"Yes," said Jim. "What about that scraggy hen?"

"She's getting married!"

" 'Struth! *That* rat-bag! Who's the happy man?"

"Her father!"

I'm afraid we howled with laughter at Jim's expressive face, even the "Jungle Man" half smiled. Old Mick smiled angelically down at the fire.

"Come on, Jim," coaxed Garnet, "was that the pub you cleared out from because the lady cook put jollop in your soup?"

"No," answered Jim bitterly, "that was across on the Stannary Hills side. I'd been down on the Tate, doing a horse out of a job. I had one of those mates who believed in calling a spade a spade, but he didn't believe in handling one. So I rolled up the drum and mounted Shanks's pony. It was some walk those times, too, between job and job—tin was down. At last I landed a job shovelling mullock for the tightest skinflint I ever knew—always swearing money isn't everything, but he was too mean to spit on his shadow for fear of giving it a wash. He'd never have any but married men work for him, he could blackguard them to his heart's content, they daren't walk away from a job. But the single man would roll up his swag, maybe show fight as well. I told him I was camped with the wife down the creek. He asked if she was a black gin. I told him it didn't matter, I had four kids to keep anyway. That satisfied him. He introduced me to a shovel and heap of mullock a team of horses couldn't have shifted in a month. He told me to shift it in a week with a wheelbarrow or roll up the drum and go. He stood over me toiling at that mullock until even the pack-mules gave me away in disgust. When I fastened on to my first pay I rolled the barrow down the gully—and him with it —then rolled up the drum and went.

"I came on the pub in a little place in the hills, near Stannary. It was a civilized place, they even had a doctor in it. But if the poor devil *was* a doctor he was only there because he'd drink rum from an oily rag. The pub was an up-to-date pub, it had a billiard table in it. You know those crazy tables that were built when Adam was a boy? The green was in patches, where there was any green left. The balls were all of a fly-blown red colour; you had to learn to tell the red from the white by the shape of the balls—

some wobbled a bit more than others. The cues were home-made, the nigger rouseabout made them when he wasn't toiling at the woodheap.

"However, it was to be home to me for a week, anyway. My boots were worn out, I was dog-tired. If I couldn't get a job in a week at least I'd have a spell before hitting the track again.

"Just to make a show, I breasted the bar for just one drink; no matter how broke you are you're not accepted in polite society unless you do. There was one flea-bitten customer sprawling over the bar, and a publican built like a sack of horsemeat was sprawling towards him. By the nasty look on that baboon's face his customer was making some complaint.

" 'Yew carn't git better beer *anywheres*!' snarled the publican.

" 'Carn't I!' snarled the customer. 'I got my beer here larst week and I aint got better yet!'

"It was the same with the coffee," went on Jim mournfully. "They called it 'cawfee'. But you had to drink the whole flaming teapot before you got a taste of the 'cawfee'. Same with everything else. Even the fleas on the dog had taken to the scrub."

Jim filled his pipe in mournful retrospect. Reaching down to the fire, with expert fingers he lifted a live coal to the pipe bowl, puffed deliberately and resumed. "In what they called a room, my company was a fellow guest, a lucky one who had a job down at the Come-by-Chance. He didn't bother me—he drank himself to sleep every night so he wouldn't feel the mosquitoes biting.

"The cook—" Jim frowned—"was a cackling old hen who thought she was the Belle of New York. She had her eye on that poor devil of a doctor. She had a face like a horse-radish all mildewed through lying outside in the wet season. But she doctored it up with pig's grease and a touch of red ink, dolled herself up in her glad rags, sent for the doctor, and when she heard him coming sort of collapsed in the kitchen. And I'm blessed if she didn't show half a yard of lace strides. I know—because I was bo-peeping in on the old she-cat.

"Well, the doctor came. He would have been quite a decent sort if only he could have left the grog alone. He unfastened **her** duds, examined her in what seemed to me a real professional sort of way, thumped her scrawny ribs, pummelled her in the brisket, squeezed her navel—it was big as a salt-cellar—looked more and more puzzled. At last he doused her with water, and she come to. Groaned like a horse with the gripes, sat up, and yowled, 'Oh, what's *wrong* with me?'

" 'Nothing,' said the doctor quietly. 'You've got nothing to worry about. It's only a slight attack of faintness—merely a sign of advancing years.'

"She was on her feet with a yell, grabbed a saucepan and donged him. He went down like a pole-axed steer." Jim paused, glaring at the fire.

"Well?" queried the interested Garnet.

"Oh, there's nothing much more," said Jim. "I felt sorry for the doctor, and I was fool enough to start telling her what I thought of her. She didn't let me finish—I poked my bib outside that kitchen a damned sight quicker than I'd poked it *in!*"

"Well?" sniggered Garnet.

"Oh, there's not much more to tell," said Jim almost shame-facedly. "I left."

"Why?"

"Oh well, it was *that* night she put the jollop in my soup!"

"Did you remember to pay your bill?" laughed Garnet.

"Well, now, I did not!" answered Jim with a surprised glance at Garnet.

"And how did you get out of *that*?" persisted Garnet.

"Oh, I just put it down to running expenses," answered Jim modestly.

CHAPTER XVII

WE GO WALKABOUT

THE Jungle Man proved good as his word, for one chilly dawn he was suddenly within the tent, shaking my shoulder and in an urgent voice commanding, "Shake a leg! Shake a leg! The owls have gone to roost, the day is half done. I'll put the billy on, and we'll see the Crater today if you've nothing doing."

And he was out at the galley lighting the fire while I sat up in bunk, dream-hazy. For to me he was still miles away, asleep in his camp along the Dry River somewhere.

That was a glorious walk over the hills, though it was a bit tough climbing a "goat-track" through dense bush away up that rugged volcanic cone. Long since a decent track must have been cut up there for sightseers. Throughout this trip my strange companion was trying me out. He led, I followed. He proved tireless, but I could walk, too, for I had been compelled to carry the swag along some pretty dry tracks in New South Wales, and had already done about three years' prospecting on foot. I set my pace to that lean greyhound ahead and just walked—he did not encourage talk. In coming trips I was often to feel thankful I was only a handful of bone and skin and sinew with that enduring ally, plenty of wind.

The Old Crater was well worth the walk and the climb. Like the socket of a giant tooth, the deep hole yawned at our feet when we had pushed through the wild tangle of scrub that almost hid it. Rather marvellous, how the tender green life that the volcano had once quenched under a roaring sea of molten lava had come again and smothered it—all but the glazed core, the throat of this deep natural chimney, falling down there three hundred feet to dim, motionless water.

"No one knows the depth yet," murmured my mate, "a problem

difficult to solve. Mazlin and Joss found this old relic while searching for cedar, just pushed through the scrub and gaped down this hole."

"If it had been in the night!" I said.

"They would have vanished."

I shuddered.

Staring down from away up here, I found it easy to picture, even without the Jungle Man's outstretched arm and quiet voice, how this dead beast had overwhelmed all the fair countryside with its merciless rain of death, drowning the very streams under a sea of molten rock, burning forests to cinders, smothering life far and wide under clouds of poisonous gases. The Jungle Man was to show me on this and other trips similar dead craters and beautiful volcanic lakes hidden throughout those mountainous miles along the divide between the Barron and the Johnstone. What an unimaginable cataclysm must have rocked the very heavens over this huge area when all those awful things were thundering their brimstone!

But now, but for an occasional low moan down there of probably some wind current, the Old Crater seemed sullenly dead. An eerie quietness here, as with all these burnt-out old mysteries, as of some lingering, ghastly memory of the dreadful things they'd done. And still at this very day, away down there, the dull throat of the Old Crater seemed nearly perfect, as if it were only awaiting a polishing up. . . .

"Like the phoenix arising from the ashes," said a quiet voice.

The aptness of the words startled me. He seemed to have—he *must* have read my very thoughts!

I turned and gaped at him. His steel-grey eyes seemed strangely bright. A little grey bird in abrupt, circular, chirpy flight came swiftly up from away down in the crater. What a place to choose for a nest, a bush clinging to the burnt-out throat of a volcano! How did that life grow there? Did the bird realize how safe its babies would be from enemies down there? But then, how on earth would its babies ever fly up, with a sheer drop and that dark water below their very nest? The shadow of a smile flitted across his lean face as he gazed down into the crater. "The aboriginals," his dreamy voice was saying, "shunned the Old Crater, as they did all the craters and even the volcanic lakes, as the abode of evil spirits. It seems their ancestors in considerable numbers were living happily here from the eastern coast to the Gulf when the volcanoes exploded one after another. A few escaped through the Terror to build up the tribes again. They've told me remarkably strange stories about those times, their story-tellers are actually links in a frail chain of primitive humanity stretching right back to those prehistoric times—stories handed down from generation to generation. Anyway, from time immemorial now the local tribes have used the terrible fear of this place to keep their women in almost unbreakable subjection. But a frantic love will at times chance even a volcano. When a woman broke one of those unbreakable laws of the tribe she was dragged screaming all the way up here. Then the old men threw her out and over down into the Old Crater—to be the prey of the 'devils' you can hear moaning away down there." The quiet voice paused.

"The natives have assured me," he almost murmured, "that any of their women thus thrown down there—never came back!"

Again I was gazing at his calm, steel-grey eyes. I shivered. It was so plain that any woman, any man, *anything* once thrown out down there would never come back!

That evening, to my surprise, we were in Herberton, and in the morning on the Cairns train to Atherton, only about fourteen miles distant. I soon realized the Jungle Man lost no time while travelling in civilization. It was quite different, though, when he was in those queer reveries of his in the depths of some gloomy jungle, or sitting silently perched on a rock on a forest peak gazing out over a vista of peaks bathed in an ocean of sunlight. Such sights had a strange effect on me also, as if a man should glide up into space and just float away out and over. . . .

Atherton was a township in the building; I am told it is a fine town now. At that time it was only a few years since the Cairns railway had reached Atherton, but already there were signs that the camping place of the teamsters was being brought to a thriving agricultural life. Here, at the foot of the Herberton Range, the teamsters used to camp before tackling the long climb to Herberton. The ceaseless coming and going of that little army of toiling teams to mining camps constantly being discovered had formed quite an important, if tiny hamlet here. And the arrival of the iron horse meant permanent settlement.

The first settlers, while clearing their land, grew that precious stand-by of early Australian settlers everywhere—maize. But now dairymen were starting in earnest, many of them experienced men from the northern rivers of New South Wales, attracted by talk of the richness of big new scrublands in the Far North. As a schoolboy I'd watched the big scrub being felled along the Richmond near Lismore to make way for sugar lands, then dairying, and had seen development along the Clarence and the Tweed. And here, years later, to see the same phase starting all over again made this little walkabout all the more interesting, especially as the Jungle Man quietly kept me supplied with information on men, animals, timber, and incidents from the pioneering days of but yesterday to now. As in other trips, this unusual mate seemed to know everything.

My boyish interest, however, was first attracted by the josshouse, an elaborately barbaric affair in the little Chinatown close by. Here lived a compact little beehive of chattering Chinese in pantaloons and quaint hats, with droves of fowls and ducks all over the place.

The joss-house loomed large in the life of this industrious community, with its hideous joss, its ever burning incense, its garish pearlshell ornamentation, brass gongs, and queer-looking offerings, its slant-eyed priests. I was to become familiar with such reminders of the Orient in the North, I suppose they have mostly vanished now. Such Chinatowns were formed by the Chinese diggers who remained in the country after the Palmer rush. Many "grew into the country", the business-men among them became trusted and esteemed. And the storekeepers, once they had proved a white man trustworthy, would stick to him through thick and thin. Later on in Cooktown I was to meet such

Chinese storekeepers who were held in the highest regard by miners, sandalwood getters, bêche-de-mer men and shellers throughout the Peninsula. Perhaps genial old Ah Yam, known far and wide throughout the Hodgkinson district, was one of the better known. Goodness only knows how many diggers down on their luck old Ah Yam "stuck to". I hope he is receiving his reward in heaven, for he had a few bad debts here.

Authentic figures are impossible to come by, but old Cooktown records stated that twenty thousand Chinese came pouring into Cooktown for the "Strange Land of Gold". Most of them were to return to China fabulously rich men, for when the Chinese teams, working in a face, cleaned up creek or river-bed they left not one grain of gold behind. And we know that gold was taken from the Palmer in tons. However, many of these industrious workers were to die in the new land, though their bones would eventually go home to rest in the land of their ancestors. It was always a sacred trust amongst their living comrades to make certain that this would be so. And that trust was always faithfully carried out, except in case of shipwreck, or of those still more luckless ones whose bones, well gnawed, were thrown to some starving native dog.

There were those who did not even reach the mysterious southern Land of Gold, but were wrecked in the treacherous waters of the Coral Sea. One such disaster is surely the world's classic in cannibalism—the wreck of the *St Paul* on the Rossel Island Group, in Papuan waters. With 317 Chinese aboard, she was eagerly sailing to the Land of Gold. The barren reef on which she struck became their hopeless prison, more frightful, perhaps, because it was open to the sky and the wild sea-waves and the stars of heaven.

By canoe, the Rossel Island men, armed with spear and club, took the shivering castaways as they wanted them, in batches of ten, to an adjoining, fruitful island. Here they fattened them, just as we fatten pigs in a sty. Daily the headman tried them out, grabbing a handful of buttock, pinching arms and legs, while growling approval or disapproval of how the victims were fattening. When they were ready, these buck-toothed natives slaughtered, cooked, and ate them.

Long afterwards one demented wretch was rescued. He had survived only because he had been "recognized" and accepted as the reincarnation of the son of an Islander.

In those days of the little ships twenty thousand men were a hefty mob to transport in a hurry, even though packed like sardines. There must have been many human cargoes unloaded at Cooktown. Then their troubles really started. In gangs they started out in the tracks of the white men for the distant Golconda, through wild bush. And it was wild, too, alive with wild men. Even in my day, long after the Palmer rush, men were speared to death in the Peninsula.

A mile-long string of these coolie adventurers would set out, each, except the leader, with a bamboo pole across his shoulders from which were suspended the two baskets loaded so heavily that the strongest white man could barely lift the weight from the ground. Yet these bowed men kept at the jog-trot across those miles and miles of hot bush. They had learnt the knack of it, of course, in childhood.

As a rule, only the leader carried a gun. The gang would carry knives and clubs. They kept together for protection, and clung to the tracks of the whites. The aboriginal warriors were close on their flanks, eagerly alert for stragglers. These were promptly speared, and sometimes eaten, the hearty old abo declaring with gusto that the flesh of a Chinaman is considerably more tasty than that of a white man. So they have assured me and numerous other men, anyway, the Palmer natives in particular. Old Chinese diggers I was to meet several years later, farther north still, on Cannibal Creek, told me the same story.

"Chinaman hunting" was considered great fun by the aborigines. They ambushed the gangs, too, when the heavy-loaded toilers were tired and slowed down in crossing the sandy beds of scrub-lined creeks, and later again when they spread out amongst the thousand and one gullies and ravines of the Palmer.

It was a number of these "Palmer Chinese" who, liking the

country, eventually settled in Cooktown and formed the considerable Chinatown I was soon to know very well.

After Mulligan found the Hodgkinson many of the Chinese on the Palmer again followed the tracks of the white diggers, who, so easily gripped by gold-fever, rushed the new find. Again the Chinese diggers came plodding along behind, southward now through wild bush, again constantly ambushed on the long, hot track—with no protection from the whites now, who had gone before. Chinese diggers have told me of some grim fights when travelling gangs were cornered; it was drop baskets then and seize knife and club and scream to scare off "the devils" while the leaders would blaze away with what firearms they had. But attacking aborigines can yell, too, and such an encounter must have been a devils' pandemonium. Both sides must have looked and sounded pretty awful—the aborigines with their spears and throwing sticks, and the Chinese diggers with their few firearms and long knives, screaming frantically as they charged the agile men of the wilds. Some gangs which left the Palmer for the Hodgkinson never reached there.

These Chinese now settled in Atherton were mostly men from the Hodgkinson, for by this time Chinese diggers from the Palmer and Hodgkinson were to be found throughout North Queensland. Here, they had leased land from the early white settlers and were mostly engaged in maize-growing.

Several years ago had come the first land boom, and now white settlers were planting grass for dairying, while a tiny butter factory had just been established.

The little railway siding was a scene of quiet energy. Enormous logs were being hoisted onto trucks; the giants among them seemed bursting at their gleaming chains. Surely a little train like that would never succeed in carrying those towering logs down the gorge; surely trucks and all would be crushed under the great weights before even arriving at the lip of the falls! Or, if the puffing little train got far enough to start on that precipitous downward grade, surely its mighty cargo would hurl it crashing down into the gorge!

Before the railway, the mighty timbers of these scrubs were the pride and despair of men from Cairns to the Tableland. In my day, there among the big scrubs, the bulk and height of those beautiful trees had to be seen to be believed. They promised wealth untold to the earliest settlers, yet it was impossible to transport such great logs down the range. At last a powerful group of timber men—Burns, Philp and Company were interested, too—decided to attempt raft logs down the Barron River.

A great quantity of beautiful cedars were felled throughout a dry season, the logs transported by team to the river to await the coming of the Wet.

The thunderstorms came and the river began to rise, choked with the trussed rafts, the great logs groaning and straining at their shackles. Then the Wet came in earnest, the Barron swelled and came roaring down, and away went the logs.

The old-timers would never tire describing what must have been an awe-inspiring, a magnificent sight, as faster and faster the giant logs were drawn into the roar of the falls. Then they were over—avalanche upon avalanche of mighty logs hurtling over the lip of the falls. Vanishing in foam clouds to reappear in hurtling masses, drowned again in curtains of spray, seen for a moment falling at terrifying speed in water and foam, to reappear yet again like helpless matches in that green sea thundering down in its eight-hundred-foot fall into the maelstrom of Devil's Pool, far below in the jungle-clad gorge.

Very few of those magnificent cedars were swept unscathed down the river to Cairns. Some were splintered into matchwood, nearly all were badly damaged, some were tossed far up on the lower river banks. Even at this time, years later, a number were pointed out to me, hopelessly stranded. Some were caught in pools and would never work their way out, would be swirled round and round in the wet seasons of years until they were ground down to pathetic little sticks.

The disaster was never repeated. But now the railway had come.

CHAPTER XVIII

THE MAKING OF TOWNS

UP ALONG the dusty road came slowly toiling team after team of bullock-wagons, each wagon under a mighty log. Experts indeed were the bullock-drivers of Atherton and Tolga, Malanda, Millaa Millaa and the varied districts of coast and all the great hinterland. I never failed to stand and wonder at the bullockies parbuckling a great log to load the wagon, hauling it from the ground up the sloping skids to the stationary, securely chocked wagon. That rounded log would be tons of dangerously rolling weight should it break loose. The whole manoeuvre always had to be a masterpiece, with perfectly regulated movement to the very inch on the part of the team and judgment of time almost to the second, of balance and strain and movement to the inch, on the part of the bullocky. I always held my breath till the huge log was securely chained in place.

As we strode out along the road—it was then only a scrub-lined wagon-track—to Yungaburra, we saw again and again among the clearings in the timber the settler and often his wife busy among a forest of stumps, planting maize with the hoe, or planting grass-seed, or burning off, or building the first new home. As we walked along the Jungle Man mentioned, if my memory is correct, that settlers were encouraged in all ways possible, and were given 640 acres, with rights to the timber. Numbers of settlers, he told me, paid for their first crop, their horse and cow and fowls and fruit-trees and house, from the timber they felled and sold from the selection.

Because this settlement began in much later years, there was not here, Back o' Cairns, the destruction of untold millions of pounds' worth of beautiful timber, sent up in smoke, as happened in the settlement of similarly rich timber lands in southern Queensland and in all the southern parts of Australia—although, alas, quantities of lovely timbers had been burnt off before the railway came. There was a hungry and growing market for timber now, and the logs could be trained to Cairns whence ships carried them to Brisbane, Sydney, and other markets. But it was only the cream of these beautiful timbers that were sent to market. Much timber that would be invaluable today still had to be destroyed in the clearing of the land.

Thus were the scrub lands of the great plateau being opened up. Thus, too, the big scrubs of Tumoulin and the Evelyn would be cleared. Even now Mick the ganger's one-time mates were toiling out in the hot forest lands past Nigger Creek, laying the rails slowly but so surely to the Tumoulin scrub, bringing the iron horse—and the axe. But development also. And, years later still, so would the great Tully scrubs be opened up.

We strode along in happy mood, at least I was happy, not realizing my companion was hating what also brought a passing regret to me—the muffled crash from within the scrub as some giant was brought to the ground, tearing down an acre of trees with it. Again and again, too, came the sharp crack of a whip as away in there a bullocky cleverly manoeuvred his team along a narrow track hewn through the timber. To me, those cool, dark, leafy tunnels creeping into the great scrubs were beautiful. Now and again a loaded team passed us, toiling towards the railway, straining under some great log of cedar or pine, walnut or hickory, maybe of lovely satin-wood.

The beauty of the old volcanic lakes is still fresh in memory; I hope they will ever remain as they were. To me, they were breath-taking and mysterious in their wildness, with their haunting atmosphere of aboriginal superstition. Writing these lines, I hear a ghostly whisper, and there comes faintly to me the Jungle Man's voice as I gazed almost in awe down upon each lake in turn. Wherever he is—he may still be alive for all I know—wherever he went after our last meeting, I'll swear he never again visited the lakes once they became well known. As they are now a beautiful tourist resort I'll write no more about them—just visit them yourself.

We were travelling light. Carried a week's tucker at a time, billy-can and blanket each. Didn't notice the load. Slept where evening found us. The whole trip cost us only a few shillings each. I was learning how to travel surprising distances on a shoestring.

Along a bush track we made for Mareeba; my quiet mate wished to see old Pat Molloy, discoverer of Mount Molloy, on some business or other. From the cool depths of the scrub we stepped out into sunlit forest country of bloodwoods and tall spear-grass through which stretched a deeply rutted road red with red, red dust.

"What's the story of Mareeba?" I asked my moody mate.

"John Atherton, Jim Mulligan, Herberton, or the teamsters," he replied. "Take your choice."

"Which means?"

"Mulligan found the Hodgkinson. Which brought men swarming out into this then unexplored country. John Atherton, seeking pastoral country, found all this land out ahead of us, came along with bullock-wagon and buggy, wife and young family and cattle, plodded along round the Great Scrubs, struck the Barron and followed it down to the junction of Emerald Creek. Built their slab hut, reared the family, and formed the present Emerald End station from which you can see present day Mareeba. Just after the Hodgkinson, Jack and Newell found Herberton. Christy Palmerston, with McLean and Mullins, then blazed a track from Herberton through here across the Barron to cut the track from Port Douglas to the Hodgkinson. It crosses Granite Creek within sight of Atherton's homestead. That crossing is midway between Herberton and Port Douglas. Because of that, and the water-pools and grassy flats, it was just the place for a big camping ground. Which it became, the Granite Creek Coach Change, as soon as the pack-teams and wagons, then the coaches, began carting goods and passengers to the new Herberton tin-field. That camping ground became the township of Mareeba, which is going to grow into a big town. John Atherton built the first building there, a rest-house for coach passengers at the Crossing. As field after field was found it quickly grew into an important junction for the teamsters and carriers and Cobb and Co., for the camps and townships springing up practically from coast to coast. It quickly grew into a real town when the railway came a few years back. John Atherton has been active in the development of the entire district to this day, and his son Paddy is carrying on the good work. John Atherton is known far and wide as the founder of Mareeba. So there you are."

"H'm. Surprisingly flat country."

"Yes. And yet it is the divide between the Barron waters and the Mitchell, the crown of another tableland. The divide is so level, though, that the citizenry swear that when it rains along this road the water in one wheel-rut runs east into the Barron, while the other overflows westward into the Mitchell."

"So one wheel-track runs away east into the Pacific, the other runs west into the Gulf of Carpentaria and the Arafura?"

"Yes," he replied, "that's about it. Though your friends Mick and Jim would assure you you had water on the brain if you put it that way."

What my mate's business was with Pat Molloy he did not say. Fortunately, I did not ask. Knowing he was a "strange man", I had fallen in with his moods as best I could and we were getting along quite well together. There was plenty to interest me, anyway, in the constantly changing scenes through which we were steadily passing, and in yarns with the old hands when we came to some little township. He was never so patient on any other trip, as I was soon to learn.

The favourite yarn of that grizzled veteran of the roads, Pat Molloy, was how he found Mount Molloy.

It was soon after Jack and Newell, Brown and Brandon, had found Herberton. Molloy was a teamster carting stores from Port Douglas up over the Bump inland to the Hodgkinson goldfield. When the Herberton rush developed in earnest and the track was made through the Atherton scrubs to connect with the track between the Hodgkinson and Port Douglas, teamsters were offered big money to cart loading to the new tin-field, urged on by the energetic John Moffat. He had bought out Jack's share of this unusual discovery, the Great Northern, and shipped from the south a stamper battery to crush the stone. Maybe the team hauling that "old-time" machinery along the rough track freshly cut through the virgin bush was the largest team of bullocks ever yoked up in Australia, I cannot say. The old-timers assured me there were eighty-one bullocks in the team. And they and the wagon and the teamsters got the machinery there, a little epic of engineering in itself, just one page in the fascinating book of the development of the Tableland.

Pat Molloy's job, though, was with stores. With a fellow teamster he set out with both wagons loaded, safely they negotiated the Bump. One sundown they camped at Chinaman's Creek. Next morning half of Molloy's team was missing, having strayed away during the night. He was "pretty mad", for the teams were making good time, and Pat was anxious to strike the growing camp at the Granite Creek Crossing while the weather held good.

Several days later, still searching for the strays, very anxious now lest the natives had driven them away and speared them, Molloy rode up onto a ridge near Rifle Creek. Standing in the saddle, he shaded his eyes with his hand and gazed out over the country—a green ridge! He stared closely, for there was something strange about it; it did not appear to be the green of grass or shrubs. The harder he gazed, the queerer looked that ridge. He rode across to it and unbelievingly stared down at the bluey-green copper carbonate capping the ridge.

Thus was found the Mount Molloy copper-mine.

Pat kept the secret for several years, for copper then was at a very low price. Then for some years it was worked intermittently by different parties as the price of copper fluctuated. John Moffat and friends had erected a smelters on Rifle Creek now, a little railway would eventually creep out to this little mining township from Biboohra, a few miles down the line. Behind Mount Molloy, beginning at Mount Fraser, a range runs north to the Mount Carbine wolfram field. In a future trip to the Tableland I was to work right along that range, for a time on a mixed tin-wolfram reef on Mount Spurgeon. It was somewhere within the deep gullies of that sombre old mountain that Jim Bell's tough-faced old moonshiner had worked his illicit still. However, that trip was in the future.

Old Pat Molloy was to prove tough, like quite a number of the old-timers. He had quite a number of years stretching ahead along the track yet, he would not cross the Last Divide until 1923, eighty-three years young.

Ted Troughton, the bullocky who took the record load to the Hodgkinson, was another who lived to a ripe old age. He quietly started out on the Last Long Road at the age of one hundred and three. Genial old Ted was a dozen books in himself.

What books I missed in the yarns of those old prospectors and timber men, the packers, and teamsters, the drivers of Cobb and Co. and the earliest settlers! But shyness, alas, robbed me of all chance of a few little yarns from the women-folk, who were gamer than the men. For, after all, the men had the incentive of helping to "break in" a new country where the rewards could be golden to the lucky ones, and there was almost certainly a cheery security to all who stayed and worked—though this fact could only be realized at the time by the dogged, far-sighted ones. Whereas all that a woman had was the hope that her man might succeed in carving out a home, while she had the doubtful pleasure of looking after the brute. And some took a bit of molly-coddling, too. However, at the time all hands and the cook looked upon the job they had done and were doing as all in the day's work.

It was with regret that I heard my mate quietly say, "Right. This little trip is finished. We catch the train for Herberton tomorrow."

I'd seen quite a lot, missed learning a very great deal, on our "shoestring" trip. And I'd filled half a dozen notebooks with tightly packed scribblings—fuel for the "Bullerteen", and, though I never dreamt of it then, for this book.

Back at Herberton, I naturally was for stepping out for the camp at Nigger Creek. My strange mate, seemingly about to say, "So long, be seeing you", drawled instead, "How about a walkabout to the Dry River now? Then we can follow right up, cross the divide, and drop down on Stannary Hills or Irvinebank. An easy walk, then back along the Herberton road."

He seemed looking out over the distance, not at me.

"Right-oh!" I agreed, somewhat surprised.

Before I knew it I was following him across to Jack and Newell's buying "a bit more tucker", and, grudgingly, a few more notebooks. Then I was following him out into the hills, already shadowed by sunset. We camped "cosy" on a patch of warm sand sheltered by big grey rocks down in the quiet bed of the river, which is a raging torrent in the Wet. Sprawled on our blanket, smoking, my mate lapsed into one of his "quiet" moods, staring at the fire which reflected back from the rocks, throwing his cleanly featured, sombre face into bright relief—a thin-lipped chap with perfect teeth firmly gripping the pipe-stem. I quietly thought he would be a good-looking cove if only he would smile just a bit now and then. He was thinking about goodness knows what, that steely look in the hard grey eyes quite noticeable in the firelight, which was dancing playfully on the big grey rocks. However, I could be quiet, too; there were plenty of things to think about to keep a man company. Had I not fitted so naturally into this unusual mate's moods he never would have asked me on a trip again.

Rough country, the Dry River, growing rougher and rougher as we trudged up towards the watershed. Every here and there we came upon a camp where mates were stacking wash-dirt by bank or flat. Each such party ceased work to pass the time of day and ask the news. I soon sensed by their restrained, almost solemn manner that all these different parties, like my friends at Nigger Creek, did not feel quite at home with the Jungle Man. They had nothing at all against him, it was just that to them he was a bit puzzling, he was a "strange cove". The same reaction exists among boys at times, should a lad have a quiet nature and not mix in with schoolboy life. That the Jungle Man quietly resented this feeling about him I eventually became sure. But he got some queer satisfaction out of it, and retaliated inwardly with a feeling that was almost contempt.

These parties we passed at every mile or two were gully-raking and dry-stacking—that is, working the river-bed, bank, or terraces, digging out the wash-dirt and stacking it near a water-race—a narrow channel cut by hand—to shovel it into the race when the Wet came. For the Dry River heads in a belt of country that is dry indeed except during the Wet. That dry-stacking work is sheer, continuous navvying. I was soon to be very surprised to accidentally learn that my travelling mate, while working in a dry-stacking river, did not work by those backbreaking methods that sometimes yielded such poor returns. As Tim Ringwood, whom I later met away north on the Cooktown side, was so fond of saying, "It's all in the head, Jack, not in the back. A man can turn himself into a working bullock and hardly make enough to pay for his grass. While a little fox can lie low, bask in the shade, and nose out a fat feed with just no trouble at all."

The Jungle Man worked when necessary, but he certainly "worked with his head" also. I was to learn lots more about him.

CHAPTER XIX

I'VE GOT PLENTY TO LEARN

His camp was pitched in a snug spot near the mouth of Woolooman Creek, sheltered from storm winds by a rocky spur, a cool spot in summer, warm in winter and well above the reach of sudden floods. It was on an "easy" level, nicely drained. His bunk would be dry, no sleeping over sodden ground that would mean discomfort and maybe fever and rheumatism. There was something clean and efficient about that neat little camp, all that a man required, yet easy to pack up quickly. The same applied to his working and cooking tools. Well cared for, light to handle, all that was needed yet nothing cumbersome, certainly no lumber of any sort. His saddlery, sheltered from weather, was in apple-pie order. This man could pack up and move off at a moment's notice —though I did not notice this all at once.

From across the river somewhere came the tinkle of a horse-bell. He nodded in a satisfied way.

"My horses," he said simply. "A riding and a pack."

"Is that all you need?" I asked doubtfully.

"Yes. I can travel anywhere with two—a thousand miles if necessary. As a rule, unless I'm moving a camp, I only use the pack. It's easier in rough country, and especially in scrub. I don't mind walking. I do a lot of prospecting on foot, though, simply carry a few days' tucker."

We camped there that night, in the tent, for it was a bit chilly. While spreading the blanket I commandeered from the tent-side a couple of neatly folded bags for extra nap. Under the bags was a neat four-foot length of tin trough, very similar to a short length of roof guttering. What caught my eye, though, was that one end of it was neatly closed in, like a sluice-box. Under the hurricane lamp the bottom gleamed bright and shiny, as if worn smooth like the bottom of a well-kept, constantly used streaming box. Lying in

151

it was a flat piece of tin shaped just like and not much larger than a playing card.

"Sorry," I said. "Didn't know you had anything under the bags."

"It's all right," he replied quietly. "What do you think it is?"

"Blessed if I know," I replied doubtfully, "unless it's a toy sluice-box you've made for some youngster in Herberton."

"It *is* a sluice-box," he said. "I stream all my tin in it."

Sitting cross-legged on his bunk, hand cupping chin, pipe between lips, with not a flicker on his face, he seemed quietly enjoying my disbelief.

"Fact," he went on. "I stream all my concentrates in that box. As quickly and cleanly, perhaps more so, than you could with a heavy, twelve-foot wooden box and shovel. Also, I can carry it anywhere, any distance, and a bag of tin with it as well, if need be. Can put it in anywhere, creek, bank, terrace, ridge-top. To run a race into it I've only to dam up the creek water with a couple of handfuls of sand. Then again, a mere trickle will work *this* box, where the usual box would be hopeless. If distant from water, I merely scratch a race to this little beauty with the pick or—" he nodded gravely—"with the streaming shovel." And I stared down at the little oblong of tin lying in the box. "When I travel," he resumed and did not even smile, "you can see that the box is no weight for the horse to carry."

Blessed if I knew whether he was joking or not. Those tight-closed lips, that clean-cut face wore no tell-tale expression at all.

"I'll show you in the morning," he said. "Then you'll see it *can* be done!"

Laying down the pipe, he pulled off his boots and lay back in his bunk, hands clasped behind head. I rolled into my blanket on the floor.

"I work my claims a little differently, also, " presently came the voice from the bunk. "Never bother with dry ground unless, as happens very seldom, I wish to be near a town for a few months. Always work ground with, or very close to, running water—which is power. Choose the shallowest ground, never work deep.

And, even then, pick the eyes out of it. Prospect it. And only work those little patches here and there that carry good, payable ground. Then pack up, and look for another claim."

"That means you never waste time and labour working dead ground," I said haltingly, "but you'd never find a Deep Lead that way."

"I don't want to," he answered simply.

"But," I protested, "on one of these prospecting trips when you're roaming around you might drop on a rich claim, a good-sized claim rich through and through. You'd have to settle down and work it then."

"No, I wouldn't, I work it until I get tired of it. Then sell out, pack up and look for another. There are thousands of square miles of country still to be gone over here—there will be mineral still left in these ranges a hundred years from now."*

He reached up and blew out the hurricane lamp.

I lay there in the darkness thinking, it seemed, for hours. Thinking is the hardest work, but here was something to think about, how to make an independent living without being a "working bullock", as Jim Bell called it. When I thought of all the "dead work" that Jim and Mick and Old Brookes and Tommy Turley and I and many others bullocked through—and down there in the darkness of the earth, too! When I thought of the box we used—it took two men to carry it a few yards! When I thought of the sluice races we had to dig, of the heavy tools we used, of the often scarce, precious water we were so dependent on!

But I had a very great deal to learn about tin-mining yet. However, in years fast coming what I did learn from this strange man was to save me incalculable labour. And especially in gold-mining.

Birds were still squawking their joy of sunrise when we were plodding on "up the divide"; bird life in fascinating variety enlivened all those great tablelands. Steadily we climbed well out from the rocky banks of that now so dry Dry River. I was follow-

* That was fifty years ago. There still is mineral there.

ing the Jungle Man, though this was lightly timbered forest country with rugged outlines softened under early morning sunlight. Soon the lightening shadows still lingering in gorge and ravine would reflect bright sunlight from grey, hot granite walls, then dreamy coolness would give way to heat, the busy calling of birds gradually quieten to the hushed restfulness of midday.

It was glorious, this steady walking on and up past rock and tree over fallen branch and coarse grass where man as yet had made no track. Ever ahead, bold hilltops reached challengingly up, to right and left the steep fall-away of rocky ravines fairly shouted to the prospector an invitation to try their shaded, mysterious depths.

I was eager to do so, but, glancing at the ever advancing back of my now quiet mate, I instinctively hesitated to call out, "Shall we try this one?"

By the end of several days' tramping I realized he had no intention of trying; this little trip was merely a try-out to try *me* out, though he was carrying the prospecting tools that had interested me so much. As we climbed higher and the way grew rougher my eyes were watching the ground and continually rising to that little pick slung so easily at the back of his belt. It was no weight to carry and was not in his way; he could reach behind and whip it out at any moment. And yet we walked over reef after reef and he never knapped an outcrop once.

Any prospecting I had done so far was with a heavy, cumbersome five-pound pick, with a thick handle nearly three feet long. His slender handle was only a foot long, that toy pick and handle combined would not weigh two pounds. There was something else. One end of the pick had been cut off and fashioned by the forge into a hammer-head.

"A knapping hammer," he had explained, "for knapping a sample of rock from a reef."

Any knapping hammer I had yet seen had been several pounds in weight, and quite separate from a pick.

The other end of his pick was as delicately shaped as the beak of a crane, but slightly curved. I was to find that it was efficient for its work as the beak of a bird is to *its* job. And tempered to an amazing strength.

"For digging out a sample—anywhere," he had said simply. "On hillside, gully, or river. Particularly good for crevice raking."

Only experience was to teach me how efficient it was.

Up above his belt, his pack-swag rested easily over the sturdy shoulders; in a pocket on that pack was the prospecting dish.

I could not believe it. The usual large, wide, deep prospecting dish would hold a dozen such as this—dozens, should they be stacked together. A prospecting dish would hold ten, fifteen, twenty pounds of wash-dirt. This dish would barely hold a pound.

This dish was a baby, a *small* baby frying-pan, with the handle cut off. We could, and did, use it also as a frying-pan when we needed to.

"Why carry heavy weights of earth often long distances to water," he had asked the evening before, "when a few handfuls, if selected from the most promising ground, will do as well? When you're prospecting away from established workings tin in this district must be fairly rich to pay. If you cannot root out wash-dirt that will show a payable result for the quantity of dirt you can put into this frying-pan, then it is not payable. Not to me, anyway. As a matter of fact," he had added, "when bush prospecting, I rarely bother to use it. If I cannot *see* tin, whether 'dry' or 'wet', then the ground is not good enough for me to waste time over."

Seeing my complete mystification, he had almost smiled. "I'll show you one of these days how it's done—if we take a trip or two together. I use this dish mainly for gold."

At that magic word I was all ears—luckily, because too much tongue would have spoilt everything. In a dreamy sort of way the evening before he had spoken of gold, of "silent" prospectors, of hidden gullies, of mullocky leaders heavily studded with "golden plums", until well into the night.

And now the sun was blazing from a cloudless sky and he was climbing on just ahead, seemingly quite without effort. And also without a sign of showing me one prospecting secret, or how to use those baby tools I still could not quite believe in. How burdensome the usual dish and pick, let alone a shovel, would have become by now! I knew well how they seemed to grow weightier with each mile—just as a man's iron-shod boots would drag over the long, rough miles. I wiped a sweaty forehead with the back of my hand, staring again at that moving back, those long legs just ahead so effortlessly carrying not only prospecting tools but swag, blanket, and tucker!

All this man claimed for his methods and equipment he would prove true during other trips. In years fast coming the knowledge I gained from him was to mean never riches, but an independent living for me. And one regret—that through stupidity, or the exuberant carelessness of youth, I had not learnt ever so much more from my strange mate.

A brazen sun had passed just overhead when he called a halt, merely by turning round. As I came up to him he inquired, "Boil the billy?"

"You bet! But where's water, up here on top of the world?"

He merely glanced down by his right. And there, under the lip of a gully head, in a hole in a big flat rock gleamed a tiny pool. Cool nectar. Not until I had thirstily drunk did I notice the water was seeping from a spring in the bank.

"You've been this way before?" I called up.

He merely nodded. Bending, he already had lit a fire. I filled the billy and put it on. The sun-dried sticks, crackling briskly, were already at fierce heat. This man knew how to prepare a fire. He was gazing back.

"Which way would you say Herberton lies?" he asked musingly.

I turned around, stretched out an arm, and opened the big mouth. Then abruptly shut it.

Behind us stretched a vista of descending hill-crests, gullies and ravines far as the eye could see, a serrated maze of broken country going on and on. But the gullies, only partly visible here and there among the ridges, surely seemed to be running in the wrong direction! Hastily I squinted towards the sun. Even the dashed sun seemed to be "travelling wrong"—walking lightheartedly behind this man, I had failed to register direction. Warily now I noted the direction of my shadow, then turned again to gaze back over that country.

The silent devil must have taken a sharp turn when coming to that spring, just to confuse me. He had!

It took quite some moments to trace where those seemingly criss-crossing gullies must drop down into the Dry River, then carefully follow the lie of the country where the river would twist and turn on its fall for miles and miles among those ridges to join far away down there with the Wild River, then follow the Wild River to Herberton.

Slowly turning, I stretched out an arm.

"About there!"

"Not bad," he murmured and, turning to the fire, dropped in the tea and lifted off the billy.

To hell with *you*! I thought.

CHAPTER XX

MY STRANGE MATE

Hot billy tea without milk. The simplest of meals sauced by ravenous appetite. Purest air carrying a lingering whisper. The tang of trees surfeited with sunlight taking their midday doze, insects busy in their struggle for survival in their great forest, the stunted bushes and warm grass-tufts.

I leant back against a rock—there were rocks everywhere—lazily taking out the pipe. Yes, it was good to be alive. Curiously enough, in the clearest of skies three big white fleecy clouds were majestically sailing just overhead, one following the other, slowly changing shape.

Three old-time ships, I thought, quietly taking in sail, manoeuvring for a cosy anchorage in the Coral Sea. And if the waters are bluer than that sky, then I'm a Dutchman.

He was slowly filling his pipe, gazing away out over distance. I remember idly thinking he might be a much stronger bloke than he looked—he was built for endurance, anyway. A few cheeky birds, despite the wildness here and the heat, were twittering near by, hopping gradually closer, cautious yet clearly expectant. I glanced round, feeling mean—we had not cast aside a crumb.

"Oh well, remember next time," came a murmuring voice.

He was filling his pipe. I gaped at him.

"I was dreaming," I said uncertainly. "I didn't quite catch what you said."

"You felt nice and sorry about the birds," he replied quietly. "You were thinking we were greedy pigs. Oh well, we won't disappoint them."

Coolly he threw them a couple of crusts of damper. He'd kept those crusts out of sight behind him. It was days later before I became firmly convinced that this cunning devil had deliberately tested me to learn whether I felt kindly towards birds.

He had lit his pipe and got it going well. Eyes half closed, I waited for him to say something.

"Better be going," he said quietly. "It'll be rough going before we make camp."

He reached for the billy, tipped out the leaves, hung the billy on his pack-swag, slipped it over his shoulders, and seemed to be standing up in the one movement. Surprised and disappointed at having been done out of a midday smoke and yarn, I slung on the swag, too. The birds hopped warily aside, the greedy ones protesting.

He faced south and pointed almost west.

"Mount Misery!" He nodded vaguely towards hill-crests that might have been left-overs from the moon. "Deserves its name, too. Woolooman Creek heads near there. We'll soon be up on the divide now. A bit of rough country before that, though!" He started off.

That bit of rough country *was* rough, just a sea of ravines, Nature's deep-scoured furrows of millions of years of wear and tear. A man with a careless foot could easily break his neck here, let alone a leg. I took care not to, with a wary eye now on direction. Back there the curious thought had struck me how easily this man could slip a man up, back there where he had tried to bamboozle me as to the direction of Herberton. From there, I would have had enough bush sense to have found my way back, it would be much more difficult now. If a man were a new-chum, and had a row with this man, why—he could simply disappear! In a case like that an inexperienced man in this deceptive and terrifyingly rough country, nearly waterless as it now was, would probably panic within a few hours. I began wondering yet again at my strange mate, while carefully now memorizing direction. Steadily he climbed on, and down, and up again, and never once suggested we try this fascinating country all around us. The rocks, the reefs, the deeply scoured ravines were simply crying out of minerals— perhaps gold! And he was to have shown me—I realized now that was only the *impression*—how to prospect even without water. Surely he must be making for some even better-looking country farther ahead!

Suddenly he turned with a warning finger to lips. Motionless, I watched his finger point down towards his feet, then back slowly out across the bush.

His finger traced a wallaby pad leading faintly yet distinctly through the grass, then over bare rock into grass again, such a constantly used pad as undisturbed wallabies make to and from a watering place or favourite shelter. Motionless we stood. Plain now the murmur of the bush, only the faintest whispering of air currents rising up from the ravines, faint hum of insect life, screech of a parrot. Distantly then, but distinctly, a soft "Thud! Thud!"

In amazement I realized this man had heard that wallaby moments before, and even while he was walking!

Came that "Thud! Thud!" again, a little closer. I could picture that lazily contented wallaby day-dreaming as he came leisurely hopping along. I grinned at the silly thought that he might have a meet on with a girl-friend.

His ears, head appeared, his forepaws, then the little hunched-up body slowly hopping towards us amongst the tall, coarse grass-tufts.

He came hopping to within six feet of my mate, who hissed loudly.

That wallaby's forepaws hit out as if warding off a blow; he jerked back upright on his tail, his whole body swaying agitatedly, prick ears outstretched and twitching to every air current, his nostrils dilated and sniffing, his eyes big with fright.

He simply did not *see* us! He was staring straight at my mate, then his pretty head jerked towards me. I though he was going to fall back over his tail as he sniffed agitatedly to locate the very danger his dilated eyes were staring at. We were dressed in grey flannel and grey dungaree trousers like the grey granite rocks, faces, arms, chests, sunburnt like the sun-baked earth, and we stood utterly motionless. The shock was so unexpected he seemed to have lost power either to see or smell us. My mate said, "Hullo!" and the wallaby's head jerked back to the sound, then it plunged uncontrollably forward straight against my mate, bounded sideways, struck a rock, bounded aside again, and was away down a gully in frantic leaps that I thought would break its neck at any moment. At that volley of sound of swishing bushes and stones rolling down into the gully I broke into a peal of laughter. And my smart mate, who must have had the wind pretty well knocked out of him, laughed too, a quiet laugh, but the first one I'd heard from him.

Still laughing, I squatted on a handy rock and pulled out the pipe.

"This is worth a smoke-oh!" I chuckled. "Best laugh I've had since I put the billygoat in Old Mick's bed."

With a bit of a smile, he sat down and pulled out the pipe.

"Yes, that wallaby got a shock," he said casually, "as did Mick when he woke up to find the old billygoat breathing across his face. A worse shock, though, was a joke that gave Paddy Garland the fright of his life a few years back. Paddy was a cedar-getter on his way to Cairns for a spree. He put up at the Riverstone Hotel one night, about fifteen miles out of Cairns. Paddy had the local reputation of being a great joker. So had a character he met at the pub, a wandering sort of cove who'd taken on a job collecting native curios for Baron von Mueller the naturalist. He'd come in from the scrubs the same night, with natives carrying a load of curios he was going to ship from Cairns. He and Paddy chummed up right away, they had a lot in common. They played jokes half through the night, got hilariously drunk together. Paddy staggered away to bed in the small hours. He awoke at sunrise hazily aware of an awful smell. He groped out with an arm and found a man in bed beside him—the sleeper felt as hard and cold as iron, but as Paddy just then could only feel his own head it took him quite a time to realize this. Indignantly he threw off the blanket and roared at his bedmate—then nearly bit off his tongue. With a yell that woke the hotel he was out of bed and the window in one bound.

"You see, the sleeper beside him was an aboriginal mummy, somewhat beetle-eaten, and atrociously smellful."

"Good Heavens! How on earth did it get there?"

"Paddy's boozing partner of the night before put it there, of course. It was the prize of his collection for von Mueller. He thought it would be a great joke to slip it into the bed of his fellow joker."

"What a beastly joke!"

"Maybe that's what Old Mick thought," he said slyly.

"At least Old Mick woke up to find a live billygoat sleeping beside him. But your cedar-getter found a dead blackfellow."

"Yes," he admitted, "a lively difference, indeed." And blew a smoke ring to encircle an inquisitive March fly.

"I've never heard of the aboriginals mummifying their dead," I said doubtfully.

"I've only met two tribes who do. Away farther north, it is more common. It is only a very rough mummification, anyway; they actually only smoke-dry them in a hollow tree."

"H'm. Anyway, how on earth did you hear that wallaby all that distance away? Why, it must have been minutes before he came along! He was hopping slowly, and softly, too, and he came from away down to the left side of us, and you were walking ahead at the time!"

"I've got pretty good ears," he puffed.

"And you use them, too! Why, you must be able to hear even an aboriginal's footsteps."

"Not quite," he replied. "Not unless he was walking carelessly."

"I thought I was pretty good. I've done a lot of wallaby hunting among the hills around Broken Hill, but you can beat me by miles."

He was pleased, for he quietly told me things about animals until our pipes smoked out. I could have listened through "many pipes", for all bush lads prided themselves on knowledge of animals. All too soon we were walking on again.

Barely half an hour later he turned round with the same warning signal. From a patch of stunted forest we had stepped out onto a gully head that fell precipitously before us. Abrupt ridgetops scarred by gully heads and crowned by stunted timber stretched on up to the divide. He stood leaning forward, left hand resting on the side of a granite boulder nearly as big as a house. He put his cheek to the boulder that, half embedded in the earth, sloped out over the gully side. He turned and beckoned with a sign of extreme caution. When I crept down to his side he whispered, "Do you smell anything?"

I sniffed the air carefully. "No. Only the bush."

"Put your cheek to the rock, and smell again."

I leant to the hot rock, smelling all I knew how. But there came only the "granity" sense of the rock, the faint tang of vegetation warmed by heat. I straightened up, shook my head wonderingly. The faintest expression of satisfaction seemed to flit across his face as he whispered in my ear, "Creep down along the side of the rock ever so carefully. Turn with it, creep along it. If you are quite noiseless, you may see something!"

With the hunter in every youth aroused in me, and intensely curious, inch by inch I crept down along the side of the boulder. Hardly breathing, I began to move round it; it sloped overhead now like a veranda over the steep gully bank, throwing a cool shadow upon the coarse grass at its base. Though now I was staring straight along the base of the rock and could plainly see the markings on the granite, see every tuft of grass, the few dead twigs, every pebble in the cool shade cast by that overhanging boulder, still I could see "nothing". Inch by inch I crept along, then in a flash froze to the granite as there stood erect, not six feet away, a full-grown dingo, sniffing nose straight at me, ears pricked, eyes not wide like the wallaby's, but half closed as its nostrils wrinkled in intense concentration. I could see the bristles twitching and feeling around as if each were a live thing; like the wallaby it could see me, but as yet its startled instinct could not register the fact. Every ginger hair on its taut body seemed standing erect in questioning alarm. Gradually its green eyes widened, glaring up into mine; it simply *must* be smelling me now, surely it could even see the movement of my breathing as I crouched frozen to the granite.

For long moments we stood staring thus at one another; I could hear birds whistling with a clear distinctness, hear the hum of insects, seemed to see every hair on the taut red body as its sharply cut, suspicious muzzle sniffed up at me. Then—I smelt it so distinctly—"He has lit his pipe!" and in a flash the dingo had wheeled round and vanished down the bank.

And in another moment the Jungle Man stood beside me.

"A dingo," I said. "He was sound asleep under the rock—he smelt your tobacco smoke!"

"A cosy possy for a warm afternoon's siesta."

"How on earth did you know it was there?" I asked.

"Smelt it," he replied simply.

"Smelt it? From away back there?" I said unbelievingly.

"Farther than that," he answered, "but this was so simple." With the pipe-stem he pointed to the gully head. "As you know," he explained in that casual tone of his, "heat and atmospheric conditions draw up air from the valleys." I did *not* know, not then. "From the valleys it seeps up into the creeks, then the gullies, comes creeping up the ravines. Here is the gully head where it seeps over, overflows as a flooded river does its banks. That air current breathed up against this big rock face, crept round its corners, then up along its sides, from where my nostrils got a whiff away back there. Such air currents, as they creep along over the earth, carry the scent of animal with it, any animal or man that the current just there passes over. And that's that!"

Gazing at him, I pulled out the pipe and sat down.

"I'm learning things," I said. "Stone the crows! Then you can smell distant animals, as well as hear them?"

"If conditions are favourable," he answered. "But I can hear a long way farther."

"Well, I wish I could do the same!" I said admiringly, and meant it.

He sat down. I'd said the right thing again, I could smoke my pipe out now.

"Well, then," he said calmly, and nodded towards the rock, "go and smell where the dingo was lying—you'll register the tang of it then."

Not over-willingly, I did so. I'd smelt animal dens before, and was not keen on the perfume.

"I can smell him now," I called, "that is, where he was lying down."

"Right. Get a good whiff of him. But don't linger *too* long—if you get a dingo tick on you you'll know all about it."

I was up and away from that spot almost as fast as the dingo had gone. It was through poking about in kangaroo caves that I had learnt very agitatedly of the kangaroo tick. And they're hideous things.

"That's queer," I said, nodding over the pipe-stem, "what you just told me about air currents."

Dreamy voiced, he told me other "queer" things then, about air in valley and mountain-top, in forest and jungle, in heat and cold and wet. And scents from flowering trees in forest and scrub, and of lovely, elusive perfume lingering in the jungle from some scented bark or hidden flower or, strangest of all, from some poisonous, phosphorescent fungus. In no time the pipe was smoked out and he was standing up there, slinging the swag over his shoulders.

That night we camped almost atop of the divide. As usual, seemingly by instinct, he'd walked straight to a snug spot. A wee spring handy, a grassy hollow cosily sheltered from wind. The earth would remain warm for quite a while here, for the hollow had collected concentrated sunlight throughout the day. Nights can be bitter cold in that area, and we only had one blanket each. With a rock face at our back and a cheery fire, down in this snug hollow we were warm enough. I noticed he did not waste wood, though there was a forest of it all around us. But his fires were not like the wary blackfellow's fire; they were always cheery and seemed to throw out just the right heat, and he chose wood that always lasted until well on into the small hours. It was always I who shiveringly awoke then to make the fire up again. He would have lain there without sound or movement until daylight otherwise.

Plodding along that afternoon, we had been silent ever since seeing the dingo. And now each was lying on his blanket within the warmth of the fire, smoking and gazing up at that everlasting wonder of the stars. But for the cheery fire the night seemed as silent as they.

"Do you ever think there may be men up there?" I ventured at last.

"Why not?"

"H'm, I dunno. Never been up there."

"You can easily do so."

"How?"

"Imagination. Pick out any star. Imagine you are there—and you *are* there! Imagination travels faster than the speed of light."

"H'm, h'm. There was no imagination in that dingo smell this afternoon."

"That is only because it is earthy—like we are."

"H'm. I'm a bit puzzled why you suggested I smell it and 'register'."

"So that you would know a dingo scent again. And if at every chance you smelt one, or *any* animal, and were always alert to air currents, your nostrils would begin to register. Your sense of smell would gradually wake up, you would begin to smell the presence of an animal, and identify it, farther and farther away."

"H'm."

"Same goes for hearing, and sight, too. And other things—instinct, and intuition for instance."

"H'm. Is that how *you* learnt?"

"Mainly, yes. Though as a very young boy I noticed at times I seemed to 'know things' better, or sooner than grown-ups. Saying nothing to anybody, I began to develop these senses. I soon could smell my own father when he was angry—that is why he could never find me when he was coming to give me a hiding for doing something he did not understand."

Covertly I glanced towards him. Lying there with hands cupped behind his head, he was smoking up at the stars, firelight bathing his serious face with an expression of quiet serenity. He could be a likable chap if he wanted to, and would only smile a bit more. But—there was that cold grey look in his eyes. I turned back to the stars again.

"Have you ever been a primitive man?" the quiet voice inquired.

"Why, no, of course not!" I replied in surprise.

"Yes, you have—as truly as those stars are above! You carry countless cells in your body that come from your most primitive ancestors, and, to come nearer home, from those who lived only a few thousand years ago. Even then, most men's lives depended on their 'primitive' senses and abilities, which, after all, are the same as those we are made up of today. Eyesight, hearing, reasoning, acuteness of smell, touch, speed, instinct, endurance. You've inherited a fair endurance, which your fathers must have had before you, and ever since you were a toddler, as you've told me, you've knocked about the bush a lot, been keen on hunting and bird life, which to the bloodthirsty youngster means long walks and tree-climbing and all the rest of it. And since boyhood you've been kept fit by physical work—and I notice you've kept jogging along pretty well since we started out from Nigger Creek. But your senses of sight and hearing are now only moderate, while those of touch and smell are nearly dormant. As for wariness and intuition—you've simply never used them. But they're only rusty. They're still there."

This reasoning was getting beyond me. I turned back to the stars; they seemed a bit closer somehow.

"Well, then," I said after a pause, "by now you must have the senses of sight and hearing and smell developed as keenly as an aboriginal!"

"Not quite," he replied. "Remember, the wild aboriginal is born to his primitive senses. Above all, he lives in the environment and is trained from babyhood to use those senses."

"H'm. But you said you trained yourself from near babyhood."

"Yes. But I had no one to train *me*!"

In the silence, for the first time in life I vaguely began to realize what such early training might mean.

Presently he said, "Among aboriginals, as among all men, there are degrees of 'knowing'. Some are better than others. I have proved I am as good as some of those 'others'. Quite often, too, especially in the Big Scrubs, I've smelled aboriginals *before* they've smelled me."

In time soon coming I was able to believe this from my own experience of aborigines—only because, of course, of their habit of smearing their bodies with rancid oils, and worse. Though my aboriginal friends with a disgusted sniff, swore they could smell me, or any white man, a mile or more away. However, on plenty of occasions I was to prove them wrong. Or else they were just mooning along dreaming, as we do.

CHAPTER XXI

HAPPENINGS IN THE NIGHT

For some time we smoked in silence. A silent night, one of those listening nights when the world seems bathed in a quiet beauty.

"Well," I admitted a bit enviously, "I'd like to have my bush senses developed as yours are. Must come in handy at times. In the country away north where they say the blacks are still bad it could save a man's life, too."

"Of course. Much more than that, though. For a man who trains his senses is constantly seeing more, hearing more, knowing more. Far more."

"How is that?"

"Because it is by his senses that a man *knows* things, of course—otherwise he would be a *real* animal. Because again, the senses interact. Compare it in a way to the compound interest the teachers tried to hammer into us at school. If you strive to cultivate your hearing then your eyes come into play, too, they try to see farther, to see what you are hearing. Mind or instinct or experience gets busy, too, trying to build up a mind picture to show you what you are seeing *and* hearing. Each sense strives to help the other, thus each sense becomes sharper—and grows, too! Until suddenly, but only after a long time of constant effort, you begin to *know* things."

He's leading me into deep waters again, I thought uneasily. "What animal has the keenest sight?" I asked.

"Man. Easily. He sees farther, much more distinctly, and of course in incomparably greater detail than any other animal. I've proved it many a time. So far as Australian animals are concerned, anyway."

This surprised me, for until that afternoon I had believed that animals could see as well, if not better than men.

"You believe man to be an animal, or not?"

"So far as the body machinery is concerned, though fortunately he does not walk on all fours. But his power of using brain and mind and hands and tongue makes him something very different. So different that, of course, there can be no comparison."

"What *is* man then?"

"I don't know," he replied dreamily. "You must seek that answer out among the stars."

"H'm," I murmured. The stars away up there seemed suddenly so very, very far away, like the ages of time behind us. But the ages of time *had* been here, we could see it for ourselves in the old buried river-beds. And we could see the stars, too—the Past and the Present! If there *was* any Past and Present! Was the answer away out there? Or right here?

Vaguely uneasy at these strange thoughts, I broke the spell.

"So man can see best of all?"

"Of the animals, yes. But the eagle beats us, in one way. So does the owl—at night. Which is when night-prowling animals can see better than us also."

"Ah! Night-sight!"

"Yes."

"Can night-sight be developed, too?"

"Yes."

"Have you trained your sight by night also?"

"Yes. Not too successfully. But I can see far better now at night than when a boy."

Curiously again I glanced at him. He had put aside the pipe, and just lay there gazing up at the heavens where his thoughts seemed to be wandering. What secrets of nature did this strange man know?

As if in answer he said quietly, "There is a wallaby being hunted for its life by dingoes away down the ravine. It is racing up this way. Do you hear it?"

Deep silence told my straining ears, "No."

"Listen then."

A moment later there came the sharp tinkle of a falling stone bouncing on bare rock down along the gully bottom—a stone dislodged by frantic paws. Soon I heard "Thud! Thud! Thud! Thud!" in urgent haste. I sat up as the wallaby came swiftly, body sharply outlined by starlight, across on the gully ridge, a speeding ghost along the silvered skyline. He was going all out as he bounded past and vanished over the slope. And now followed the wild dogs, a pair, one behind the other in silent, merciless pursuit, their lean bodies flecked by starlight as they, too, vanished.

I settled down on the blanket again, amazed. "What marvellous hearing you must have! How far down the gully were they before you heard them?"

"Some little distance. I heard them while we were talking. Waited awhile to make sure they were coming this way."

"Well!" I declared. "I just would *not* have believed it, had I not been here. I can hardly believe it now!"

Somehow, I felt I'd said the right thing, and inquired, "Have you developed your sense of smell as keenly as hearing?"

"Nothing like it. It is far more difficult to wake up, our ancestors let it go to sleep for too long. Once the civilized man no longer needed to fear tigers sniffing around for a meal he thankfully gave his sense of smell away, as it were."

"I never thought of that!" I grinned. "No doubt a keen sense of smell would be mighty handy if a hungry lion came prowling about. I say, it's lucky we've got no man-eating lions and tigers in Australia."

"We wouldn't be camping here like this if there were," he replied grimly, "nor would thousands of others who will enjoy a peaceful night's sleep under the stars tonight. About the only chance of a man being eaten tonight in Australia is if someone foolishly camps too close to the bank of a crocodile infested river."

"H'm! A grim awakening! Still, you must travel a long way to those rivers, and the very few white men there would know the danger. So I still cannot see the benefit to a civilized man in developing such an acute sense of smell."

"Your friend Long Stewart wishes he had it."

"Why?" I asked in surprise.

"Because then he would not sleep at times with death-adders."

In the deathly silence I stared, bewildered. He chuckled up at the stars.

"Surprised you?"

"Sort of took my breath away. What's the joke?"

"No joke at all. At least, not to your friend Stewart."

Fumbling with the pipe, uneasily I glanced at him, not knowing what to say or think. Complacently he blew a smoke ring up to encircle a star. Taking his own time, presently he said, "Has Stewart never told you, around that Council Fire of yours, of his affinity for the death-adder?"

"No."

"Well, it is fact."

After a pause, he said quietly, "You don't believe me."

"Well—er—"

"It is fact. The death-adder seeks Stewart, seeks to camp with him, to coil up in his very own blanket. I don't know the cause. But I do know of similar instances. Anyway, when travelling in death-adder country Stewart becomes very uneasy towards sunset; he must reach water, of course, but must get to camp in ample time to scout around and find a clear spot to camp, clear of all possible chance of a death-adder—you know how they lie about in that sleepy way of theirs! Have you ever awakened in the morning to find you had spread your blanket on a death-adder?"

"No."

"Stewart has. And the evening before he has examined every inch of that ground, and away beyond it, *before* he spread his blankets."

Too puzzled to say anything, I smoked awhile in silence. When next he spoke, I listened most uneasily.

"You still do not believe me. You believe that if what I said was true then Stewart would surely have brought it up as an interesting topic for the Council Fire, some time when you have all been yarning about snakes, for instance."

He had read my thoughts—which now became too muddled to reply.

"Oh well," he said, and I could swear his voice had a grin in it, "Stewart may tell you all about it some time, and he may not. You see, he may not be at all happy about this attraction of the death-adder to him. But come now, admit that in the case of a civilized man like Stewart, he would be glad indeed of a sense of smell that would detect a death-adder near his camp."

"Too right," I admitted. "I agree with you there. These things are strange to me—I was a bit puzzled, that's all."

"There are many strange things in life," he said quietly, "but they are only strange because we do not understand them."

A speck of mica was glittering like a diamond in the granite rock.

I do not understand even that, I thought. It is but a flake of mica reflecting light from a starbeam. Now I think of it, that starbeam must have travelled millions of miles! This cove must be making me think things—

"Everything has a smell," he was saying lazily, "call it a scent if you like—from a flower to a rock. Did you ever imagine that rocks possess a smell? Of course you never have. Well, prove it for yourself. Every time your pick breaks a different kind of rock, smell it. Sooner or later, you'll be surprised. Rocks have their own feel, too, if you would only develop another sense—the sense of touch. Some feel rough, others smooth, oily, cold, warm, dry, moist, heavy, light, greasy—you've felt a 'slippery-back', and surely soapstone, and that distinctive feel of a powdered manganese seam. That feel, too, of molybdenite. Just wait until you feel your fingers fondling your first nugget of gold! Ah! I see response there!" And he was not even looking at me. "Then again," he went on, "different rocks possess another power of smell, as surely you know. Heat iron pyrites, and what do you smell?"

"Sulphur," I said wonderingly.

"Of course. Heat arsenical pyrites, but take care you are not poisoned by arsenical fumes. And so on. Do you see now that even rocks have their smell?"

"Yes. I just hadn't thought about it."

"You ask me of what real use is this more or less well developed sense of smell of mine. Well, for one thing, it is great company.

If I were lying alone here in this bush tonight and a porcupine came creeping along, I would know—always providing some vagrant air current came drifting over him towards me. You could not hear him, could not see him. But I would know he was out there, very earnestly engaged in his porcupiny business—sniffing, snout-rooting, a prickly business at times, too, at times again even a matter of life and death. And his life is quite as valuable to the porc as yours is to you.

"I could lie here quietly smoking, and follow his every movement out there in the dark; I'd know all he was doing. And they are very quaint little things, believe me, with quaint habits. And like getting their own way—they are dogged little brutes. Quite bad-tempered when upset, too, and can be very nasty about it. You've never seen, I suppose, the antics of a really bad-tempered old man porcupine! You, of course, would never believe, because you don't know, these things of quiet old Porc when you meet him out in the daylight and lever him over with a stick. All he seeks to do is swiftly burrow himself out of your sight. If the ground is too hard he 'sucks' his under body to the earth, spreads out his quills, and with a motionless tenacity hopes for the best. But when he's out on the prowl at night in his own little world he's quite a different fellow—thinks no end of himself, too. Which, after all, is only running true to form—if we *all* are of the animal kingdom."

He paused, put down his pipe, cupped his head in his hands, and silently gazed up at those stars of his.

"Go on!" I said eagerly.

"I'm talking too much."

"No, you're not! I'll bet you've never had a more interested listener. Go on—where you left the old porcupine out in the dark!"

"Oh well—of course, it would not be dark to him, the mystery of night is the breath of life to him. He would be company to me, I would lie here dreaming up at the sky and yet be watching every movement of Porky's little game away out there in the grass, for as long as the air currents told me. Particularly if it were mating season, and then I would know, too, whether he were 'he', or 'she'. And I could lie here and watch every movement of his, or her, or their little game. And, believe me, at times it is comical, the path of true love does not always run smooth even for the spiny ant-eater. 'She' may be suspicious of his intentions, not much interested anyway. Which works him up into a perfect porcupiny fury in trying to impress upon her what a fine porcupine he really is. Of course, we are merely speaking of the animal kingdom!"

"Yes," I answered somewhat hazily, "seems to me I recognize something about it."

"You'd be surprised!" he replied, and I could almost swear to a fleeting smile.

"Well, this sense of smell often is great company before I turn in of nights. I can smell wild pig, a prowling old boar—savage, bad-tempered old brutes they are—or sow and litter, goodness knows how far away. Naturally it depends on favourable atmospheric conditions, and air-current direction. You can understand that a man can smell a pig, of course!"

"Oh yes, but I never dreamt you could smell it for any great distance."

"Distance only comes with development of the sense. Anyway, the smell of wild pig is surprisingly more distinctive, and 'animally', than that of gluttonous, overfed porkers in a piggery. And to me, anyway, much more cleanly."

"And can you tell what the pigs are doing, too, 'see' them as you can the porcupine?"

"Of course. And much farther away, naturally so, and more vividly than shy little old Porc, whose ways are more difficult to understand. I've seen, that is by smell, some savage fights between two wild boars that have met away out there in the night. Generally, they'll just pass one another—warily, I can easily imagine, probably with a contemptuous grunt. But if somewhere handy there happens to be a fine young sow in contemplative mood— well, then it is a different greeting altogether! Neither boar will give way. Little eyes gleam green, they glare piggish hate at each other, root the earth with those murderous tusks, grunt and squeal in primitive fury, and shake their ugly heads until they're fairly slathering at the snout. That 'mane' along the back of their neck stands erect, fairly bristling with rage. Then they lower their heads and charge! And it will be a savage, all-in fight, believe me. I can 'see' all this because at times of mating and fight the animal smell increases with a hot intensity. And then, of course, in the big scrubs I've been hidden and watched them fight in daylight many a time. I can 'see' such a fight just as plainly at night when lying in camp, by sense of smell alone!"

"I thought I knew a fair bit about the bush," I said wonderingly, "but I never dreamt of these things."

"It helps let me know lots of things," he said dreamily. "For instance, that at this moment there is a wild-cat spying down upon us from a cleft in this very rock wall below which we are camping. And its sharp little nose is sniffing *our* smell, and the smell of the fire. It is actively curious, but fearful, too. We would feel just the same at sight and smell of something big and frightening which *we* did not understand. However, when I'm alone in the bush, especially at night, particularly if in jungle country, this sense of smell is great company. And it tells me of inquisitive company near by in the jungle darkness which I may not even see, or hear. It even tells me when the snakes are making love."

"What!"

"Did you not know that snakes make love?" It seemed in the firelight there was almost a smile at the corners of his mouth.

"I've never heard of it," I replied doubtfully.

"Well, they do, sometimes silently, intensely. Mostly, though, with surprising noises, swift movement. Generally, too, with quite a lot of showing off."

"I've never heard anything at all about it," I said wonderingly. "And so you really can smell snakes?"

"Yes, of course. Especially during the mating season—that's how they advertise their presence to one another. At least, some kinds do, I'm certain. For snakes have to meet one another, just as we do. But at any season, should a crawler be near the camp I know he's there. Especially in the big scrubs. There, in jungle country, after a hot day over the 'outside' forest, the jungle at night is often humid from the decayed vegetation and moisture so often dropping from the leaves above. At such times I can smell a snake quite a distance away. There doesn't seem any air in the deathly quietness deep in there, but of course there is. And it's always moving, though you can seldom feel it among all those tree-trunks. And this carries smell very distinctly—of animal, of bird, of a scented bark, but particularly of snake. To me, anyway." He paused to fill the pipe.

"What does snake smell like?" I asked curiously.

"Not pleasant. A man would dislike it if he were foolish enough to be prejudiced. It's a mixture of animal and stale earthy smell, you could nearly say it was 'beastly'. But it is distinctive snake all right, immediately you smell it you can 'see' the crawler. In your mind's eye, of course, but there's no mistaking it."

"Can you tell the different snakes?" I asked curiously.

"A number of them—now. But it took me quite a time."

"How do you mean?"

"Well, for some years, every time I saw a snake—and later as I developed and could smell the crawler when he was out of sight —I'd walk to him and smell him thoroughly. A carpet snake, for instance. Seeing him, I'd know him, of course. By smelling him and registering his smell, then eventually a developed sense of smell would tell me what he was without me seeing him. Same with the black snake, the brown, too. I very soon learnt to smell them in the mating season, naturally. As I said, they smell strongest then."

"Good Heavens! But aren't snakes particularly vicious at that time?"

"Of course."

"And you'd go out and smell such a snake!"

"Yes."

"Stone the crows! How?"

"Pick him up with a tight grip at the back of the neck—grip the butt of the jaws. Haven't you ever done it?" he asked half scornfully. "It's simple. Then hold him up to my neck. He'd wind himself round my neck and nostrils and I'd take all the smell I wanted. He'd be quite vicious, of course, and the madder he got the more he'd smell—he'd smell like a pole-cat, as the saying is."

"Good Heavens!" I said, and just gazed at him.

There seemed almost a sneer in his faint smile.

"To find out things, to learn things, you've got to *do* things," he murmured, "and do them thoroughly."

I lay back, silently promising myself I'd never learn the smell of snake. Not as he knew it, anyway.

"It must be a handy gift to develop," I ventured at last somewhat lamely. "You could smell a snake around camp and go out and belt the daylights out of him before he came dangerously near."

"Why should I?" he answered quietly. "I never interfere with them, and they never interfere with me. I've had them crawl over my chest in my bunk at nights, lots of times. Did not move, while they crawled on and away." (The same experience was soon to be mine. I didn't move either—because I was scared stiff.) "Besides," he went on, "what would be the sense of learning to know the presence of things if you were going to chase them away just when they would be company, and of interest, too?"

"H'm! What kind of snake can you smell the farthest distance away?"

"That is difficult. It depends entirely on the season, whether in scrub or forest, and conditions of atmosphere. And, of course, whether a man is in the mood! But, for instance, I can smell a python on a still, warmish day quite a distance if he is sleeping off a meal with a young wallaby inside him."

"Yes," I said dubiously, "I s'pose they'd hum a bit more then. Anyway, where on earth is the interest, let alone company, of a mob of snakes around a camp at night?"

"Have you ever camped in the big scrubs—alone?"

"No."

"Well," he said grimly, "if ever you do then you'll know what loneliness really feels like, and you can *feel* that loneliness! Then don't let the pitch blackness, and that creeping silence, and that drip-drip-drip of water-drops from the leaves get on your nerves.

Or the whisperings going on among those millions of tree-trunks —often I've been near certain that trees whisper among themselves. Anyway, that sense of smell can be very maty when it lets you know some quaint thing of the scrubs is coming to keep you company. However, so far as snakes are concerned, in some portion of a jungle here and there the place will suddenly become alive with them—maybe only in that one particular little area." (I was to find this to be quite true, too.) "If it happens to be the mating season and your camp is pitched right there then without that sense of smell, look at all the lively things you miss! At night time I'd smell them coming swiftly, slithering around from all over the place. And those urgent hissings, and other queer little sounds I can hardly explain, have shown me lots that was going on, kept me company for hours on end. The swift meetings, the rising up of the agitated heads on long, quivering necks, the swaying and parrying, those black tongues flickering in and out fast as lightning, then in places those demon fights with two snakes locked together until one kills the other. Elsewhere, the rising and swaying until the glistening necks glide across one another as in a caress, then all around there is a perfect orgy of love wrestling. I've had them writhe right into the very tent, despite the light of the hurricane lamp; they simply know nothing but one another—and the mad urge. I can assure you I've never been lonely on such nights. Such an orgy a man sees seldom, of course, and only if he happens to have camped in such a spot during the very nights that this particular snake-life is going on. Well, it is this developed sense of smell that has both brought me company and shown me things on such nights, on many and many a lonely night. For although I actually miss nearly all of such interesting happenings, still I 'see' quite a lot indeed."

Which left me too amazed to reply. It is an uneasy feeling to be listening to something you vaguely realize must be true, yet cannot understand. Something like being awake in a nightmare.

But I slept as snugly as a bug in a rug.

CHAPTER XXII

THE TOWN THAT MOFFAT BUILT

COLD dawn came to the lively crackling of a fire.

"Billy's boiled!"

With sleepy rebellion I slung off the blanket at the second call and sat up. We slept in our clothes, of course, much warmer that way, besides dodging the necessity of carrying another blanket. That fire hummed nice and warm, the billy was steaming, and I was jolly hungry.

Rippling fire lifted the wild peaks to eastward up out of a sleeping world. Flaming fingers quivered heavenward towards a lightening sky.

Protestingly, a bird attempted a sleepy squawk here and there. By the time we'd wolfed a simple breakfast and slung on the swags a crimson sky was warming the dark face of the earth, and we stepped on into a noisily growing aviary as another day was born.

Once over the divide we dropped down into country that reminded me of some old picture of Dante's Inferno, my mate trudging on hour after hour without a word. Barely a grunt, even when we boiled the midday billy. And morose that evening. Yet again he had not stopped to try one dish of dirt all day, even though trudging over country fairly shouting for the prospector's pick. And my mind was warm with dreams of stumbling upon a fortune in tin, a new Great Northern, a Vulcan, a Lyee-Moon, a King of the Ranges. I even dreamt of sinking the pick into a Golden Gully. But sundown came softly and he had not tried one dish. It was a silent camp. I left him to his thoughts, whatever they were, and took my disappointment to the Land of Sleep.

And dreamt of finding another Palmer, and a kiss from Palmer Kate. Such a kiss used to cost the old gold-diggers an ounce of gold, a golden kiss indeed. Such a reward would have sent me clean broke at present. But it was a golden dream.

Next day, deep among arid-looking hills, sounded the rumbling of explosives. Soon, here and there on rocky hillsides, we saw the grey dump of a shaft or the black of a tunnel mouth, and toiling men burnt nearly black by the sun. Irvinebank made itself heard well before we saw it, a murmur growing into the roar of forty head of stampers. As we strolled along the deep-trodden mule-track I could not help thinking of my mate "seeing" things by "hearing". For it was easy now to visualize this lively mining township.

The roar of the batteries, now fading away to roar again as the big iron stampers crushed down and their song was carried along the gullies by the breeze. Dull thunder of heavy explosive charges. Then, sharp and clear through a break in the hills, the clang of steel upon steel. Sharp echo of an axe, throaty roar of a boiler letting off steam. Then a slowly drifting cloud of dust and smoke showing where the smelters were on Gibbs's Creek, machinery transported to this wilderness and erected by the foresight and indomitable will of one John Moffat. From the rock-girt hills around the township pack-mules laden with ore from outlying mines were cautiously snaking their way round precipitous tracks, warily working their way down to the dusty road and the battery. No chance of wheel traffic up in "them thar hills", even a mountain goat would need to be an athlete to climb some of them. And now a lazily rising cloud of dust showed where pack-mules and horse-teams, wagons and loaded buckboards met to roll on towards the scattered township, its iron roofs glinting under sunlight among the scrubby hills and gullies.

"The Vulcan!" The Jungle Man pointed, and I gazed across at the "Big Mine" up there on its hillside, pride of John Moffat, of all Irvinebank, the Vulcan already developed into the biggest, deepest, and richest tin-mine in all North Queensland. High up, stretching right down to the creek by the battery, were aerial ropeways down which suspended trucks laden with Vulcan ore were dizzily swishing down to the battery. The stacks at the near-by smelters were belching smoke. And—lovely sight in this hot, often thirsty area—the sunlit water of a large dam made a sanctuary for wild ducks by John Moffat. Overlooking the dam was a home that caught the eye immediately, in a little oasis of greenery.

"Moffat built it," said my mate. "He built the dam, too. Without it, both life and work would be impossible for a township here."

Facing the precious dam was a long, dusty street; it was really a road lined with shops and hotels, very hot-looking. Citizens on horse or foot or in carts were going quietly about their business along this street.

"That town is all made of tin," said the Jungle Man. "Just tin, there is nothing else. Just tin and rock, sweat and heat and mules and horses. And the energy of men. Gathered together and cemented into a busy town by the brains, foresight, and energy of one man."

"Moffat, you mean?"

"Of course."

Snaking out from gully after gully among that sea of hills appeared laden teams constantly plodding down to the township and battery, while now the road from Stannary Hills was a dust-cloud under plodding teams. A busy scene, and of warm interest to me.

"There must be hundreds of shows back in those hills," I exclaimed.

"There are. I wouldn't venture to guess how many hundreds. All made possible to work because of Moffat and his battery, and now the smelters. Otherwise only the very richest of the lodes could have been worked. Even then, only for a short life."

"Who found the Vulcan?"

"No one knows. One of the early prospectors, who abandoned it because he could not find rich surface ore. With no battery, let alone a smelters, and with an impossible transport problem, none but the richest of surface ores was payable. Yet the Vulcan is the richest tin-mine, even richer than the Great Northern and Wild Irishman in Herberton. The lode was really opened up by a party of Italian wood-cutters years later. They went broke on their first crushing, but sold the show to the Vulcan Tin Mining Company —Moffat's crowd. Irvinebank was originally found by Gibbs and Donoghue's party, seemingly two parties rode into this country at about the same time. Thompson, Green, Pollard, McDonald and Eales were with them. About two years after Jack and Newell's party found Herberton. Gibbs's party found the Southern—you see it away up there overlooking the creek. Quickly then the Adventurer, Comet, Tornado, Star of the South, Agnes, Valetta, Forlorn Hope, Perseverance, and many other shows were found, still are being found today. The old-timers, though, had a lot of trouble with the blacks, not so many years ago either. A number of prospectors have been speared among the hills between here and Herberton. The early diggers here, as on all the early fields and on the Russell, too, down on the coast, always had to work with a revolver on their belt. However, Jim Bradshaw and other early arrivals following the tracks of Gibbs soon found other good shows. This place in the wild hills soon became known as Gibbs Camp. It was not until Moffat came with his idea of transport, of that fine big storage dam for water, and a battery on the spot to crush the ore, that Irvinebank was really put on the map."

"Why was the name changed to Irvinebank?"

"Because Moffat was born in Irvinebank, Scotland. The people would much rather it had been called Moffat's Hills, because he really made the place. They almost worship him here."

Lengthening rays of the western sunset were lighting up the little houses clustered to the hills. Something in his voice made me glance at his sun-tanned face, I caught a fleeting glimpse of a most human smile.

"They *do*," he was saying softly, "for I have seen youngsters on their knees at their bedside ending up their prayer with 'And God bless mum and dad. And please, God, bless John Moffat, too!' "

"They must like him very much," I said.

But his mood had vanished. "Well, *this* is Irvinebank," he said shortly.

"It is well established now."

"It is—a little human ant-bed among these grim old hills. Just fancy a railway actually coming creeping out here!" And I could have sworn there was a tinge of regret in his voice.

"Who built the railway? The Government?"

"No, Moffat, of course; he wasn't satisfied until he'd connected the Stannary Hills line to here. It is only a tramway, of course, the two-foot-gauge line these energetic mining companies have built out north and south and west from the main Cairns-Herberton Government Railway. From Boonmoo on the Cairns line the Stannary Hills Company built the line out to Stannary Hills. John Moffat then carried it on to here. Last time I was at Irvinebank the first 'train' arrived, about three years ago, crowded with people from the Stannary Hills end, a funny little Puffing Jinny crowded with waving, yelling human ants. You'd have thought the very hills had suddenly sprung alive and gone crazy—of course, it was a great day for Irvinebank. John Moffat had six hundred men on his pay-roll, a tremendous number for the small population of these isolated areas, I suppose Irvinebank and the hills can muster about three thousand people, counting children of course. Well, from near-by townships and outlying camps people just poured into Irvinebank by horse, by buggy and buckboard and camel and Shanks's pony. That was about the wildest week I've ever seen. And by far the gayest. And certainly it must have been the greatest collection of whiskers from the hills ever seen in North Queensland, and that is saying a lot. And as for dog-fights, I'd see more in an hour than I'd see in a year otherwise. With, of course, the old abo and his wife and piccaninnies enjoying themselves mightily on the outskirts. A wonderfully good-humoured crowd though, a week of meetings and greetings and dances and feastings, while the young girls saw more men than they'd ever dreamt existed."

"I'd have loved to have been there," I said longingly.

"I suppose so," he replied, "but just remember that the old men of these hills are handy with a shot-gun."

"Have you ever seen a shot-gun marriage?" I said, with a grin.

"I have!"

"So have I." I grinned again. "At Lightning Ridge."

"Well, let that be a lesson to you. Looking down the barrels of a double-barrelled gun," he added grimly, "is very different from looking into two smiling blue eyes. Oh, well, that tiny railway has meant a great deal to Irvinebank. Practically ended isolation, enabled hundreds of mines to be developed that it would never have paid to work otherwise, made living conditions much easier, solved a heartbreaking transport problem."

"It will be a godsend to the poor old horses and mules," I said. "There must be thousands of them toiling among these thirsty-looking hills?"

"Thousands and thousands—you've got no idea, not only here, but the teams plodding back to Herberton, the teams working between here and Stannary, let alone all the outside camps. Moffat has some beautiful teams of draught-horses, known throughout the North. I'll show you some lovely animals tomorrow, the very best in Queensland, I believe. Oh well, without the horse and mule and bullock this country could never have been opened up. Come on, we'll go along down into town. It's pretty lively—it's booming."

Livened up by the mere sight of the activity down below there, I stepped out beside my now taciturn mate and tried to keep the conversation going—up till now he'd hardly spoken a dozen words in the last two days.

"And how about Stannary Hills? Is it booming, too?"

"It is—always does when there's a fair price for tin—and of course it's got a great go-on now that the tramway's arrived there. Then again, your friends the railway navvies have been painting the place not only red, but every colour of the rainbow. We may go along and see it while we're here, it's only twelve miles or so farther on. If we do, I'll introduce you to Peter the Pig."

"Who on earth's he?"

"Oh—" and he almost smiled—"that gentleman is the fattest, most cunning, most gluttonous pig in all Queensland. The only time he'll condescend to move is when someone calls him for a beer. He may have drunk himself to death by now, though—it's some time since I've been in Stannary."

"He seems to be a bit of a character."

"He is. Nearly as well known as Townsville's boozing goat. You seem to have a fancy for animals. You put that disreputable old goat into Mick the navvy's bed, but I'll bet you couldn't put Peter the Pig into *any* man's bed—not unless you rolled a barrel of beer in before him."

Not feeling over-enthusiastic over meeting Peter the Pig, I held my peace until we strolled into town.

By then the afternoon shift was already knocking off, and groups of men were strolling along the deeply worn footpaths from mines to township, to the little homes among the hills, the camps by hill and gully. Laughing voices, a bit of horseplay among the young fellows here and there. A full mile away a figure high up on a rock silhouetted in fire from the setting sun stood yodelling in a voice that rang piercingly yet musically away out over hills and gullies and broken flats. My mate strode silently on those long, tireless legs of his, speaking now only when spoken to. And I was fairly bursting with questions.

The long straggling street was already growing lively, though of course no one was in a hurry. Folk strolling to shops, others for a knock-off beer at their favourite among the four hotels. Horsemen calling greetings as they rolled by, teams making for their camps. A few women were shopping, my wandering eye spied nearly half a dozen shy-looking girls; boyishly I guessed the competition must be fierce, a handful of women in this ant-bed of hungry men. It was always so among these little mining townships scattered far and wide amongst this sea of ranges, comparatively few people in the township by day, but at week-ends especially they came streaming out from among the hills until there seemed a little army of them. Especially so now where "the line is coming through"—any township within reach of the navvies where the little railway lines had and still were creeping out from the main Cairns-Herberton line, to north and south and west, linking up mining camp after camp. Right there, from Saturday afternoon until Monday morning, day carried on throughout the night into day with a liveliness that must have astounded the silence of the age-old hills.

Of course, picture-shows and radio and television and pastimes like that had not been invented in those days that were but yesterday. I was to see my very first motor-car in Mareeba, imported by the very progressive local doctor. I believe it was the first motor vehicle in all the hinterland.

I had not even time to gape around me before my mate strolled out of Stillman's store, nodding, "Come on!" and we were trudging out of town towards the creek.

Blast him! I thought unfairly. Too unsociable to buy a cooked meal even when we strike a town!

Though every shilling those days meant a shilling to me, still what a luxury a "bought feed" would have been. For a shilling you could buy at any pub a meal that it took a buck navvy all his time to wolf through. And we might even have been served by a waitress! But never once, in our little wanderings, did my strange mate ever buy a meal at a township hotel.

And this evening he cussedly walked a mile away from the township, passing sheds even where we easily could have thrown down our swags for the night, would not even camp by Gibbs's Creek. Picked an out-of-the-way sheltered place that even cut out almost all sound from the near-by township, though grudgingly I saw it was an ideal camp.

There was the usual simple meal, quickly cooked as the shadows fell. But we were as hungry as hawks, goodness knows how many miles we'd walked that day over rough and trackless country. After the meal he spread out his blanket, lit the pipe, then stretched out to gaze up at his everlasting stars. Surely he can leave them alone for *one* night, I thought grumpily.

"Coming for a stroll into town?" I asked.

"No, you go if you want to—I've seen it all before."

So there was I trudging back to the "bright lights". Under that vastness of night amongst the black shadowed hills those few dim lamps today would be thought a very dim show indeed. But, as a little candle shines like a good deed in a naughty world, as some poetic chap other than Mick Moore wrote, those lights were a symbol of the enterprise and dogged determination of man, and to me a big town full of warm-hearted human beings in a wilderness of hills.

Shy in my young days, I mooched quietly up to a group of men sitting smoking and yarning by Ledlie's store. Sat down, and listened. There were other such groups along this dusty road, "street" just here. Slow-moving figures by the scattered, busy pubs; from the nearest came a hum of voices, laughter drowned in a rollicking chorus of song. Probably there would be a few fights along the street before morning.

The yarns were all of "shows", of course, of percentages of tonnages and crushings, of prospecting and the price of tin, of good and bad country and water, of the Vulcan and particularly of the "Tin King", John Moffat.

Of the doings of well-known prospectors, of returns from rich crushings that fairly took my breath away. Yet another group were yarning "horsey" talk, teamsters and packmen—these yarning of roads and tracks and "loading" and feed and camping places, of Barney Lesina with the largest team of mules on the roads, 130 of these sure-footed, sturdy slaves of man. Of Donny MacDonald, whose pride was his beautifully outfitted team that could carry almost unbelievable loads. Of the feats of Manny Borghero, who seemed to be the "gun" packer of them all. And they yarned just as glowingly of horses and mules as well-known as the drivers, particular animals famed for their endurance and work. They drifted then on to yarns of daredevil drivers of Cobb and Co., still in the limelight, though the coming of the iron horse was fast wiping out that colourful era. Still another group were interested in the construction work of the mountain tramways, the problems and triumphs of a work that was a living romance in itself. I could have listened throughout the entire night. It was in a grumpy mood that I returned to my uninterested mate, sound asleep.

CHAPTER XXIII

MEN OF THE HILLS

THE twelve-mile tramp to Stannary Hills held plenty of interest for me though my again non-communicative mate spoke only in reply to questions, never pausing even for a yarn with passing horsemen, which just isn't done in that country.

"I bet these blokes have no fleas in their whiskers," I ventured.

"Why?"

"Because their foliage is so smothered in dust a flea couldn't breathe."

"Huh!" he grunted.

The road *was* dusty. No wonder. For this was the hottest period of the dry season, and this particular area misses out on the heavy rains and cooler climate of the Tableland while for years past this road had been cut up by the teams and buckboards, ceaselessly pounded by the hooves of an army of horses and pack-mules. I really wanted to sulk, but couldn't. The day was bright, every step was taking me into new scenes, the world was big and wide and smiling. This moody walking machine beside me had done me out of a few glorious days "looking around" Irvinebank with no other explanation than "Come on! We must get moving!" To *hell* with him, I'd come back here again on my own. Meanwhile I'd just soak in what my eyes could see and keep my own company. At which very thought he chose to surprise me. A way of his.

"You mention you've worked as a rouseabout down south in New South Wales."

"Yes."

"And were promised a learner's pen next shearing season, but you went digging for opals instead."

"Yes."

"Sheds you worked at were still using the blades, except the last shed, which had just installed the new shearing machines?"

"Yes. The Wolseley," I answered, wondering what he was coming at.

"Ever heard of the Moffat-Virtue shearing machine?"

"Yes. It was just coming on the market, a number of sheds were installing it when I left New South Wales."

"Well, the Moffat-Virtue sheep-shearing machine was invented and made in Irvinebank."

"What?" I exclaimed in sheer disbelief.

"You've heard of John Moffat."

"Of course," I growled surlily.

"Well, *there* is the connection! Virtue was the inventor, he had the idea, so far as my not very interested knowledge goes. He came to John Moffat who is interested in just about anything he calls 'progress'. Moffat backed Virtue. They went into partnership. Moffat gave Virtue the use of the Vulcan machine shop, and all the help he could. Virtue made and successfully completed the first successful Moffat-Virtue shearing machine in the Vulcan Mine Workshop, Irvinebank, North Queensland."

"But," I protested, "there would not be the machinery, the special materials, let alone specialized tools in a little mine workshop to make such a modern, intricate machine as a shearing machine!"

"Wouldn't there! You have not seen inside the Vulcan Workshop. And the Vulcan is the biggest lode-tin mine in Australia. And, until three years ago, anyway, the Vulcan Workshop was generally believed to be the most modern machine shop in Queensland."

Which I would not, simply could not believe, in those happy days not realizing the woeful extent of my own ignorance. However, he strode on, had said all he was going to say.

No, I thought surlily, I did *not* see inside the Vulcan, nor anywhere else, simply because *you* were in such a dashed hurry to drag me away from the place. And you only spoke just now to shut me up, to give me something to think about! May your fowls never lay eggs!

And he *had* given me plenty to wonder about. To think of coming all the way from New South Wales where, in every pastoral district the name of this marvellous sheep-shearing machine was on everybody's lips—to come all the way here into a little, isolated, tin-mining township to the very spot where it had been invented and actually made! I could easily have had a row with him. Nothing could have dragged me away from Irvinebank before I had at least ventured to approach John Moffat himself, and asked could I see inside the Vulcan Workshop had I known.

Yes, he is a strange mate, all right, the grumpy devil, I thought as the old hobnails bit the dust. And why had he not yet tried one dish of dirt, knapped one reef upon all this country we had gone over?

Why, we might have walked over another Herberton, another Irvinebank, even another Palmer. The last thought was just too heartbreaking to contemplate. Well, I would still keep up with him, anyway.

And the doing of it calmed hurt feelings somewhat.

Stannary proved to be more hilly even than Irvinebank, with the homes of married men scattered far and wide wherever they could find a spot level enough to build upon. The little township itself clung to Eureka Creek and now was under a dust-haze from the teams of horses and mules and the lively feet of a thousand people, brown as sun-baked earth. For this was pay-day, the place was "lively". The stores, the four pubs doing a roaring trade, the good-humoured crowd on holiday bent, quick and lively betting as a dog-fight broke out, boisterous cheering on of the snarling combatants. Outside Jack and Newell's crowded store half a dozen tyke-fights broke out in as many minutes. After the silence of the hills a lively scene like this made me eager to see more. But soon he had me trudging behind him like a disappointed puppy to the "Big Mine", the Ivanhoe perched up on a hill overlooking the tramline. Three hundred men were on the pay-roll here, which meant a very big concern "way out in the hills" in those days, a veritable sea of precipitous hills. A harsh roar came down from the mine where ore was tipped into a hopper to chute down into a truck by the line.

"The tramline snakes among the hills to the Walsh River miles away," explained my mate, "where the ore is crushed at the battery. Thirty head of stampers—you can hear them miles away. Across there is the Eclipse, across there is the Kitchener, there is the Kitchener North—they are making them into a maze of tunnels. The Arbouin is across on Iona Creek. These are the main mines, but there are hundreds of shows back in the hills—some are pretty good. Rich tin is being won, big money is being made from them—and in lesser degree from the hundreds of smaller shows for miles and miles like wombat holes within those hills upon the moon."

"Must be pretty big wombats!" I said, in a feeble attempt to dig up a bit of humour.

"Yes," he agreed evenly, "and you won't see these human wombats any more than you'll see those on the moon—we haven't the time. Anyway, when the price of tin booms it's these shows that make Stannary Hills and Irvinebank the liveliest townships on all the tin-fields along the Walsh and Tinaroo watersheds. And it would take you quite a time to travel over that area of country, believe me. Come on." And he was striding down a goat-track with me following behind bursting with a hundred and one questions as to this fascinating country and a form of tin-mining so different to the Deep Lead alluvial at Nigger Creek. In a flash I guiltily remembered I had not thought of Mick and Jim and Garnet and Old Brookes and little Tommy Turley for days and days.

I wondered how they were getting along in that placid backwash, as I now regarded it, little realizing that years later Wondecla was to boom and become the centre of a big timber industry. I wondered whether Mick had written any more "pomes", but the grin changed to a clutch of alarm as a pebble slipped under my heel.

"Just as well you grabbed that rock!" he said calmly as he turned round. "You could easily have broken your neck down there. Better watch your step!" And he strode on.

"Down there" was a sheer drop of three hundred feet into a rocky ravine. It looked a horribly hard, hot, merciless death-trap to pitch headlong down into. All thought of the placid ways of Nigger Creek vanished from a now alert mind.

The Arbouin appeared like a landslide away up a steep hillside, a dark tunnel mouth below, busy 'nts that grew into men as we climbed.

"The ore only goes one and a half per cent," my mate was saying, "but they work it cheaply by open cut, and transport to the battery is easy, so it pays—"

An eerie shriek cut through his words, followed by another spine-chiller. Almost immediately I saw what it was. Heavy tramway trucks loaded with ore were being pushed out from the "face" to the head of an aerial tramway, a great steel cable like a spider-web stretched far away out over a dizzy gorge. When the rumbling truck was pushed to the top station only three men handled it. The loaded truck, minus its undercarriage, was simply hooked to a trolly, head fitted over the cable, a lever was pulled, and the next second that truck was shrieking down and away over the gorge, flying hell for leather out over space and down, while up screeched empty trucks hauled by the weight of the loaded one whizzing down.

"There's only one man down there at the bottom station," came the voice. "He pulls a lever, the truck drops down onto an empty undercarriage and with others travels along to the battery at Rocky Bluffs on the banks of the Walsh. Thus the earth's cheapest power, gravitation, makes this otherwise poor mine payable. Come along."

And he was off again, with me following behind and growing madder and madder. Here were another hundred things I wished to see and learn, a hundred questions to ask of the brown-skinned men who bade us a curious "good day" as we tramped by. They would good-naturedly have answered any questions I asked, been pleased to explain things. And here were we just walking past!

We had barely left the Arbouin when a murmur growing into a roar fading into a murmur came thunderously through the gorges—the battery of thirty stampers somewhere in this maze down by the wild Walsh. The battery crushing the ore continuously pouring from the tramway cut so wonderfully around and through and above these hills and gorges and ravines, among which but a very few years before there had been only the winds and the precipitous pads of the wild aboriginal hunting the wallaby.

With the rhythmic "Thud-clank! Thud-clank! Thud-clank!" of the thirty head of stampers thundering among these rocky passes, I stood staring in boyish pleasure, in admiration of the men who had got these iron masses of machinery into such a place, all the way from Cairns away back east on the coast. Those to me huge boilers, those miles, it seemed, of water-pipe lines, those pumps, all that scaffolding and troughing, all the iron for the battery sheds, the rails for this wonderful tramway, that staunch little engine even now coming puffing along with its long line of clanking, heavy-laden trucks, a "train" I had already seen snaking round a precipice edge as nonchalantly as if the awful gorge dropping away beside could go hell and bang for all *it* cared. From the battery a hiss and roar as a cloud of snowy steam shot skyward, letting off excess energy, the rumbling of a tramway hauling ore up to the hungry stampers by endless rope and by no visible means of power, all those men serenely at work, this wild river that must roar in the Wet plunging its way through the gorges past camp after camp on its mad journey to the sea—

"Come *on*! We'd better be *moving*!"

He must have spoken before, but I just stared at him—surely he would pause at least to boil the billy at such a place as this.

"We'll visit the town of Rocky Bluffs."

"Town?"

"Yes." He almost smiled. "And remember—while we're wasting our time sight-seeing you're not working that claim of yours at Nigger Creek!"

And in an instant I was brought back to reality, the ever-gnawing urgency of "knocking out" a few pounds at least to pay the tucker bill. It was on the tip of my tongue to ask him to leave me here—by now I knew he could find his way alone anywhere— to leave me here and I'd take a job. I would not mind working for wages until I learnt all about this "new" kind of mining *and* saved enough to go out into these wild hills seeking a show for myself—

If I'd let the words tumble out, I realized later, he would have merely turned abruptly on his heel with a "So long!" and I'd never have seen him again.

We scrambled down a mountain-side along a mule-track, I pitied those poor slaves of man.

"This track is as rough as blazes!" I growled at last. "How on earth can a town be down here?"

He had wheeled as I spoke, almost a smile on his face. "You've said something!" and for the first time I'd known him he really grinned. "But there actually *is* a township down here, the township of Rocky Bluffs. Into this town there has never come a cart even, a buggy, a wagon, no wheeled vehicle of any sort. And there never will!" And, leaving me to chew over this, he strode on and now down.

Rocky Bluffs! I thought sulkily. There's no township here at all, can't be. But it's a good name, anyway.

For the place was a lost world of sun-baked bluffs and rocky mountains wild as the hobs of hell.

And suddenly we entered the place—by a mule-track. Just a tiny level space of ground among those bluffs, and in amazement I stared towards a low-built pub, a store, a score of shacks—homes of the battery men.

"Rocky Bluffs township! Welcome to Rufasell Street!" My strange mate stood aside and held out his arm invitingly.

"Rufasell Street?" I murmured, for there seemed nothing else to say.

"Yes."

"Rufasell?"

"Yes, you can read it on the board there!"

"What on earth does it mean?"

"You've said it! Back there when you nearly went head over heels. Rufasell Street—Rough-as-hell Street!"

I laughed and good humour returned.

"Come on!" he said, and turned on his heel.

"But aren't you at least going to walk along the 'street?'" I protested.

"Not on your life. You see every bit there is to see. Remember, we are a long way from Nigger Creek now!"

Silently I followed him. We boiled the billy down by the Walsh, all alone. My legs were aching. But I would not have mentioned it for worlds.

Soon we were on the move again and kept on until midafternoon. Upon a peak he stopped to sit on a boulder, pulling out his pipe. Thankfully I followed suit. The bush was still and quiet. Far away up, on effortless wings, an eaglehawk soared like a jewel delicately set in an intense blue sky. In the hushed quietness we seemed as remote from life as that airy bird of prey.

"He can see us as clearly as we see him, though he only looks the size of a pigeon. There appears to be only he and ourselves in all the world. But at any moment we may hear an echoing blast from men toiling in the hills."

I nearly dropped the pipe, staring into those cold grey eyes that now turned to the hills again.

"You seem to have read my thoughts," I said at last.

"It's quite easy at times," he replied.

"But you weren't even looking at me!"

"How do you know?"

I didn't. And was silent. He lit up, puffed, then, elbow on knee, chin resting on hand, stared away out over distance, motionless as the rock upon which he sat. I followed his gaze out over a sea of range tops, of peaks, of dark gorge and countless ravine.

"You can see out over near a hundred miles of country," he said quietly, "if you've got the eyes to see. As we're not as high as the eagle you'll have to see it in imagination. Away out there—" he pointed eastward—"over some pretty rough country is Mullaney's Pocket—they call it Garrumba now it's begun to develop, though the first tin was found by Tom Roberts years ago, long before a track was formed, of course. There's three hotels there now and about five hundred men working good tin in the hills. There's the Dalziel out there, and Boulder, the Ballot Box, Village Blacksmith, a big show, too, that John Moffat's crowd runs, and hundreds of smaller shows. Some of the hills are honeycombed with tunnels, many a king's ransom in tin has already been gouged out from those hills. The Gilmour group of mines are out there, too, the Dolly Grey and Midas and California Creek, a rich alluvial field on its own."

For nearly half an hour, easily the longest smoke-oh I'd yet enjoyed, he held me entranced, turning to every point of the compass describing mining fields and camps near and far. Presently I vaguely realized what a vast district this was, impossible to visualize if a man knew only that handful of townships up on the Tableland along the Cairns line. A man could easily spend a lifetime seeking minerals in this district if he wished. And again came that ever-present, unhappy thought, But how *can* a man move without horses, without the few pounds to buy them to carry his tucker and tools?

"Come along! We'd better get moving!" said the voice.

"The old hands must have been great bushmen to find their way into all this country," I said as we stood up, "and to find all these scattered fields."

"Yes," he answered, "some of the best. Prospectors mostly, and cattle-men. Good men among the timber men, too, they *had* to be good. But one man was the great pathfinder, one man's tracks opened up sugar lands and timber lands and mineral fields. Christy Palmerston was the greatest bushman of all time."

And he was striding away down the spur. Thus did I gain the first inkling that my strange mate worshipped the deeds of that elusive character, Christy Palmerston.

CHAPTER XXIV

THE THOUGHT-READER

THAT night we camped yet again beside the shelter of a gigantic rock. Like wallabies in the grass, I thought morosely.

"There's one out there now!"

Startled, I wondered whether I had really heard the Voice.

"Do you hear him?" I asked hesitantly, then added, "*or* smell him?"

"Both," he replied quietly, "and see him also. He's been poking about down there for quite a while."

I could hear, see nothing but the mysterious shapes of the night.

"You must have the eyes of an owl!" I declared.

"Infinitely better—for I can see clearly and a long distance by day. However, the owl beats me by night. There he goes! Away down there by that clump of granite!"

"Thud! Thud!" Silence. "Thud! Thud! Thud!" Distinctly now I could hear a wallaby leisurely hopping his way out of our lives. But as for seeing him—! I could but vaguely make out the outline of that "clump of granite"—and massive boulders indeed they were.

"You must have marvellous night-sight, all the same," I said enviously and settled back on the blanket.

"Reasonably so. With years of constant training, and night-sight will grow *within* a man. The awakening of a sleeping gift from our ancestors!" and I seemed to feel him smiling. "However," he said, "there is far more light at night, even on a dark night, than our civilized life is aware of. It is a matter of realizing this, then by constant practice training the eyes to 'collect' the light rays—I suppose you would call it 'focus' them."

We both were silent. I was but little more than a lad, the world —our world, anyway—was still in its horse-and-buggy days, this subject was a little too deep for me.

At last I doubtfully ventured, "You seemed to read my thoughts again!"

For the second time I heard him laugh, a soft laugh, up at the stars.

"The 'wallaby' thought? Yes. But you're not bewitched," he quietly reassured me. "It's really simple, because it's natural—but only, of course, at times—when the necessary conditions are perfect. After all, I know quite a lot about you, far more than you realize. But quite naturally so. I love the bush. So do you. Animals, trees, birds, hills, plains, rivers, minerals, prospectors, settlers, distances, are all of interest to you. Your thoughts are filled with what little you know of the bush, you are eager to learn much more. Rocks and gullies, reefs and rivers and creek-beds are of particular interest to you. Your mind is a whirlpool of 'Gold! Gold! Gold!' 'Water! Water! Water!'—at present shaded by 'Tin! Tin! Tin!' Such thoughts in the men of the mining camps are nearly as close to me as the air I breathe. Well, here we are, two men alone in the night bush. In a shadowy way of speaking, our thoughts—some of them, anyway—are almost common property. We are resting. You are tired. Your thoughts die away a bit, then momentarily concentrate on one simple subject of common interest to us both—and I am lying here in a *receptive* state of mind. You thought—a bit touchily, because you'd rather be sitting by some campfire listening to the boys yarning about minerals—you thought 'camping here like a pair of wallabies'. My mind, for it too was concerned, quite naturally received that thought. It was only that I'd been watching that wallaby for some little time that I mentioned it—it just seemed to fit in, as a little joke."

I could not see that joke, perhaps because of a sort of creepy feeling. And in the silence I could almost have sworn he was lying there amused.

Then he was saying, "Try it! See if you can receive *my* thoughts. First, become receptive. Listen to the voices of the bush, absorb the night—and what it tells—into you. Then I will send you a direct thought."

But I was too startled. Staring out into the night, presently I could feel that silence. And it grew strange, as if alive. Dimly I began to smell the earth, and the grass. The ghostly granite boulders were being caressed by cold starlight. I almost felt they liked it after the heat of the day. Even the dim shapes of the trees seemed listening, almost as if "a something" were about. Uneasily I turned over and, dead tired, was sound asleep.

One mine in the Stannary Hills I was very keen to see, for its virtues were spoken of in awed tones as far away as Herberton. This was "the Lass"—otherwise the Lass o' Gowrie.

For the Lass was much more than a good show, she was the stuff that the prospector's dream is made of. Always to be depended upon to keep the straight and narrow path as a true fissure lode should, she kept between her foot and hanging wall, clean and sweet as the tasty ham in a well-cut sandwich. Within those close-cut walls there was never any fear of the Lass skipping aside and vanishing, thus causing a frantic search to left and right, ahead and behind and below by the despairing owner in an effort to pick her up again. Alas! Such happenings were common with most lodes and reefs—here today, gone tomorrow!

But not so the Lass, not once yet had she proved flighty. When the toilers knocked off for the night the Lass, with her staunch belt of good tinstone, could confidently be depended to be there tomorrow. And the next night also. And the next year.

Sweet in such happy virtues, naturally the Lass was sweet in riches also. And here again her consistency shone true, a consistent producer. For year by year she "made" generous bunches of rich ore that were the talk and envy of township and hills far, far away. Yes, the Lass was a "sweet" mine. Quite rightfully, the lucky owner and partners strutted with swelled chests, matched by swelled bank accounts.

No wonder the Lass was the pride and favourite of all the Stannary Hills.

In wandering years I was occasionally to meet with a favourite mine, a mine esteemed by an entire district. I was already familiar with one, the Big Mine of Broken Hill, and with "sweet" claims on the White Cliffs opal-fields, and on Lightning Ridge. The little Lass o' Gowrie in far away Stannary Hills was only a tiny miniature of a mine of course, compared to the Big Mine of the Silver City. I did not realize it then, maybe lots of Australians hardly do now, but the Big Mine of Broken Hill with its ramifications was to play its part, and a big part, in the destiny of our nation.

My ever-restless mate tolerantly gave me time to browse about the Lass, possibly because his queer nature admired something nearly perfect in nature. I don't know. He was to grow ever more of a puzzle to me. Anyway, I spent fascinating hours exploring, my many questions being weclomed by the miners who quite obviously found pleasure in working on the Lass.

I hardly knew when I was aboard the "train", for my mind was still full of the Lass, and how I would just love to find such another one. But there we were rattling along behind the cheeky little Puffing Jinny of the Stannary Hills Mines and Tramway Company, quite unaware how and why I was aboard, unaware of whither I was bound. Nor did I care, for this was a hilarious experience to a lad as we rattled round precipitous curves, and puffed along the edge of gorge after gorge with wild bush towering to left and right, in whose depths and heights I wondered how many Lasses o' Gowrie might lay hidden.

No fine big roomy carriages on *this* railway, the funny little engine, the track itself, would have disdained such. These carriages were affectionately called "dog-boxes" by the boys. One grizzled old-timer squatting beside me, pocket-knife in hand, contemplatively rolling plug tobacco between horny palms, amiably advised me: "Better keep yewr head inside that what they call a winder, young feller, else yew'll git it knocked orf goin' eround them bends. An' hang orn like grim death when we're jerkin' eround them gorges or yew're liable to be thrown right out an' over. An' this train don't stop fer corpses. Wouldn't be no use lookin', anyway. Oncet a bloke went out over there no one could climb down after him anyways."

"That's true enough!" I admitted, for just then we were skirting the extreme edge of a hair-raising precipice.

"Unroll yewr swag an' spread it on ther seat," he advised kindly. "No man can sit comfortable on these seats until he's grown corns on his arse like a mule's hoof."

Sundry other advice he amiably gave me as we jerked and rattled and puffed along, deflating my bushman's pride by taking me for some lily-white product of civilization worthy of a little kindly advice and encouragement. And I had been a bush lad all my life! But then this gnarled old museum piece, like many of the old-timers back in "them thar hills", had reached the stage when they cleaned their teeth with sandpaper and trimmed their toe-nails with a blacksmith's rasp.

The old dinosaur's warning was quite correct, though, for a man with his head out of the window was liable to get it smartly rapped indeed against the sheer rock wall when the train was jerking its way round a cutting. The engineers on a job like this naturally had to save every inch. I wondered how the funny, swaying little trucks did not smash again and again against those rock walls. Just once, with long wheezy groans, terrific clankings, and clouds of steam, we came to a groaning stop—to my joyful interest. For automatically all hands began climbing out, then, warily clinging by the side of the trucks, we strolled up to the puffing, waiting engine. Some tons of rocks and a gnarled old tree had crashed down into a cutting along the mountain-side.

Axes were brought from the engine, sapling levers cut, and the tree was sawn and chopped into lengths, which one by one were levered over into the gorge. All hands manhandled the boulders, rolling them over with a cheer as each one bounced out into space, dusted their hands on their trouser seats, pulled out the pipes, and casually strolled back yarning to their seats again. The engine crew climbed aboard, a wave and a yell of "All aboard!" and the engine gave a hoarse blast that echoed defiantly up and down the gorge. A rending tremor, a cloud of steam, a creaking strain, and slowly we shuddered into movement. A few hoarse, energetic puffs, and we were smartly on our way again.

A wonderful piece of engineering work, that miniature railway—as were others built by various mining companies among the maze of ranges just here giving way to less interesting, flatter country.

"What is that big peak sticking up away ahead," I asked.

"Boonmoo, the aboriginals call it," my mate answered. "It means 'the jump-up'."

"It certainly jumps up."

"Yes. From that summit on a clear day you can see away out over a hundred miles of country. It is a pinnacle of alum."

"Alum?" I said doubtfully.

"Yes, you don't believe me again," he replied calmly. "You've seen alum used in the kitchen at home?"

"Yes."

"Well, then, alum is a rock. And Boonmoo is a pinnacle of alum, believe it or not."

"What else is there, besides alum?"

"Nothing much," he replied indifferently, "just a little bush pub. When last I was there it was kept by Bill Jackson. I suppose he's still there if no one has killed him."

"Why should they?"

"Oh, he's a notorious joker, he'd rather enjoy a good joke than a good feed any day. If a traveller is a bit timid about snakes he'll quite likely wake up to find a big carpet snake slumbering in his bed. Harmless, of course, but hardly a welcome bedmate. And not the only pet of Old Bill's, either; wild things seem to like him. If a new-chum is scared of wild aboriginals he may be 'attacked' by painted, naked, screaming savages. The tame abos love that joke. Old Bill gives them a stick of Nigger Twist tobacco each, and I've no doubt a bottle of what he calls rum; they wish he'd spend all his time playing jokes. However, as with many jokes, there can be an element of danger, just a chance that in a joke like that some nervous traveller might shoot one of those charging warriors."

"That could happen." I grinned. "This old publican must be a character."

"He is," he replied shortly. "He's a decent enough old roughneck, if it wasn't for his lunatic jokes. However, he's always been willing to give a down-and-out a helping hand."

Something in his tone warned me that *he* might have been one victim of the old publican's. This man would not take kindly to a practical joke. Suddenly I knew I'd never put a billygoat into *his* bed, as I had into Old Mick's.

It was only when we came clattering into Boonmoo, the junction with the Chillagoe Tramway, that I realized our walkabout was ended. With a little chill, too, for my hobnail boots were definitely worn out beyond all repair and it might cost as much as 7s. 6d. to buy another pair.

At Mareeba we boarded the Cairns-Herberton train, which was in no great hurry. Nor was I. But at last we came puffing up into the hills of Herberton, which then was the end of the line and meant I had to stroll out and continue per Shanks's pony.

By the little station he turned to me and casually said, "Oh, well, so long! Will be seeing you," and with a half nod turned and quietly strode away in the direction, I knew, of the Dry River.

CHAPTER XXV

OLD MICK'S "FAMILY"

I GAZED at his nonchalant back a moment, then turned in the opposite direction, returned the "Good day, Jack!" of several passers-by and was stepping out on the brown, open road back to Nigger Creek. I was happy as a lark as soon as a momentary grouch against my unusual mate had faded. After all, this short trip had broadened my local knowledge tremendously, and as I thought over things, walking along, I grew more and more surprised at all I'd learnt and vaguely conscious of lots more I'd missed. I hoped then that I'd see him again, and wondered yet again why he'd chosen me for a walking partner. Maybe because anyone else would have insisted on prospecting. On the whole trip he'd never tried one dish, had not knapped one solitary reef. He certainly was a strange mate to go prospecting with; those queer ideas of his were sometimes difficult to understand, too. But he certainly did know the country, and wonderful things about it. And he loved it. I dimly realized then that if I'd done or said anything to upset his apple-cart I'd never have seen him again.

Such puzzled thoughts faded at sight of Nigger Creek. A beautiful day, sunlight gleaming upon the hillsides, the Wild River quietly singing down there beside me, the dusty road meandering on, the steel rails so newly laid stretching on and on. And now just ahead were the two pubs, and there the Meeting of the Waters and the farther gentle slope where Garnet's tiny school stood out, there was Grigg's little store and the cottage with the flowering creepers where the pretty girl fed the gluttonous duck. There were the half-dozen other little cottages, and now I could see Old Brookes's camp. And yes, there was little Tommy Turley outlined up on his dump on the rise, with his hunched back and skinny, bowed little arms and legs, as slowly he turned the windlass handle like a spider winding a laborious web. A great little toiler, was Tommy Turley. Soon I would see Mick and Jim and Garnet, and the anticipation was pleasant. Then, from the school, a lad came running. Breathlessly he told me that Mr Aitchison the schoolmaster would like to see me before I went to my camp.

Garnet came smartly to meet me, with his ready smile, but I felt he was worried.

"Had a good trip, Jack?"

"Yes, Garnet, I've lots to tell you."

"Good, I'm keen to hear all about it—I'll be right over as soon as the Council meets this evening. Meanwhile, I wish you'd call at Old Mick's camp on your way across. Old Mick is very ill. Jim is working down the creek."

"Ill! I'm real sorry to hear that! What is the matter with him?"

"Fever—malaria. Jim has been very worried, but Old Mick simply refuses to go into Herberton Hospital. He's stubborn as a mule when he likes—you'd be surprised!"

"I'll call in and see him before I go to camp."

"I wish you would. Jim can't be with him *all* the time. Jim has been doctoring him up by night, working the claim and cooking and trying to tempt him to eat. Old Brookes and Turley keep an eye on him, too, but he's so irritable they can't do anything with him; he only wants to be left alone. You might be able to manage the stubborn old he-goat—he thinks a lot of you. Coax him to go to hospital where he can be fixed up in no time."

"Right. I'll do the best I can."

"Good, I knew you would." Garnet seemed very much relieved. "I'll come across and hear all the news this evening." And as, with a wave, the schoolmaster turned back for duty all the little heads poking from schoolhouse door and window popped back.

I hurried up along the creek towards Old Mick's camp, concerned about the sick railway ganger. Nearing the camp I saw and heard the chattering birds, that part seemed all right, anyway. Those knowing birds from far and wide so confidently "calling in" at the camp sure of more than a crumb or two if Old Mick was about. The camp was big and neat and comfortable looking as usual, Jim Bell's hand plain to see in everything he did. Soon I could see right through the camp, the big tent sides would not be lowered until night. All was quiet with the dreamy doziness of midafternoon. Approaching along the grassy creek bank, my footsteps made no sound. Then I walked slower, puzzled. Then stopped.

The sick man was sitting bowed over the camp table, he was not tossing feverishly in his bunk. In a patched old flannel, all hunched up in an attitude of painful concentration, he was slowly gnawing a pencil end and staring fixedly at a writing pad before him.

The sick man was in the throes of composing a "pome"!

For quite a while I stood there, a grinning spy. The old ganger was completely engrossed in his task, his furrowed brow nearly as corrugated as the logs bridging a creek crossing.

Those weather-beaten eyebrows of his are as bushy as a mule's tail, I thought, grinning. I wonder if Shakespeare ever looked like that!

An inexperienced fly settled expectantly on that weather-tanned nose and flew disgustedly away. No wonder. Any fly that tried to bite into that leathery beak would surely blunt its boring tool. Anyway, the old ganger was oblivious of everything but the heavy labour of digging out this "pome". He was no more sick than I was.

I stepped right into the camp and stood beside him. He became aware of my legs first, his eyes followed them up with a guilty uneasiness, then he gasped out a relieved, "Jack!"

As instinctively he reached back to roll into bunk I grinned. "Suffering a relapse, Mick?"

"Yes, Jack," and he tried to make it a weak voice. "You startled me. I've had a nasty bout of fever," he sighed.

"Liar! You're no more sick than *I* am! You're poling on your mate while you loaf here scribbling bad poetry. There's Jim Bell toiling his ribs out down the claim, worrying about you while he works double shifts to keep the tucker-bags filled. You've got the whole camp worried while you calmly squat here scribbling *this* stuff!" And I picked up the scribbling pad and scoffed at the evidence of his guilt:

> "There's a lovely maid in Nigger Creek
> Where the Wild River flows. . . . "

"Lovely maid my eye! What the blazes would she have to do with *you*, anyway? You're an old shyster, Mick—just wait until I tell Jim Bell!"

"You won't put me away, Jack?" he asked anxiously.

"Why shouldn't I? You're poling on your mate!" Sternly I frowned down at that grizzled old face, it looked awful now with a few days' growth of stubble that I knew he'd let sprout on purpose.

"But, Jack, *you* above all men know what it takes to write a pome!" he pleaded. "*Any* man can swing a pick and shovel! Jim likes it! But supposing now, just on the off chance, I *could* write a *real* pome!" He gazed earnestly at me.

I tried to scowl.

"Now, Jack, you *know* how it is," he continued ingratiatingly. "They laugh at me. The only chance I've got of doing anything is through some little lurk like this!"

Lest I burst out laughing I frowned again, most sternly. "Oh, well, for just this *once* I won't put you away. But you get up on your pins quick and lively, shave that awful whisker off what passes for a face, then get out to the galley and put the billy on and cook Jim's tea for him. He'll be knocking off soon, anxious to see how *you* are getting on—I notice he's got a billy-can of soup simmering on the galley to try and tempt your appetite—you double-crossing old fraud! Well, *you* be moving about the camp and let him see you're fully recovered when he comes back from work. If not—!"

A relieved grin twinkled in Mick's eyes. "You're the ganger, Jack, I'm only the navvy. What you say goes. But perhaps I'd better not shave, not until morning."

"And just why not, now?"

"Well—" he grinned sheepishly—"you can see how it is. Or rather, how it *will* be!"

"Oh!" I said understandingly, "you cunning old devil! You look like nothing on earth with that stubble! If you shaved you'd look as healthy as you really are and Jim would slit your throat—as he ought to. Why, I believe you've actually put on weight!"

Mick grinned happily, he had won. "Just mind your feet, Jack."

"What's wrong with my feet?" I demanded.

"They're quite all right, Jack," he explained hastily, "but those hobnails—I've been afraid all the time you might hurt one of the family", and he bent down and, picking up a little lizard, placed it on a scrap of scarlet rag upon the table. Slowly the lizard took on a rosy hue.

"What on earth—!" I began.

"Don't you recognize Jack?" he asked disappointedly.

"Recognize *what*?"

"You remember the little lizard I showed you a few weeks ago, the one I put under the tin with the jam on top to catch the ants?"

"What about the dashed thing?" I asked.

"Well, this is Jack. Don't you remember saying I ought to get a wife for him?"

"Good Heavens, Mick! Have you really called this fool of a thing after me? I ought to let Jim knock your block off! How on earth would I remember a stupid thing like that, anyway! But I *do* remember, though."

With a satisfied grin Mick bent down again and brought up another lizard, a smaller, noticeably fatter one, and triumphantly placed it beside its mate. I watched as slowly it turned into rose colour.

"Rosie," introduced Mick simply, "Jack's missus."

"I'll upset the water bucket on you in a moment, you grinning old has-been. Do you mean you actually mated these two silly-looking lizards?"

"Yes," he replied with eager satisfaction. "I had some little difficulty at first, but I remembered a look I'd caught in your eye one day when you were watching that girl feeding the ducks. But I had to catch quite a number of lizards and show 'em to Jack before he responded. It worked out all right!"

"You see more than you damn' well should!"

Hiding a grin, he bent down again and gently lifted up a baby lizard. Placing it beside the parents he announced proudly, "Jim! The first-born! Son and heir!" He bent down again and up came a fatter baby lizard. "Meet Old Brookes!" Beside "Old Brookes" he placed a skinny little baby "Tommy Turley". A lively little lizard was "Garnet". And beside "Garnet" up came another "Jack"!

"That's a dopy-looking thing you've called after me again! I thought I was supposed to be the old man," I complained.

"Ah, but we must have *two* Jacks in such a distinguished family," he declared enthusiastically, "and our baby Jack is developing into a deep thinker." He stroked the sleepy little thing with a caressing finger.

I had to laugh as one after the other he gently picked them up until eleven rose-pink baby lizards lay there beside "Mum and Dad", otherwise "Jack and Rosie". I understood Mick's concern now, for I hadn't seen his precious little brood around my feet since of course they had taken on the colour of the floor.

"And what does Jim think of this family of yours?"

"He doesn't know about them, at least not *all* of them." Mick smiled. "They keep well out of the way when Jim's in camp, they know quite well he objects to lizards about the place. Wonderful how soon they come scuttling in to keep me company when I'm alone."

"Well then, what on earth is going to happen when all this crowd find wives and husbands and bring their families into camp to be fed? You and Jim will be eaten out of house and home!"

"God looks after the sparrows," replied Mick wisely. "God will provide."

"Loading your problems on to someone else's shoulders, as usual! Oh well," I said, laughing, "I'm glad it won't be *me*. I'm off to camp now. And you get busy out at the galley—Jim will be knocking off work any time now. What a wonderful recovery you've made, Mick! And if you don't let Jim see it I'll certainly spill the beans when I come across to the camp for a yarn tonight." And I strolled away to my own camp, all the better for a good laugh. What a difference there was between Mick and my strange mate of the hills! And between Jim Bell and Garnet and me, and Old Brookes and little Tommy Turley. What a difference there was between *all* men!

It was with a feeling of wonderment that I came to my own deserted camp.

There were not even lizards to greet me.

CHAPTER XXVI

THE SECRET

THOUGH I was breaking my neck to spill the beans, I dared not tell Garnet Aitchison about Old Mick. That high-spirited prankster could not possibly have kept the secret. To think that "poor old sick Mick" had so beautifully pulled their legs while composing a "pome" would have appealed to the young schoolmaster as "priceless", he just could not have kept it to himself. I doubt very much whether I could have, had it not been for some subtle influence of my strange mate. For now, as I dawdled about camp after sunset, I was thinking of that quiet, set face illumined by the firelight upon the rocks, a face that could hold *any* secret. Walking slowly down through evening towards the Council Fire, some whimsical fancy whispered to me, telling me to prove I could be as secretive as the Jungle Man. Otherwise I'm certain I should have awaited a ripe opportunity, then with gusto blurted out the story of the old ganger's perfidy.

I'd given the boys plenty of time to gather together and unload their congratulations at the patient's amazing recovery. Now, instinctively treading softly, I paused outside the ring of firelight and listened a few moments, noting how clearly each man's voice came to me. Was this the Jungle Man whispering? I could catch the ring of pleasure in each voice, and quickly knew the sentiments of each and every one. But they had no idea I was there! Quite interested by this little experience, I stood there awhile longer. They were all present, Matt Stillane also and Tom Burgess and Gallogoly and Long Stewart from Flaggy Creek, and three friends of Old Mick's from out Tumoulin way who occasionally visited Mick and Jim by the railhead pump-car. What a gathering of the clans, drawn together in sympathy because of "poor old sick Mick"! I'd have the greatest difficulty in keeping that secret I thought as I grinned towards the convalescent sitting hunched up there with a coat on and a blanket wrapped round his knees. Jim had insisted, despite the patient's feeble protests.

"You might catch a chill, Mick, you know, sitting out here in the cool so soon. You've been a sick man, remember!"

Sick my eye, you old fraud! I thought, then, mustering a solemn face, stepped into the firelight. And I was given the cheeriest of greetings, Garnet actually preparing a seat for the returned wanderer.

"Here's the conquering hero, the doctor *par excellence*!" Garnet introduced me enthusiastically. "Poor Old Mick has had Jim near worried out of his life. Mick in the Land of Moans and Groans for the last fortnight, but no sooner does Jack appear than Mick's fevered brow cools to the magic presence. The renowned Hippocrates himself could not have wrought such a change. And here now is the patient eating almost heartily, and back on his feet again—though it's his tail at present. In a day or two he'll be composing another 'pome'."

Across the firelight I caught Mick's appealing eye.

"I'm sure I'd like to hear his last poem!" I said, nearly biting my tongue to hold back the secret.

"It's marvellous, Jack," said Jim seriously. "I don't mean his idiotic pomes, I'd just about made up my mind to manhandle him to the railway tricycle, tie him down, and pump him into Herberton to the doctor. And here when I knock off he's up and about the camp and even has dinner cooked!" And Jim, obviously very relieved, looked just as puzzled.

"He must have taken a turn for the better before I came along," I explained. "He was well on the road to recovery, for he began pottering about soon after I arrived."

"So long as he doesn't overdo it and suffer a relapse!" murmured Old Brookes.

"If he does," I said to Jim Bell, "I'll give you a hand and we'll manhandle him straight to the pump-car. Hospital is the only place for a sick man if he falls sick again!"

Old Mick kept a discreet silence.

"We thought you were a goner this time, Mick," teased Garnet.

Mick sighed. "Only the good die young."

"Then *you'll* live for ever!" declared Jim Bell.

Mick's shaggy eyebrows lifted quizzically.

"I was a pretty sick man!" he protested mildly.

"Sick maybe," admitted Jim, "but pretty—never!"

"Never mind, Mick!" Garnet laughed. "You would have made a pretty corpse. Had you written us out your epitaph, by the way?"

"No," answered Mick brightly, "but there's one I'd like."

"What is it?"

"The poet Gay's."

"And what is that?"

> *"Life is a jest, and all things show it.*
> *I thought so once, but now I know it."*

At our hearty applause, Mick beamed.

"How quickly he recovers, soon as you mention poetry," mused Old Brookes.

Jim Bell glanced in puzzled fashion towards the convalescent.

"I thought you might have been going to give us Longfellow," said Garnet. "It would just suit you, too.

> *"Life is real! Life is earnest!*
> *And the grave is not its goal!"*

"That's a bonzer pome," said Mick enthusiastically. "No, I was not thinking of that one, I was thinking—"

"Since when?" broke in Jim Bell.

"I was thinking of Shakespeare," said Mick serenely. "He's got some real good ones."

"What? Tips for the races?" inquired Jim.

"No," replied Mick, "epitaphs. Have you ever read Shakespeare?"

"No."

"Ah!" breathed Mick.

"But I *have* read!" declared Jim.

"What *have* you read?"

"Red hairs on the back of my neck!"

We sniggered at Mick's disgusted grimace.

"He's getting better so quickly you won't be able to hold him back from the windlass handle tomorrow," laughed Tommy Turley.

Mick glanced at me in obvious alarm.

"Don't you dare go into a relapse, Mick," I warned, "or it's the pump-car and hospital for you!"

"It's all right, Jack," said Mick, grinning, "I feel a lot better now. I'll be right for toil tomorrow."

Jim Bell sat with crossed legs, puffing at his pipe and regarding the convalescent most suspiciously.

"All the same," said Jim deliberately, "I think he'd better go into Herberton tomorrow and see the doctor—just to make sure!"

"No fear, I'm all right now," protested Mick. "The last time I saw a doctor he said he didn't like the looks of me."

"Who would?" inquired Jim.

"Now then, Jim, you'll have our patient taking to his bunk again," warned Garnet. "Look how flustered you've got him—I believe he's running a temperature."

"If he is," said Jim with a doubtful frown, "then it's the first time I've ever known him run hot. Oh well, I suppose the old goat *was* sick. He acted it, anyway. Pretty well, too—one night I really thought he might be going to die."

"I nearly did," sighed Mick.

"Then why didn't you?"

"I changed my mind."

"Never knew you had one," murmured Jim.

"You're a long way from dying yet, Mick," said Garnet, "though one night you *did* look extra awful."

"If possible!" said Jim.

"I could hear those angels singing," sighed Mick.

"Angels!" snorted Jim. "It's Old Nick *you* heard—in a hurry to close the gates!"

"That would be stiff luck," said Old Brookes, "to be shut out of *both* places. What would you do about it, Mick?"

Mick glanced up at the sky. "Compose a pome," he murmured. "I'd find a fleecy cloud to sit on. I'd call it—I'd call that pome—" he shut his eyes, his face screwed up in a most awful grimace; Old Mick was in the throes of the Birth of an Idea—"I'd call that pome," he declared hoarsely, " 'Denied from Paradise, Barred from Hell'!"

"Of all the priceless idiots!" exploded Jim Bell.

"Tell us about your trip, Jack," said Garnet, laughing.

Which I did.

"A strange mate you travelled with," said one of the old hands reminiscently. "Do you know that you're the only man he has ever taken on a trip? So far as the few of us who know him are aware of, anyway. He works alone, too, never been known to have a mate, either working or travelling."

"Tell me about him," I asked eagerly.

"There's nothing to tell, for nobody knows anything about him. He's here today, gone tomorrow. He was knocking about on the Ravenshoe side for a while, and I met him again north on the Chillagoe side. Then away down on the coast on the Russell River gold. He wanders about on his own. Seems to like the big scrubs, though. He disappears in there—it's rumoured he knows of a golden creek in there somewhere, but only works it when he needs a few ounces of gold. I dunno. He's been followed by good men a time or two, but he simply vanishes. Whether the crafty devil knows he's being followed or not no one knows, but he's led the boys a hell of a chase on three occasions I know of, then vanished as if the ground had swallowed him. And the boys have had niggers doing the tracking, too."

"Then he just *must* have known!" declared Jim Bell.

"I suppose so. Just the sort of thing he'd delight in doing anyway. Lead them into the most difficult country he knows of, then leave them find their way out as best they can. Two parties who sleuthed him struggled back in a bad way."

Good luck to him, I thought with satisfaction.

"He must be a Christy Palmerston if he can beat native trackers," said Old Brookes doubtfully.

"He is. The natives know him well, but they close up like a clam if you ask them anything about him. They seem to both like and fear him, just like they did Christy. Some of the boys have tried to bribe the natives to follow him on their own and find out if he really has a secret gully, but they won't take it on at all. And I don't think it's because they're afraid of being shot either. And you couldn't find a better place to shoot a man than in the big scrubs—he'd be there until Doomsday, or rather until the wild pigs ate him. No, he's a queer bird all right. Down on the Russell River the gold-sluicers call him 'the man nobody knows'."

I glanced at Long Stewart, wondering whether *he* knew that the Jungle Man knew all about those death-adders! But Stewart's calm face gave no sign, and I doubted if he knew a thing. He was simply listening with interest, that was all.

"Any news of our local dusky society?" I inquired.

At which Mick chuckled. "Yes! Big happenings—marriages, births, murders, fights, abductions—just the usual news when we are honoured by a visit from our dusky brethren, except that this occasion was something right out of the box. The *entente cordiale*, as it were."

"Cut out the bullswool," growled Jim Bell. "Spit out the simple facts."

"A Great Event!" went on Mick placidly. "A crowd of our cultured primitives from the depths of the big scrubs descended upon Nigger Creek chattering in a lather of excitement, piccaninnies and dogs and the tribal fleas included. Two of their number in the grip of the heart-throb wished to become united—in white-man fashion."

"For the love o' Mike!" declared the exasperated Jim.

"These two bashful young worshippers of Venus," Mick continued, "were Warrigal and Nellie. Our good friend Brookes here, who officiated as parson, declared them so, when the whole mob of them descended upon his camp with the demand that *he* marry these two shrinking violets white-man fashion. The groom had to have a name first, so Brookes chucked a bucket of water over him and christened him Warrigal, because he did look as wild as a wild dog from the hills. He doused another bucket over the blushing bride and christened her Nellie, because, as Parson here told us, she'd look like any other Nellie after a year or two of marriage. So Parson Brookes then prepares to officiate solemn like, threads a necklace of rum-bottle corks through his whiskers, pins a flour-bag over his shoulders, makes bashful groom and bride stand hand in hand while the mob stand round with eyes sticking out like pickled onions. Then Parson Brookes holds up his hand and holds forth with mumbo-jumbo while sternly ordering Tommy Malone and Dick Bates to wipe the grin off their faces. Our solemn friend Brookes here, with his whiskers dusted in flour, acted the part real human like. Then he waved Tommy and Dick do their piece. So, carrying a long sapling between them, they walked to a nice grassy patch fifty yards away and held the sapling between them.

" 'Hand in hand,' explained Parson to Warrigal and Nellie, 'you must run and jump over that sapling, then you will be married white-man fashion.' When at last it dawned within Warrigal's thick skull of the simple thing he was required to do his smile was the grin of a tiger. And it was reflected upon Nellie's cherubic countenance."

"My Gawd!" moaned Jim Bell. "And to think you were near dying last night! A pity you didn't!"

"It was such an easy jump," droned Mick somewhat hurriedly, "so with a happy laugh they clasped paws and ran at it. As they rose gracefully into the air the pole jerked up between their legs and they came down together with a belly-grunting thump upon the grass. But they jumped up smiling, believing it all part of the ceremony. Assured then that the knot was well and truly tied, the whole mob in high glee raced caterwauling down to the creek to celebrate in corroboree fashion. And thus, in your absence, Warrigal and Nellie from the big scrubs were married white-man fashion by Parson Brookes at Nigger Creek!"

"And if it took Brookes as long to marry them as it takes you to tell—you don't look very sick now, you grinning old hyena." And it gave me quite a kick to watch that deep suspicion smouldering on Jim Bell's puzzled face.

"Oh well," said Old Brookes with a smile, "they got their wish. Nellie's eyes shone like a cat's at night, and she giggled all the time like a pullet crowing over its first egg. Oh well, maybe the happy union will last longer than her sister's down the line."

I'm afraid we laughed at the allusion—no wild bride from the scrubs this, but a very sophisticated sister down Mareeba way. Her ambition, which would not be denied, was that hers must be a town marriage, she must be married to bridegroom Abraham by a "real" parson in a "real" church.

And she was. The white folk lent an encouraging hand. A local paper reported the wedding in style, the bouquet and dress of the blushing bride and so forth. The folk all along the line were kind to the aborigines and were always willing to lend a hand if they thought any of the local abos really wished to better themselves. But what the local rag did *not* report was the proud remark of the bride as she swept down the aisle to the triumphant peals of the Wedding March.

"Me alla same white lady now! Me married longa church! Me have three husbands before longa camp. Me married proper fella now longa church true husband!"

That bright-eyed brunette, so Jade Rumour declared, was really true to her church husband for three whole weeks.

"They're a funny people," remarked a quiet old visitor from Tumoulin who had come to see "poor sick Mick". "They remind me of us in some ways. Only a while back I was deep in the Evelyn scrubs spying out the timber. A furious argument broke out in the blacks' camp—over a lady. It appears she was bitten with the wanderlust when the moon shone bright. So hubby and Romeo were arguing about the divorce. They couldn't come to terms so in the heat of the argument hubby thrust an eight-foot spear through the wandering lady. Which ended the problem with finality, a judgment from which there could be no appeal. All parties, including the tribe, were quite satisfied—the lady, of course, having no say in the matter. But several days later the husband began to grumble a bit, he was waking up to the fact that he'd lost damages. Also a wife who, though somewhat unreliable in the moon season, was still a good worker. The damages, I understand, were to have been three hunting spears, a woomera, and a speckled cattle-dog. The husband grieved over the loss of that cattle-dog until it preyed on his mind. Then he sharpened the barbs on his war spears and went looking for Romeo. He is still looking. So that the case, which appeared to have been settled with such grim finality, is not settled yet."

"What happened to the speckled cattle-dog?" asked Garnet.

"That bone of contention is seeking distant horizons with Romeo," replied the Tumoulin man.

"They're practical people, too," remarked his friend. "I was 'way back in those scrubs down in the gorge a couple of years ago, prospecting. And taking care to mind my own business—it is a lonesome place. There was a tribal war on and the tribe near by captured a prisoner, a fine young buck, too, only a lad, and terrified. I had an idea of buying him from them when the excitement died down a bit, a tomahawk and half a case of Nigger Twist tobacco would have done the trick. But I left it too late. When I strolled across to the camp they'd broken both his legs at the ankles.

" 'What did you do that for?' I demanded.

" 'So him bin no get away!' a warrior replied, and gaped at me as if I was a fool for asking such a question. Which I was."

"What happened to the young prisoner?" Garnet asked.

"They killed him, of course. What use is a man with two broken legs in the big scrubs? Or anywhere else in the bush, for that matter?"

"Yes, they're a queer people." Paddy grinned. "They've got a great pride in their family trees, too, just like our blue-bloods. But I wouldn't be surprised if they are more scientific in keeping the old tree breeding true than we are, even though we reckon they're Stone Age savages. Anyway, old Cumbilooroo—you remember him, Jack, skinny as a crane, one-eyed, with a leer like last year's bad debts? Well, his gin brought a piccaninny into the

227

world that looked like a nightmare of the old man. The poor little wretch had a head shaped like a dingo, and its arms and legs were abnormally long, if you could call the skinny, crooked little things arms. Fingers and toes like claws. Well, old Cumbilooroo took a violent dislike to his offspring, probably because it reminded him of what he saw when he bent down at a waterhole to drink. Anyway, he waited until his woman was asleep, snatched the baby from her arms, hit it over the head with his nullah, and callously threw it away into the bush. The mother, though, was inconsolable. Thus, the 'white-man law' soon caught up with Cumbilooroo.

" 'Why did you kill your piccanin?' demanded the policeman.

"Old Cumbilooroo grinned pityingly at the policeman's ignorance. 'Him baby no good,' he explained scornfully. 'Him alla same longa grasshopper!' "

Walking up the slope to camp late that night, I realized I'd got a real kick out of this evening. All the time I'd known what no other man there knew except the anxious Mick, though Jim Bell almost suspected. Surely this must be something like the pleasure that secretive Jungle Man enjoyed: to know things other men didn't know but keep it to himself. It was quite interesting to think about. But few men could or would go to all that long, secretive trouble. I grinned at the thought of how all the time I had been longing to put Old Mick away, and when I thought of Jim Bell's puzzled, suspicious face I chuckled into the night. How Garnet would have laughed, and the others, too, had I only spilt the beans!

Entering the cold tent, I lit the stub of a candle and shoved that infernal possum off the bunk; he hissed quite aggressively as I tried to kick him out into the night.

Kicking off my boots, I rolled into the blanket, started filling a final pipe, and laughed.

I should have just loved to put Old Mick away, but I was glad I hadn't now.

But let the old fraud beware, should he ever again try to force me to write another "pome"!

CHAPTER XXVII

THE PUMP

EVER seeking variety in the search for fortune, I moved camp for the time being to Flaggy Creek, a few miles farther along the Deep Lead. Here, for some seven miles along the Lead, scattered working parties were toiling to unearth fortune from the old river-bed deep beneath the basalt. Abandoned shafts and tunnels stretched for some miles where fortunes (for those days) had been won in alluvial tin during earlier years. The men working here now were toiling under appalling difficulties—dangerous ground, drift, underground water to contend with. Generally the shafts, and every foot of tunnels and underground workings had to be securely timbered, which is an expert's job. Labour and precious time must be expended in felling the timber, cutting and shaping it, transporting it to the claim, then erecting it to hold up the often broken, sometimes rotten basalt roof, and to hold back the seeping in of the walls. Especially careful work was needed against that treacherous drift.

Drift is pure, packed sand which in places lies many feet thick on top of the gravels of the old river-bed. This fine sand, of course, is the remains of mountains washed away by great rains millions of years ago. What a buffeting from the elements this old continent was forced to battle through when all of us were but a thought in our Maker's Mind!

When working underground, with this seemingly harmless drift overhead, to tunnel on through the old bed without using timber meant the day would surely come when in a second tons of smothering sand would pin you to the tunnel floor and bury you as a falling sand-heap would bury an ant.

Broken rock from an insecurely timbered roof can fall and crush you to death. Drift can overwhelm you as an avalanche and smother you to death. An inrush of subterranean water can dash you into darkness struggling for your life. Such awful deaths *have* happened on many a mining field.

Added to such risks, foul air.

The tin-miners* had found, on sinking shafts that tapped the centre of the old river-bed, that in many places there was water at the bottom, which, when it grew too strong to be bailed or pumped out, would creep up the shaft so that all their labour and time would be gone for nothing.

Thus Nature against Man again, grimly ready to maim or kill him should he, unwittingly or otherwise, break one of her laws.

Though millions of years ago the volcanoes had sealed up her river-beds with molten rock, long since solidified, she still had water, and often slowly running water, imprisoned down there deep in the darkness. Disturb its course, and surely, though perforce slowly, it would fight against man and find its own level. Little wonder that many a miner has bitterly thought, with at long last fortune seemingly within his grasp, that a living, implacable Nature was "dead set" against him.

Nature hides her secrets well, protecting them by immutable laws.

To try to overcome this both dangerous and apparently insuperable water difficulty groups of miners, as mates, had driven and were driving tunnels where the level apparently allowed, that is where Nature seemed to allow a chance from away back "outside" the Deep Lead to come in *under* the old river-bed, and thus drain away the water.

The labour and skill involved, and the chances against success, were sometimes almost insuperable. The men had the hearts of lions—so we say, but the heart of a lion with everything on his side and freedom to run away when anything goes wrong is a puny thing indeed to the heart of a man.

* The "tin-scratcher", or "gully-raker" is the man who works up on the surface, under the open sunlight in river, creek, gully, flat or terrace. The tin-miner is he who sinks a shaft or drives a tunnel seeking underground tin. The alluvial miner seeks an old, buried river-bed (tin-scratching is alluvial mining also, but on the surface), the reef-miner seeks a tin or other mineral lode in a rock reef that goes down underground through the solid rock.

Some of these tunnels, in those days of the pick and shovel, were hacked through solid rock for considerable distances. The Herberton Tin Syndicate's Tunnel was three thousand feet long, apart from numerous side drives; Mazlin's Long Tunnel was half as long. Years earlier Masterton's party had driven a tunnel three thousand feet in under the Deep Lead, a tremendous task without modern explosives. Where mates were working they had to labour on their own, for there would be no payment until, and if, they struck tin. Mazlin's party alone had done two and a half years necessary "dead work", without a shilling return in payment. And it was in such instances, upon all these scattered mining fields, that men like John Moffat and Jack and Newell gave unstinted aid. For on all fields most storekeepers "stuck to" many such ventures with tucker—for the families, too, if the men were married. The storekeepers were paid immediately if such a party "struck it". If not—ah, well!

I doubt whether miners and storekeepers would or could work under such handicaps today.

The Queensland Mines Department was now giving aid to drive a tunnel that it was hoped would drain a large area of the old Lead. Whether this was eventually successful or otherwise I do not know.

In desperate attempts to beat the water when it defied all the slavery of man- and horse-power, some ingenious "home-made" expedients had been used by the old hands, from the bush-made Archimedes Screw and "endless buckets", to the weirdest of pumps. The heavy, clumsy machinery of those days was not like the efficient, compact little pumps of today, of course. Besides, the battling alluvial miner could seldom afford such expense. For the treatment of the wash-dirt also, in cases where its gluey, clayey, or cement-like nature defied ordinary attempts to extract the tin sands, ingenious home-made machines were devised. Some among these quaint makeshifts proved actually to be forerunners, models for portions of extraction machinery of years later. Strangely enough, three thousand miles south-west on the waterless goldfields of Western Australia, the bushmen prospectors, with a tomahawk, a few sticks of mulga, a bit of hide (cow, horse or camel), a strip of tin or a sheet of bark, were devising that remarkable "dry-blower", their "machine" to extract alluvial gold from dirt in places where water at times was worth its weight in gold. But in the Deep Lead in Herberton, as in many other mining fields, the underground water was a curse.

In tin-mining, as also in gold-mining, we used to declare it a "cussedness of Nature" that in one area ground would be richly payable if only we could get the water on, yet in another area water could be a curse, especially underground water.

One "machine" of the old-timers was a local classic. Throughout the bush for a hundred years and more men had been noted for "getting along" with a tomahawk, a sapling, a length of rawhide and, when "modernity" dawned, a bit of fencing wire. But this "machine" really was a museum piece—a pity it could not have been preserved to amuse, also to instruct in human ingenuity, our atomic-electronic wizards of today. Its base actually was machinery, a very ancient, long discarded, rust-eaten boiler that originally had come from goodness knows where. When they had patched up its holes with "plates" cut from oil-drums, tarred it and "rawhided" it and bound it round and round with wire to strengthen it they up-ended it up onto its "platform", where it stood like a prehistoric toadstool. Home-made steam pipes were fitted into it, and to give these pipes strength each was securely bound round with rolls of stringybark, just as, but much more tightly than, a soldier would bind puttees round his legs. As the live bark dried so it contracted and tightened round the pipes like a vice. Perhaps you know the power—and the awful uses it has sometimes been put to—of raw bullock or camel hide bound round an object, then left to dry and contract in the sun. Thus those pipes were greatly strengthened, so that the "bush engineers" knew more than appeared on the surface. By the way, these particular "engineers" were "Ravenswood blokes". Men from the Ravenswood side had quite a name as engineers across on the Herberton side.

The ancient boiler was now treated similarly, completely encased within sheets of stringybark. To all outward appearance the boiler was now a boiler made of stringybark. Maybe, for this particular job it was the only one of its kind in the world.

This boiler had to raise and withstand the necessary pressure of steam to provide the power to work the plant. The local men made quiet wagers as to "how long she'll last before she blows up"! And all were on tiptoe awaiting the great day to see her "bust". The plant itself was quite a good-sized concern, actually a puddler, separator, and tube mill, and a good head of steam would be necessary to operate it. The "accessories", too, were all home-made.

Well, "she" did *not* blow up. She worked—more or less in a rattling, hissing, shaking, groaning, agonized fashion at times, as if working up to one last "bang!" in a cloud of steam and flying debris to the skies. But it never happened. She groaned away at her job for quite a time, until at last the underground water beat them. But they had raised a lot of rich wash and managed to put it through and had done quite well out of it. Finally the underground water flooded the workings and engine and plant sobbed themselves to quietness, a last quietness, abandoned to the bush. But what a museum piece that stringybark boiler and plant would be today!

Not possessing the inclination or the wherewithal to settle down to such long periods of dead work, I set to with my own "machinery", pick and shovel and elbow-grease—tin-scratching in a creek-bank to overcome the one worry of that interesting, happy-go-lucky life—tucker money!

I missed Old Mick's campfire. It was pretty lonely for a young fellow of evenings, his only company the candlelight and the peeping stars outside the open tent door, the bush quietness dreamily sympathizing with his feeling that he really was still a little lovesick, though ever so hopelessly.

About a quarter of a mile down the creek Long Stewart, who used periodically to come to Nigger Creek to do the communal tin-streaming, had his claim. I'd stroll down there for a yarn some evenings, but not often. For Long Stewart regularly toiled a shift and a half. Ten hours for himself, then four hours every evening "knocking out a bit of dirt" for his father-in-law.

"The father-in-law," Stewart had explained almost apologetically, "has a heart." To me it seemed it was the son-in-law had the heart, and a mighty big one.

On my first visit I walked down the creek and stopped by the little tunnel mouth. It was visible as a faint glow up in the creekbank, the glow coming from the candlelight some forty feet back in the tunnel. In the quiet night, very distinctly came the steady, methodical, muffled "Thud! Thud! Thud! Thud!" from the pick away back in there. Curiously I hearkened to another sound, a much softer sound, but quite as distinct and clear: "Thump! Thump! Thump! Thump!" Like the candlelight confined within that little tunnel, the sound could find no way out except along the tunnel walls and through the mouth where I was standing.

Stewart must have a pump in there, I thought wonderingly. But why? He's working above water level.

At my call he stopped work and said, "Come along in, Jack." He always welcomed this chance of a pipe and spell.

I crawled in, and we settled down for a yarn and smoke. He was dressed only in dungaree trousers and the little white miner's cap to keep the dust from the roof falling into his hair, and his body was caked in sweaty dust.

"You're toiling pretty solidly, aren't you," I asked, "doing two men's work?"

"Oh well, Jack," he said quietly, "the old man can't do too much. I give him a bit of a hand to help him keep the tucker-bag full."

"H'm!" I gazed curiously along the tunnel. "Do you know, standing out there I could have sworn you had a pump in here! I was certain of it."

He said nothing for a moment, just sat there looking at me, his eyes tired in the candlelight. Then he said quietly, "Yes, Jack, there *is* a pump working in here. My heart!"

Each evening afterwards when I visited him I'd stand awhile listening at the tunnel mouth. And always the pump was pumping, dreadfully hard it seemed to me.

Of course, in no time an eager curiosity took me exploring those long tunnels, very different from the short little tunnels of Long Stewart and myself, where we sat cross-legged swinging our picks at the face, the roof only an inch over our heads. These tunnels you could stand up in, of necessity, for huge baulks of timber had to support roof and sides, every foot was timbered, boxed-in, to hold back treacherous roof and sides from squeezing down together and obliterating the human insects boring their way in. Then, too, the tunnel must be roomy enough for the truck line and loaded trucks that carried the debris dug from deep within to be wheeled away out and dumped under the blessed open skies. Often there was the "pit-pat, pit-pat" of monotonous water-drops dripping heavily from the roof. Running along the floor on one side of the tunnel was the drain, with its whispering, running water coming from the old river-bed far away in the darkness ahead, chilly dampness, smell of wet timber and dank earth, the candlelight casting dim, eerie shadows upon the timber and around Long Stewart's stooped form as he trudged steadily ahead.

The old river-bed far away in there fascinated me, for in the workings so much was exposed, after all these millions of years. It felt like a dead world, too, this cold blackness of the tomb pressing around us against the frightened little candle flame. Every here and there cross drives and large chambers had been dug out where the wash-dirt had been rich in stream tin. In the dim light of candles one portion was a devil's canyon of mighty boulders glistening with water, and wedged amongst them the compressed masses of water-stones and gravels and sands of this vast old river-bed. Slushy water underfoot was sucking and gurgling its way to escape away back down the tunnel, but in places what had once been an enormous waterhole was below the level of the tunnel floor, and here the water could not escape. And in these places all the wash-dirt possible had been most laboriously and uncomfortably dug out by long-handled shovels, the men working to their waists in the black, icy water. How deep those holes went, what riches of tin might lie on the bottom, impossible to work, no man could know.

In one place, tunnel and shafts had proved that the ancient river-bed was half a mile wide at least. What a difference between the prehistoric Wild River to the Wild River of today! Even in a heavy wet season the Wild River of today, let it roar its foaming song its hardest, would be but a tinkling creek to the inferno of waters of that Wild River of the past as it battered into fragments mountains to which the ranges of today would be like hills.

And to think that this was only a fragment—for it had been proved now that the Deep Lead was but a part of one river alone of some vast river system.

One day I found myself alone in such a place, not then experienced enough to understand the risks, though the chilly loneliness, the black depths all around, grimly hinted at it. No crouching figures illuminated by candlelight away in at the face of drives worked here today, no scraping of shovel, no rumble of truck coming from far away down the tunnel. Here was an awesome silence emphasized somewhere by the steady drip of water, a ghostly loneliness, a black cavern in which my one feeble candle was barely reflected from the black, gleaming sides of huge boulders, black mouths of side tunnels, compressed masses of ancient river gravels and grey baulks of upright timbers, which I would instantly remember in later years when a candle was lit in a burial chamber of the Pharaohs and a grey line of mummies took ghostly form. On that day when we prowling soldiers broke into that underground burial chamber in the Valley of the Dead and lit the candle, in a flash I was back under the Herberton Deep Lead staring at those shadowy baulks of timber. Strange indeed at times is the flash-back of memory in the mind of man. But now I dug the candle spider into an upright, sat upon a fairly dry place, and sought to see around as far as possible. I must not lose my sense of the direction of the main tunnel—awful to get lost in these black drives! I hadn't given it a thought. What was it the Jungle Man had said? "He who uses his ears hears things! He who uses his eyes sees things!" Why on earth was I thinking of him? Thinking, too, strange thoughts that came flooding in when I was working down in my own tiny claim by Nigger Creek. . . .

Sounds were growing—the drip of water so close, and other drips, quite far away, yet so distinct. Then came every now and then a whisper—and now a long, shuddering sigh that brought me up, alarmed. Some distant baulk of timber had groaned under the strain of helping support those millions of tons of rock pressing down from above. Why, the whole cavern was whispering—plainly, too, away in the black side drives, all these stout timbers straining in their task to hold up the mighty roof that was pressing down to fill in again this huge cavern gouged out of the old river-bed. This was Nature working—Nature ever against Man. I could smell it now, too—the clammy smell of seeping water everywhere, the smell of mouldering timbers, the dank, earthy smell of these cold boulders, these shadowy masses of solid, this disturbed wash-dirt. The Jungle Man had been right—

Splash! And I jumped, though instantly realizing it was only a "slide", the falling of some fragment of wash-dirt into a pool—there was dangerous ground close by.

For quite a time I sat there while the candle beamed without a flicker in the motionless air. And as the Jungle Man had said, things "came" to me—if only a man could keep a receptive mind! I'll swear the spirit of the river came to me, all those faint sighings and whisperings and moanings took form as if the song of the great river had been overwhelmed and crushed and sealed off from the skies by the land, but was still moaning for life under its imprisoning walls of rock. The tunnel coming deep under the ridge had opened the old bed up at this one little spot and let in the faintest of light and air again, and its choked voice was whispering away down the tunnel in awakening reply. Could these whisperings be magnified, there would burst out the voice of a river, as in the open air.

It was a most strange experience until a sudden grinding, ending almost in a shriek, scared the daylights out of me. I snatched at the candle and made for the tunnel and escape. That splintering rock told so loudly of the rock masses above pressing down upon the straining timbers to imprison yet again the whispering river—and me!

CHAPTER XXVIII

THE DEATH-ADDER

DURING our evening yarns in Long Stewart's wombat burrow under the creek-bank he held me spellbound with accounts of the remarkably rich tin won in those tunnels and shafts in the places where men had been able to work the old river-bed. For the bottom wash-dirt was often black with stream tin—forty pounds to the yard was common—what a fortune today!

"Like shovelling up black sand, Jack," said Stewart dreamily, "in the Ocean mine particularly. There, the wash-dirt was almost fit to bag—fifteen hundredweight of tin to the yard! Yes, Jack." Stewart smiled at my amazement. "Makes my mouth water, too, just at the memory of it. Three-quarters of a ton of stream tin to every yard of wash-dirt in one patch, £75 worth of tin at the present price in every yard of dirt! It would be a rich gold-mine indeed that would give a return as juicy as that! You can guess how they slaved night and day under heart-breaking difficulties to get out all the wash-dirt possible before the whole place fell in on them. For the Lead there was really a little ocean of underground water."

With pipes alight, Stewart's chest gleaming with sweat beads under the candlelight, we would sit and meditate on those rich finds. One evening I asked him to tell me some of his own adventures.

"Oh, I haven't had any," he answered in surprise.

"You *must* have, you were in at the opening-up of this country —and what a tough country it must have been but a very few years back! With all sorts of things happening—prospectors finding new mining fields, timber lands, new country, new rivers, wild blacks, new ranges! Come on, tell me some of the things that happened to *you*!"

He passed his hand over his brow in a puzzled sort of way.

"But nothing much happened to me, Jack. I was just an ordinary knockabout bush worker. Until I got married in Herberton, I suppose." He smiled slowly. "That was my one and only adventure. However, it hasn't panned out too badly. But nothing much else has happened, all has been in the day's work. I've been near drowned crossing flooded rivers, like many another man. I was trapped once under a fall of rock, lay there in the darkness slowly being suffocated and pressed to death until three hours later my mates dug me out—*that* was a close go. Once a blackfellow near took my scalp off with a boomerang, but then he'd mistaken me for another man who'd done him a bad turn. I tripped once when scrub-cutting and was pinned under a falling tree, but got away with that, too. I've had a horse somersault head over heels and roll over me when galloping full pelt after cattle—oh, a few little things like that have happened, Jack, but it's all been in the day's work."

"Have you ever been bitten by a snake?" I asked.

Slowly he took the pipe from his lips in a surprised sort of way.

"That's strange," he said. "No, I've never been bitten by a snake. But what makes you ask?"

"Nothing in particular. But as nothing seems ever to have happened to you, I thought there must have been something."

"I'm not the adventurous type, Jack." He smiled. "If I had anything interesting to tell you, I would. And willingly. But my life has been mostly hard toil, with very little play. Plenty of travelling, but mostly just trudging along, looking for a job."

"Then why were you so surprised when I mentioned snakes?"

With a half smile of uncertainty, finally he answered, "Because I'm the Death-adder Man."

At my expression of surprise he laughed, a pleasant laugh. I remember thinking, This man must be a real decent cove!

"There now, Jack," he said, "you asked for it! And now you must think I'm a hidden terror of some sort. You won't come strolling along of evenings to have a yarn with me in the tunnel any more."

"What nonsense!" I said eagerly. "I'll never leave you alone now until I hear all about it. Come on, out with it!"

Almost bashfully, he began filling his pipe, speaking with a slow smile that reminded me of a recent schoolboy friend caught out in some mischief.

"There's really nothing to it, Jack, just the merest chance. But wherever I've been, in death-adder country and in season of course, I've seemed to be always running up against the brutes. So much so that I've carried them about with me in my swag. Have you ever unrolled your swag at sundown, Jack, to find a big, fat, brown, sleepy death-adder in it?"

"I have not!"

"It gives you a bit of a shock," he said, smiling, "especially if you've trudged a good distance on a hot day along a dry track. Of course, I'd spread the blanket on the wretched thing when I'd camped late. Or else it had crept into the blankets for body warmth. In the morning, I'd simply roll up the swag with the adder in it. It only happened a few times like that, of course, before I'd give my blankets a jolly good shake in the morning. And at nights, if forced to camp late, I'd light a blazing fire and examine the ground carefully before I'd spread the blankets."

He paused, lighting his pipe, then said thoughtfully, "Have you ever noticed how difficult it is to see a death-adder, Jack, if you're not looking for them?"

"I've only seen two in my life—and they were pointed out to me."

"You haven't started life yet, Jack." He smiled. "There's a long track stretching ahead of you. A long and pleasant track, I hope. Anyway, the adders blend so well with the dull brown soil when the bush is parched, or the dull grey. The short, squat devils lie utterly motionless, too. And they love to choose a pad to bask or sleep on. I suppose a well-worn pad beaten down by hooves of horses and hobnails of men collects the sun's rays by day and retains some warmth by night. Anyway, if ever you pick up the billy-can after sundown to fill it at the waterhole, never go without your boots. Or when you go visiting camps at night. On different evenings I've stood stock still with one foot held up, then stepped smartly back. Lit a match—and there was an adder lying there just where my bare foot would have trod." He paused, puffing thoughtfully.

"A man would be in a nasty fix," I said, "if he was bitten like that, and distant from help."

"I've seen a man die within a few minutes from death-adder bite, Jack," he said, "so don't forget those boots! I know it's much easier to walk barefoot down to the waterhole than to go to the trouble of putting on boots, but before you do so next time just remember what might lie in wait for you. Anyway, they'll lie out anywhere in the bush, not only on a pad. That is, if you happen to be in adder country, of course."

"But if you've slept with a death-adder in your blankets, you must have rolled on him in the night!"

"Yes, and he's never bitten me. And more than once I've had one as a bed-mate. You remember the fright you gave Old Mick when he woke up with that old billygoat's snout under his chin? Well, I suffered a much worse fright than that when I woke up cold sober with a death-adder asleep beside me."

"Then what is the attraction?" I laughed, but I knew it was no laughing matter.

"Blessed if I know," he answered in a puzzled way. "There's no attraction, I'm sure, it's been just chance, just one of those things that happen. The trouble was that it happened to others, too, when they spread their blankets beside me."

"Ah! And that's how you got the name!"

"Yes, but, Jack, only because of one particularly bad death-adder season, as we called it when a few of us were drifting through a dry district seeking work. And work was very scarce. Now, don't you go and put me away to your friends at Nigger Creek or I'll never hear the end of this. Worse than that, Mick would be sure to write a 'pome' about it!"

"I promise not to be responsible for putting you in the annals of fame." I laughed.

"You put a billygoat in Mick's bed!" he said dubiously.

"But I thought how cosy they would look sleeping together!" I protested. "Why, the billygoat didn't like it—I had to wait until he was staggeringly drunk first. He couldn't even hold his head up!"

"H'm!" he replied doubtfully. "You get such bright ideas, Jack."

"I promise faithfully I won't breathe a word," I coaxed, "and I'm real interested. Come on, tell me how the adders came to get into your friend's blankets, too!"

"They just crawled there, of course. But why, I don't know. Once I was with a prospecting party 'way down south near Stanthorpe—wonderful patches of tin were found there, too, Jack, by the lucky ones! There were ten of us. We had a big tarpaulin we used as a tent during the rains. But in dry weather, when travelling about, we merely spread it out on the ground, spread our blankets on it, and camped on it. Used it as a mattress.

"One morning, on rolling the tarpaulin up, we found, to our uncomfortable surprise, a death-adder jammed tightly beneath it. The beggar had been there all night, and couldn't get away with our weight on the tarpaulin. Well, that was all right, you could be sure my mates examined the ground carefully before spreading the tarpaulin after *that*. But a week or two later the same thing happened. So the adder could not have been there when we spread the tarpaulin. And it could not necessarily have been the weight of our bodies that kept him there. My mates were very puzzled."

"Did you tell your mates about the little death's-heads' partiality for you?"

"Would you like your mates to believe you a hoodoo man, Jack?" he asked quietly.

Only then did I see what a worry this strange thing had been to the quiet man sitting with his back to the tunnel wall before me.

"If you wake up and find yourself sleeping on, or with, a death-adder more than once you grow more and more uneasy," he resumed. "You begin to wonder if you'll wake up alive next time.

I remember a mate of mine. He left his swag half rolled up while he borrowed some tobacco from me. He was fed up, decided to walk out to a show back of Elsenmore in the morning and look for a job. That night he slept in the hotel at Elsenmore—no need to unroll the swag, of course. The next morning he was on the track again, and at sundown unrolled his swag beside a lonely waterhole. To his horror he found a death-adder neatly rolled up in his blankets. He was a man afraid of snakes—some men have an unreasoning horror of them. And this was a death-adder! He didn't wait to boil the billy even. Just filled it, shook out his blankets, hurriedly rolled them, and walked on all night. He missed the track."

Stewart paused and sighed as at some unhappy memory. "Oh well, Jack, the country then was very dry, and a hot summer. They found him ten days later, but he was all in, perishing of thirst. In delirium he was moaning about a death-adder in his swag. He'd long since thrown it away, of course, but he thought it was still strapped to his back, he couldn't get rid of it. He must have raced around screaming in circles, trying to throw off that imaginary swag until he fell exhausted—then crawled away with that swag still on him. They managed to piece the story together. But he was too far gone. He died. He was a good mate."

CHAPTER XXIX

I CANNOT KEEP A SECRET

THOUGHTFULLY walking back to camp from Long Stewart's tunnel that night, I was glad I had my boots on even though the saying "death-adder country" merely meant some area where the death-adder might appear noticeably during some favourable climatic season. However, anywhere in the bush on a summer's night a man walking barefoot always risks a long-shot chance of treading upon some prowling snake.

How far south of Herberton was Stanthorpe? Away down near the New South Wales border, about eight hundred miles or a trifle more. And yet—the Jungle Man had known all about Stewart and the death-adders. And I felt certain Stewart knew nothing at all about that bush wanderer. Long Stewart obviously had kept this little experience very quiet, and now asked me not to mention it even at the Council Fire!

I had fully intended to ask Stewart how it was that the Jungle Man knew all about him and the adders. But he had seemed quite upset about the death of his mate. I was glad now I had kept my mouth shut at the Council Fire. But this keeping of secrets was becoming a bit of a burden.

The very next evening I was down there sitting under the candlelight in Long Stewart's tunnel again. In that slow drawl of his he yarned about the Chinese diggers, their fatalistic gameness, their hardihood and industry and cunning, their clannishness, their unshakable "No savvy!" when in trouble, or "on gold". And other secretive ways of theirs.

"I believe my new friend could keep a secret just as well," I remarked casually, "perhaps better."

"Who is that, Jack? Oh, the chap you went walkabout with, the Jungle Man?"

"Yes."

Thoughtfully Stewart refilled his pipe. "Maybe you are right, Jack, now I come to think of it."

"Have you known him long?"

Stewart glanced at me in surprise. "Why, no, Jack. I don't know him at all. The first time I ever saw him was when he strolled into the light of the Council Fire that first night."

"He knows you very well."

"But, Jack, he can't! I'd never even heard of the man until I met him that night!"

So then I told him, word for word, what the Jungle Man had told me about "Stewart and the death-adders". He listened in growing surprise. I could distinctly hear his heart now softly thumping, beat by steady beat within that deathly quiet little tunnel.

"You amaze me, Jack. I simply cannot place the man, I'm *certain* I've never met him before. And those little incidents happened years ago, and a long way from here, and were only known to a dozen men all told. And not one of them has ever come north. Then again, we treated those little happenings as some queer sort of 'natural' joke among ourselves, though a very unpleasant joke to me. And I have very rarely even mentioned the matter. As to this complete stranger away up here in the north knowing such details, well—I just can't make head or tail of it."

"I'm sorry I spoke about it now."

"It doesn't matter in the least, Jack. You've given me something new to think about, which will do me good. A man's own company becomes a bit lonesome at times. His thoughts are liable to wander in a circle, like a dog chasing its own tail. You've just sort of taken my breath away, as the saying is." And that slow, quiet smile of his came back again.

Again I walked thoughtfully back to camp through the starlit night. Obviously Long Stewart had something to puzzle and think about tonight. But I quite definitely knew what *I* knew! And that was that *I* could not keep a secret like the Jungle Man.

It was while camped at Kalunga that one dawn I opened sleepily protesting eyes to, "Billy's boiled! Shake a leg!" and there was the Jungle Man looking down at me, with that shadow of a smile that passed for a grin.

"Where on earth did *you* spring from?" I demanded.

"Oh, I just blew along with the sunrise. Care for a walkabout?"

"Where?"

"Oh, the big scrubs. We might try a dish or two."

"Sure," I agreed and threw off the blanket. "How long will we be away?"

"Oh, a few weeks, maybe more. It all depends. Time doesn't matter."

"I've only got about a fortnight's tucker here."

"Doesn't matter. I've got the rifle this time, we'll shoot our meat as we travel. Roll up what flour and tea you've got, the tent-fly and blanket. What I haven't got we'll get along the track if we need it."

"Right. But I must tell Long Stewart or he'll think I've fallen down a shaft or wandered into some old tunnel and been pinned under a fall."

"Right. I'll roll up the fly. Then breakfast and away."

And old Sol had not really shaken the mountain mists from his rosy crown before we were striding along the track towards Tumoulin. My unusual companion did not explain whether he had camped close by, or whether he had walked through the night. I felt too cheerful to ask, if he did not feel like explaining then he could do the other thing. The air and the birds and the physical effort of striding out seeking unknown scenes made me feel it was good to be alive.

Tumbling creeks every few miles, the banks of some a red blaze under flowering bottle-brush setting off the pure white of lilies and the vivid green of ferns. Magnificent timber everywhere, and the early morning air would make a mummy sit up and yawn. I hope civilization has not driven away too much of the beauty which made life sweet in those enchanted districts.

Here, still farther "back o' Cairns", development was taking place like that which led to the formation of Atherton, Tolga, Malanda, Mareeba, Gordonvale, Babinda and Innisfail, since

247

these huge scrub areas had been thrown open for settlement as the railway crept slowly farther west and south-west. It had taken twenty-four years, in stages, to reach from Cairns to Herberton. And now it was coming creeping on again. Here and there, just within the scrubs, there appeared acres of mighty stumps where settlers were clearing their blocks of virgin land. Rich red ribbons leading into the cool of primal forest were the wagon-tracks of the timber-seekers. Little selections now being cultivated were showing a treasure house of deep red soil.

"You know," I said, when that first night we were camped snugly sheltered between the flanges of a gigantic fig-tree, "in this new settlers' land this really *is* a *new* country in this old world. In Europe and Britain I suppose every acre of soil has been turned over and planted for a thousand years or more maybe. But here, until a year or two back, apart from an isolated cattle station, not even the pointed stick of savages has ever tilled the soil. I'd never thought of it like that before!"

But he merely grunted, staring morosely at the fire. Glancing at his set face, I gradually realized that what had thrilled me in this struggle of Man against Nature brought only despondency to him. I remembered now that all day we had walked along hearing the steely song of the axe, and now and then the shuddering crash of some timbered giant deep within the forest. Now in the deep scrub silence, cosily sheltered by that great tree, I felt sorry, too. This sturdily buttressed grey giant had probably lived for a thousand years, was good for a thousand more. And now it, too, would soon fall to the bite of the axe. But what to do about it? The country had to be developed!

Our first night in the big scrub was a silent one.

A settler's home here and there was built upon the open forest land adjacent to the scrub edge, others were being built within the cleared scrub. These were of beautiful cedar, just two or three rooms, to be added to with the yearly increase of crops and stock. The earliest of the settlers already had fine gardens and orchards, the land was eager to grow practically anything. There were shy youngsters, too, the picture of health.

He was "quite good" for a week of rambling, allowing my eager curiosity full play over a considerable area wherever settlers were active. I still have the warmest memories of those helpful, kindly folk. And the women-folk fed me as if I had been a clumsy puppy nosing his way about, but then they would do the same for anyone, let alone a shy bush lad. Yes, I had my own way for a wonderful week and more. Until one night came a most strange feeling, an almost lonely feeling, that the Jungle Man was quietly saying farewell to all this—the big scrubs. I stole a glance at his face reflected in firelight from the butt of a lovely silky oak. But his thoughts were only for the night mystery and murmurous whispering of this mighty forest. A miracle came floating on glorious wings into the firelight glow and hovered over the Jungle Man; the two were gazing at one another. A moth, but *such* a moth! As large as a dinner-plate, its body of black and brown plush fat as a young mouse and much longer, its wings larger than many a bird's, magic wings like broad leaves of a light-brown plush upon which were painted enormous eyes of gold centred with a black pupil fairly shimmering in the firelight. It settled on the Jungle Man's boot, its wings softly pulsing. In delight I stared at it, estimating its wings must surely span a full twelve inches.

"What is it?" I whispered.

"A moth," he murmured.

"What a wonderful thing! Why, it must be the father of all moths that ever was!"

"It is about the largest," he murmured. "There are plenty others near as large—and plenty others smaller, and more beautiful."

"What is its name?"

Lying there, he merely shrugged.

To hell with you! I thought. In one of your moods again!

The moth rose on effortless wings, for all its size it moved as if it were but a breath of life. It had taken no notice of me at all, but I'm blessed if it didn't hover over the Jungle Man a full minute, gazing down at him. Then it glided out through the firelight into the darkness.

"What a lovely visitor!" I ventured.

He replied neither by word nor by sign.

A blackness dark as the deepest cave squeezed us in right to the little campfire. But I knew that somewhere far up above a velvet sky was specked with star-dust. The time must surely come, was coming fast when starlight would gleam down here upon little homes, and cattle, and crops, and the family watchdog, while the green-eyed cat prowled about at night.

"Would the giant moths be able to live under open starlight?" I wondered drowsily.

I turned over in the blanket and breathed the breath of the trees until sleep came.

He woke me for breakfast next morning by firelight. Sleepily I knew that away above this tree-blackness a rosy dawn was kissing the hungry roof of tree-tops, countless leaves were eagerly opening out to drink their life from the sun. It was still practically dark when he stood up, slung on his swag with a curt, "We're leaving civilization behind us for a while now!" and we were walking through the scrub with the ring of some lonesome axe growing ever fainter—fainter.

He was a different man in the big scrubs, my strange mate, he was happy, too. He belonged here, he was a Jungle Man. I later came to really wonder whether he had a lot of those "ancestor jungle cells" in that lithe body of his. He seemed to glide along as noiselessly as a shadow, as effortlessly, too, while clumsily I kept up with him. Fortunately, here the scrub was free of that entangling trap of lawyer-canes and undergrowth that fights you every foot of the way. Here it was but a maze of tree-trunks canopied by their intertwining branches and leaves shutting out the sun and enclosing us in a luminous gloom, with underfoot a dense mass of interlocking roots carpeted by untold years of fallen leaves. All sense of direction quickly went from me, I merely followed close behind that lean, wiry figure ever moving ahead. Memories of favourite boyhood stories of the pathfinders and redskins of the American backwoods returned to me, and soon I had clothed him in buckskin with a coonskin cap and long-barrelled gun. In growing amazement then I wondered how it would be possible to prospect such country. Why, you could not even see the ground! There was none! There were only tree-trunks and roots and leaf-decayed loam. Not one sign of a rock, let along bare earth. And yet I knew that back on the coast, just south of Cairns, in dense jungle by the Russell River, some wonder men of the scrubs had found gold and were working it even now!

But this man was never to lead me to a "golden creek", he was almost afraid that we might actually stumble upon gold. For that would mean a gold rush, the axe, civilization, and bushfires—the end of his trees and birds and wild animals.

But I would only realize this as the weeks flew by.

With a startled croak a scrub-turkey ran almost from under our feet, then, rising, flew clumsily up to a branch, staring down upon us with an agitated croaking that ended with the crack of the rifle and the heavy thud of the fallen bird.

He picked it up, hung its neck through his belt, and walked on. We would have turkey roasted in the ashes tonight, or would it be boiled? I noticed now he carried two billies to his knapsack, one within the other. Trust him to save space and weight and bulk! His rifle, too, was only a light .22, the cartridges of no weight.

We would not lack for meat in the scrubs, there were plenty of turkeys, turkey eggs also. Scrub-hens, too, and plump, gorgeously coloured pigeons. You had to know about these things, to learn their habits in their environment before you could even see them, let alone shoot them in that tangled maze. Out in the open forest there were wallabies, of course, and by the jungle edge the climbing kangaroo. But we never shot any of those quaint little things. In fact, the Jungle Man never used the rifle except to secure needed food.

CHAPTER XXX

LIFE IS EVERYWHERE

THROUGH this green world we pushed on next morning to no sound but the wail of the cat-bird deep within the jungle. Difficult to believe it is the same feathered terror when his piercing challenge defies rivals to dare trespass on his playground. A cunning mimic, that lively bird, a gay deceiver, too. Later in the day I gazed entranced at what must surely be one of the loveliest of all things on wings. Pushing out from the riotous foliage lining a creek, we paused by the moss-grown rocks to gaze up at the bright ribbon of blue far above these dense walls of greenery. The gleam of sky is beautiful indeed when you step thus from the jungle gloom. And a ball of living gold was fiercely vibrating before our eyes, just up there where the blue of sky filtered down between the green jungle walls. But a little bird with a little golden crest, a quivering ball of energy and life, its body a-sheen in living gold, even its eyes were shining beads of gold, and just to emphasize the gold its body was shimmering in flashes of golden green. A flash, and it had darted to a palm-tree, it hovered within an inch of the trunk, its wings vibrating gold, its outspread tail shimmering gold and green. For a full three minutes it vibrated there as if in intense concentration, the speed of its golden wings must have been wonderful to have thus held it poised. In a flash it was gone.

"What *was* that beautiful thing?" I almost whispered.

"The few who have seen it call it the golden bird," he answered, and his calm face showed that he, too, had gloried in the beauty of the thing. "It is a bower-bird, like the cat-bird, there are different kinds of bower-birds. This is lovelier even than the regent bird. It is the smallest, too, but it builds the largest playgrounds—tunnels and runways and gunyahs, with walls of sticks and grasses

253

and shrubs. You would not believe what a massive building is the playground of the little golden bird unless you actually saw it." And he was stepping over the slippery rocks to push into the wall of damp fernery opposite.

If there is gold in the bed of this unnamed creek, I thought as I followed him, it could never be as beautiful as that lovely bird.

Evening falls within the big scrubs while sunshine still brilliantly bathes the forest lands "away outside". We camped by a tinkling creek overgrown by palms and tree-ferns heavily draped in the silvered gauze of moist spider-webs. My mate lit a fire from the damp wood of a living tree, and put both billies on to boil within a few minutes. Before the turkey had cooked he had slashed out a space from the undergrowth, rigged the tent-fly, covered the wet ground below it with a two-foot depth of tree-fern fronds ready dried before that fierce fire, spread my fly over them, unrolled and spread the blankets, and there was a dry, cosy camp in the heart of a water-soaked jungle. I would not even have been able to find wood for a fire.

How very different the big scrubs to the sunlit bush forest, how very different even merely to camp in!

"You'd think that yellow wood was soaked with kerosene," I said, amazed.

"There *is* a kerosene wood," he replied, "but this wood is full of some rich, volatile oil. You'll smell it yards away soon. Billy's boiled. Put the tea in."

Hungrily devouring boiled turkey by that fierce, scented fire I puzzled over the new bushcraft I had to learn. Suddenly I realized that the stars had gone! Only dense blackness was here, above and around the short reach of the firelight. Near by giant tree-trunks were vividly illuminated in their dampness. That invisible creek singing near by, a whispering "drip-drip, pit-pat" of moisture drops from the foliage above. And, apart from the hum of the fire, a deathly silence, a black stillness slowly growing overpoweringly pregnant with a sense of some vast Life.

Where on earth were we?

Chewing the last morsel from the turkey leg, I stole a glimpse at him, now feeling for the pipe at his belt. His lean face, bronzed by many suns, sharply reflected the firelight; its air of restlessness had vanished, leaving a harmony of body and mind. This was some baffling intuition stealing upon me; it could not have been conscious thought, it was something born from these overpowering surroundings. As his fingers gently filled his pipe, his glance strayed through the firelight to the trunk of a magnificent kauri pine. Ruddy gold in the dancing firelight, that lovely giant towered up into mysterious darkness into which, some queer sense whispered to me, his eyes could see much farther than mine. It grew upon me that he loved that tree.

"It is a thousand years old," his voice said softly. "Yes, it is beautiful—and only in the bloom of its youth."

Too surprised to answer I watched as he lit his pipe.

"Yes," he said roughly, "and if cut down and sawn up it would supply timber for three houses."

"You must have read my thoughts again!" I blurted out, only realizing with the words that I must subconsciously have been thinking so.

"Yes," he replied, "quite simply."

"How so?"

"Because we are two men all alone in the heart of a primitive jungle, thinking practically the same thoughts. The big scrub! Gold! Tin! Development! The future! All this jungle around us is breathing softly as our thoughts are flowing. But, believe me, it is a mighty breath. Under such conditions a receptive mind can read thoughts easily."

Seeking to pull the conversation back to earth, I was about to speak, when the night was rent by a piercing scream, long drawn out in gurgling, gasping agony.

I had sprung up with head bouncing the tent-fly into a shower of water-drops. Hair on end, heart hammering painfully, I glared down at him open-mouthed. Even he was startled, but he laughed up at me.

"It's all right," he said quietly, "it's only a jungle owl. Better tie up that corner of the fly where you've broken the cord before the damp gets at our blankets. It startled me a moment when you jumped up like that. But it is only a jungle owl."

My fingers were trembling so that I could hardly tie up the fly. I crawled in under again, knees wobbling so that I was glad to flop down on the blanket.

"I thought—I thought—"

"Yes, I know. That some struggling woman was getting her throat cut! I have never heard that sound fortunately, sincerely hope I never will. But that seems exactly what it must sound like."

"But," I breathed, "are you sure it was only an owl? A bird?"

"Of course. There is not a human soul within a good many miles of us, no aboriginals. We are quite alone—except for the life of the big scrub."

"My God! And you actually travel at times through these places—alone!"

"Quite often," he answered seriously, "and love it! That cut-throat bird at times can give a man a nasty fright, but not when he knows what it is."

"You can have these dashed places all to yourself then," I said feelingly. "I wouldn't camp in a place like this alone for any-thing—not even if I was to find a gold reef."

"I believe you'd risk it," he smiled, "when you calm down. I think I know you a little. The chance of gold would lure you any-where. That's the reason why you're camped here with me now —a man you are puzzling to understand—a long way away, a very different setting to Old Mick's homely campfire. And you know in your heart that you've very little chance indeed of finding gold! And I believe I know why."

He looked steadily at me a moment, it was almost a kindly look, again I experienced that eerie feeling that he could read my thoughts.

"Anyway—" and he started to fill his pipe—"that was only a jungle owl, in love, telling his mate he had made a kill."

"A jungle owl in love?" I murmured lamely.

"Yes." He smiled quietly. "The most natural thing in the world. Quite human. Just as a married man would do if he struck a rich patch of tin, just as a business-man does when he makes a good bargain—rushes home to tell the wife all about it, to throw out his chest, preening himself to win her admiration and show her what a great man he is. That blood-curdling shriek was merely old man owl telling his wife he had made a juicy kill and she needn't worry about the cupboard being bare, as he'd assured her all along. He was merely blowing out his chest, telling her what a fine fellow he is, before hurrying home with the family bacon. You see, she'll be sitting at home on the nest in some cosy tree in the scrub near by, feeling pretty hungry and grumpy as to what the old man is going to do about it. She daren't leave her warm eggs to the cold of night; if she's got very young chicks she wouldn't leave them either. She'd be much more pleased than you when she heard that blood-curdling screech." And he chuckled.

"I wish he'd broken his wretched neck," I grumbled. "He scared the very daylights out of me. Why couldn't he have made his kill in peace and just flown home to her quietly with it?"

"Because that wouldn't be natural," he replied gravely.

Still a bit uneasy at that awful scream I growled, "I still wish the wretched thing did his love-bragging less horribly."

"Sweet music to him and her," he replied simply, "the music of Life. They have to eat to live, if they cannot eat to live they cannot love. Even worms make love."

I took the pipe from my mouth, gazed at him a moment, then in the reaction, I suppose, burst out laughing.

"Now tell me," he said sharply, "just what *you* would do if your pick unearthed a nugget of gold?"

"I'd yell out to my mate!" I replied instantly.

"Of course," he grinned, "and that would be natural."

"A dashed sight more natural than worms making love!" I protested.

"Why not?" he replied simply. "Why, only this morning you watched an energetic turkey dressed in his wedding glory showing off his paces while making love to his mate! Ah! You had not thought of it that way."

"No," I admitted, "it didn't strike me at the time."

"And yet they were even building their home and doing their courtship before you. You must train yourself to become ever so much more observant, else you will never make a bushman. Well, everything makes love, worms included. Or at least, one certain species does, I don't know about them all. These particular worms, in season and when atmospheric conditions are correct, and only during full of the moon, come up out of their holes in the ground and seemingly stand on their tails and dance crazily, twining themselves around one another in a very crazy, Merry Widow waltz. I see you don't believe it, but I have actually seen this happen, though on only two occasions, in widely separated areas of the bush."

Of course I did not believe him, but I was wondering at this new side to the Jungle Man; I had not known him so "human" before. I was puzzled whether to laugh or not.

He half smiled towards the fire. "You simply will *not* believe. I have heard it declared," he said musingly, "that if Christ came upon earth again, people simply would not believe him. I wonder."

Many years later, as man's puny lifetime of years is measured, in the Kimberleys, nearly three thousand miles westward, aborigines guided me one brilliantly moonlit night to a claypan flat, sparsely tufted with spinifex. Here, from innumerable tiny holes in the sun-baked clay, emerged a species of worm in unknown numbers. Standing on end, the tail clinging by some means to the lip of the burrow, each worm began to sway gently, slowly increasing speed until in twisting, frenzied contortion. In that brilliant moonlight in that lonesome place it was a most fantastic happening. I gazed amazed, hardly grinning in reply to the aborigines' shrieks of laughter at the white man's expression at this Dance of the Worms. I had learnt many things throughout the years by that time, but only then did I realize in a flash that what the Jungle Man had told me so many years before, away back in the Evelyn jungle, was true. And now, this very night in the big scrub, again he was to tell me something which I could not believe until eventually I saw it for myself.

"Have you ever seen the mulga snake?"

"No."

"Well, he is a real snake, believe me. A very nasty customer if startled or interfered with. The male grows to a length of five feet, a little over, maybe. Fully as thick as a man's wrist. Strong, savage, swift. A brownish yellow colour which merges so well with the parched earth. I am not a man of the mulga, I very nearly left my bones there on a prospecting trip north-west of Townsville. By the way—" and he looked at me quizzically—"there will be big mineral deposits found some day in that God forsaken country,* an area where settlement would not destroy beautiful scrubs. But don't venture out there unless with one of the very few bushmen who understand the country there, or you'll never return. We lost our camels. They ate poison-bush, filled up with water at a rockhole, and swelled out with gas like enormous balloons until they burst. And it takes something to kill a camel, believe me.

"Well, out there is where I met the mulga snake, and in the mating season. When I saw the two of them I stood in my tracks. Neither reptile took the slightest notice of me. Both were violently agitated. She had come up from a hole under the spinifex. I first saw him slithering along in an urgent flurry to hiss her at the hole. It was then she had come up. They stood fairly up on their tails, swaying there at one another, hissing all the time. He swelled out to near twice his size; his distended scales had a ruddy glow where sunlight caught them between the scraggly mulga. They were oblivious to everything but themselves. Violently then they began see-sawing their thick necks across one another, hissing furiously. They grew passionate to madness—a weird sight. It lasted quite a long time."

Thoughtfully he refilled the pipe, the hum of the fire, the tinkling of the creek musically clear now above the monotonous dripping of the trees.

He lit up and resumed. "Out of this overwhelming curiosity of mine I passed that way the next morning; the lady's home was

* He was right. And today witness Mount Isa and the Mary Kathleen.

quite close to camp. Sure enough, there they were at it again. Next morning I came earlier. Presently he appeared slithering out of the mulga, again in a desperate hurry to hiss down in her doorway. She must have been waiting just below, for her snout popped straight up and knocked his head back right smart. But it was only a love kiss, they were swaying all over one another and sawing one another's necks as if very life depended upon it. Which I suppose it did, in a way. However, that evening my mate, returning to camp, came upon them and blazed at them with a double-barrelled gun. He hated snakes, was almost terrified of them, as some men are. Next morning I passed that way again, the male had been blown into shreds and was hanging limply across a mulga branch. But *she* was still alive, though blown almost in half. There she was, half in, half out of her home, swaying weakly, hissing weakly too, her head peering this way and that, waiting for her mate. She was wounded to death, but she was still waiting for her mate. I shot her quickly, I felt sorry for her."

He was silent, the creek was softly crooning. I crawled outside for more wood, the jungle blackness was fast closing in on the fire.

CHAPTER XXXI

KING OF THE PATHFINDERS

Wɪᴛʜ the fire blazing cheerily again I crawled in under the tent-fly.

"I was just going to ask you about Christy Palmerston when that wretched owl burst his bagpipes," I said.

"You don't appreciate the love call of the Killer Owl." He smiled. "Oh well, Christy Palmerston was the King of the Pathfinders. Though some very good men gave a hand in opening up this country.

"Christy first appeared in these parts with Mulligan on one of his exploring trips. It was Mulligan who reported payable gold on the Palmer, you know. The sort of river you dream of finding, a real river of gold.

"I've never been across on the Cooktown side, so of Christy's adventures there in those hectic years I can't speak of at first hand. Wild and woolly by all accounts, he seems to have been a real Bully Hayes of the bush across on *that* side. No doubt all manner of startling things could and did happen in a wild land where they actually dug up fifty-four *tons* of gold within three years.

"Christy suddenly appeared on this side as a quiet stranger with a savage blackboy called Pompo, who thought the world of him. No one knew or cared about his first coming. Along the coast then were but a few small camps called settlements, scattered groups of pioneers battling for dear life to make a go of things when Mulligan found the Hodgkinson. However, from the coast Christy plunged into the jungle and cut a track that opened up the Russell River goldfield. It was a jungle hell, but there was gold there, bringing desperately needed encouragement to the early coastal settlers.

"For fifteen years Christy was a pathfinder throughout this area. His tracks opened up the way to the Mulgrave, Beatrice,

Tully, Russell, Barron, and Johnstone rivers. And then the country beyond, big areas these of forests and scrubs. His tracks opened up mineral, timber, and sugar lands. And at last he found a track from Innisfail right up the escarpment to the great Table-land. Thus at that point of the range the way was opened right down to Mourilyan and the sea. Another great pathfinder was Oswald, who found a track from Millaa Millaa to Innisfail, and thus the sea at Mourilyan. Surely you have heard of Oswald's Track? Of Fred Warner's Track? Of Douglas, of Smith, of Jim Robson opening up the Pack Track to Herberton? Of Atherton's Track? Of Jim Sturdie and Charlie Davis? Of Doyle's Track, all the way from Herberton to Georgetown—imagine a man finding and marking a track over those difficulties and distance in those times! These, and other men were the pathfinders.

"When Jack and Newell found tin away back in the ranges at Herberton, it was Christy who found a track, and a wheel-track, to connect up with the wagon-track from the Hodgkinson to Port Douglas. It was he who suggested the possibility of a railway track up along the Barron Gorge. The railway, of course, made Cairns. And the hinterland, too. You won't recognize the port of Cairns in another thirty years."

Prophetic words. I did not. Let alone the lovely city of Cairns of today.

"Christy was a silent man," he resumed. "He would vanish into the jungles, to reappear most unexpectedly. And rarely spoke of his adventures. They were told by his native followers, and by those lonely settlers and prospectors he had rescued or befriended. For he had the uncanny knack of turning up just at the right time, when a settler was besieged in his hut, a timber hunter crippled under a fallen log, a prospector dying alone of fever. It's surprising the number of isolated people he rescued thus, mostly at the last moment. The only explanation the settlers could think of was that he must have received news from the blacks, who feared him, sometimes tried to ambush him, yet who held him in some strange regard. He would shoot a blackfellow on the instant at the first sign of hostility, he was quite ruthless, he had to be. Yet he would save a blackfellow in danger regardless of risk to himself, just as he would a white man. And he was often a rough doctor to their women and piccaninnies, which may in part help explain their queer regard for him. There was nothing frightening in his appearance, either. Maybe a bit calculating, determined looking. But he had savage eyes. Some of his wild bodyguard told awed stories of those eyes."

He filled his pipe, he had been talking steadily.

"Perhaps in time," he resumed, "the track Christy will best be known by is the Palmerston Track. It lies south of us, running from Mourilyan Harbour to Innisfail, then right on to Cedar Creek, and across over these ranges to Herberton. You can form a vague guess as to what he went through to find, and cut a track over all those difficulties of primitive range and jungle, where most men would become hopelessly lost before they had gone a mile. This particular track of Palmerston's has been, is being, and increasingly will be in the future the means of opening up new, big areas of sugar, timber, agricultural and mineral lands."*

He paused, his voice had almost seemed to sadden. It flashed upon me that though he obviously admired Palmerston so, he feared the change the pathfinder's work must bring about—wild bushlands steadily going under cultivation, sawmills, the vanishing of these magnificent timbers and wild life, clear mountain streams muddied and silted by debris from mining camps. Whereas I looked upon Mulligan, Atherton, Palmerston, Oswald, Moffat, Jack, Newell, Doyle, and Mazlin and the other pathfinders like them with admiration for the townships and many homes their lifework had and was increasingly providing in these wilds. How I longed to find a mineral field and thus be the means of opening up country to support the homes of men and women!

Yet here before me was the very man who could do it, who I felt would love to do so, yet his very love of these lands in their primitive state forbade him.

In the chill of a now deathly jungle silence I gradually became

* Today that beautiful track, now a scenic road, is becoming increasingly known as the Palmerston Highway.

aware of the singing creek. Was it imagination that brought a note of sadness to its song as a quiet voice spoke? "Yes, I suppose work and towns *must* come. But all this life and beauty throughout which we have walked all this day and will tomorrow, and for days afterward, for weeks, nay, months if we wished, will vanish for ever."

Feeling decidedly chilly now, I muttered, "I'll stoke up the fire!" and crawled out to throw on more wood, thinking as the flames hummed up, This man can read my thoughts like a book! What on earth can I do about it?

"Well," he resumed abruptly as I crawled back in under the tent-fly, "Christy used to plunge into the jungles with blackboy Pompo, a blanket, a rifle, and cane-knife. He lived on the country —he had to. Easy enough in the big scrubs to the man who knows how, except in the wet season. Rain falls in feet and yards here during a heavy Wet, not in ridiculous inches. And during the Wet most game seem to hole up, even edible vegetable life seems to vanish. With every creek a raging torrent you can faintly guess what life would be like in these big scrubs. However, Christy could survive even a wet season away from the civilization of the day, though he would never tell how he did it. He lost a priceless friend, though, when Pompo died. Thereafter, he took with him on his trips several Chinese and six blackboys. He picked them for intelligence and endurance, and from different and antagonistic tribes so that they would be unlikely to conspire against him. He trained them how to handle a rifle. They proved to be an efficient, savage bodyguard. I cannot see how, in that life he led, he could possibly have survived without them. For the wild aboriginal is not a fool, believe me. And they had realized that the work of such men as Mulligan and Jack and Newell and Palmerston was opening up their beloved tribal grounds to increasing rushes of white men, with their diseases which must surely mean extinction to them. At the same time, Christy had some queer affinity with the wild aboriginals, he was a wild man himself, anyway. And he held some control over them, for which they both dreaded and admired him. So the scrub aboriginals have told me, anyway. I have often wondered, too, whether it was through music he held some further control over them. For both he and they loved music."

"Music!" I exclaimed.

"Yes," he answered, and looked at me queerly. "Yes, music. Even here, in the depths of the jungle. I notice you have been listening to the music of the creek!"

I just stared. He smiled and knocked out his pipe against a root.

"There is music in the scrubs and the forest," he said softly, "anywhere. At any time. And the voices are different in the night and the day and the seasons. You can hear the trees singing, if you have the ears to hear and the something inside which translates into music. There are countless voices in the bush, especially in these wonderful areas. As for the aboriginals, you may think their idea of music is of the crudest. It is not so, if in the right environment the rhythm can register in your blood, bringing vaguely the meaning, too. Their life, their legends, their beliefs are bound up in their dances and songs—chants you would call them. Well, Christy's blood reacted to the mystic meanings within those age-old chants, he was one with them when he sang with them. For all were wild men of the woods. You see, there is a lot more in life than we dream of."

He gazed out at the fire a moment. I thought I caught a murmurous rustle of the palm fronds overhanging the creek merging with the hum of the flames. Many nights alone in places such as this had developed his wonderful hearing, taught him the music of the bush voices.

"It takes years," he said and gazed at me, "and you must never let up. But it comes to you."

"You have read my thoughts again," I said uneasily, "and clearer than I had thought them out!"

He half smiled, with a trace of pleasure. "That also comes to you," he said. "However, in this environment, under these conditions, it is easy. Well, Christy Palmerston foresaw that in the opening up of these lands, with increasing population, the wild lands must go. And he was a man of the wilds. So he sailed for

Malaya where the big jungles are. He accepted exploratory work from some Malayan Sultan. He died a few years back of fever. Alone in the jungle, as usual. And there his bones lie tonight."

"Perhaps his spirit roams the jungles," I said in quiet surprise at the words.

He glanced at me sharply, a strange expression in his eyes.

"There is no such thing as death," he said slowly, "as you'll realize whether you live long enough or not. And now suppose we turn in—we've got tough travelling ahead tomorrow."

"What if I put the billy on?" I suggested eagerly.

"A bright idea," he answered in a pleased way. "Watch out you don't tumble into the creek—it will be cold down there."

Timely warning. Pressing through the blackness of undergrowth down to icy-cold water taught me that even to fill the billy in the big scrubs can be an awkward job. Warily I hurried back, to keep this man talking while possible.

In no time that fierce fire had the billy singing and we were under the tent-fly again, sipping steaming hot tea.

"It tastes good," he declared, and carefully laying down his half-emptied pannikin, felt for his pipe.

"Maybe you would not have been quite so keen to grope your way down to the creek if you'd known there was a python out there!" His half smile looked grim to me.

In the chilly silence I heard myself saying, "A python?"

"Yes, a scrub python. A big fellow. He's slithering about his business out there in the dark near by."

"How do you know?"

"I can smell him."

When I did not reply he said, "You doubt me again. I told you I can smell snakes!"

"Oh yes." I remembered.

"Well, this is a perfect night for the scent of wild things to linger. He was quite close, too, he had stopped to peer at the fire-light when you went out for water. But he is crawling past on business bent now."

"Are you going to shoot him?"

"Of course not. He is doing me no harm, he has just as much right to live as I have." He lit up, the match illuminated his expressionless face until a whiff of tobacco smoke clouded it.

"I thought that pythons and snakes and things liked to keep in out of the wet and damp," I said doubtfully.

"Of course they do, but it's regulated by season and environment. The scrub reptiles naturally have to be immune to dampness, there is plenty of that in the scrubs. However, the big fellow out there must be on urgent business, for he is taking a risk in crawling over this sodden depth of rotted leaf mould on a humid night. He would feel more comfortable and happy coiled around the branch of a tree overlooking a wallaby pad."

I leant over and refilled his pannikin, asking, "But why is he taking a risk?"

"Fungus."

"What?"

"A phosphorescent fungous growth."

I gaped at him. He smiled, sipping at his pannikin.

"This tea was quite a bright idea of yours," he said. "Have you ever thought that tea, such a solace to the human race, is grown by a plant? Have you ever thought of what plant life means to all of us? That it is a fact that without plant life the human race would become extinct?"

I glanced "outside"; to my boyish imagination the firelit trees seeming listening in a brooding silence. I answered dubiously, "No."

"It is a plain fact. Without grass, nothing, as we know it, could exist. Not even fish."

This was getting too deep for me.

"Tell me about this fungus—and the python."

He half smiled. "Yes," he murmured, "better these silent trees, that so often are *not* silent, than the whine of the circular saw. Oh well, you will see plenty of fungi, of numerous sorts, before our little walkabout is over. You have not seen then, in the jungle at night, an itchy, very unhappy python crawling along as if he were on fire?"

"No," I replied unbelievingly.

He half smiled. "Well, I have on a night dark as this. I followed him quite a way. Believe me, he was on fire all right, though not exactly as we understand fire. He was luminously covered by a phosphorescent glow. Much was already growing alive upon him, but from the moist leaves he was picking up more as urgently he crawled along, much more. By some natural attraction, I really believe. It was a remarkable sight, fascinating too to follow along beside him and watch that ghostly film glowing and fading and glowing again as his writhing coils picked up more and more. His big body was fairly quivering as he urged himself across that bad patch with all speed possible. He could have crossed that bad ground much quicker, too, but he panicked, twice he reached the very edge of that sodden ground only to writhe himself right back into it again. I suppose the fungus he had earlier picked up was beginning to eat into him now, in between the scales probably, maybe something like tiny, fiery insects biting in under your toe-nails to the quick. I suppose you've seen a worm or a caterpillar being attacked by ants when crossing a roadway?"

"Yes."

"Well, just as more, and still more ants attack the caterpillar so it writhes and turns and loses all sense of direction until finally it's overwhelmed. Well, that is what seemed to be happening to the python, and he grew frantic. When he did break across into clearer country he was in a bad way, believe me. I stood there in the dark and watched him travel to safety. And he was covering that ground with all the last speed he could now muster, leaving a trail of fading phosphorescence until he vanished. Of course, as he writhed over this clearer, firmer ground he was scraping his coils upon the earth and thus scraping off a lot of the loosely cling-ing stuff from his belly."

He drank the last of his tea. Slowly he filled the pipe again while I sat silently, still disbelieving, far too inexperienced as yet to know that what he said was truth.

"So far as reptiles are concerned," he resumed, "they are subject at times to a parasitic fungous disease, according to seasonal vagaries and environment and luck. For, like humans, many escape, while others are unlucky. The fungous growth, or spores, or whatever it may be attaches itself to the underpart of the snake, its belly scales, as it passes over the moist leaves, and spreads and grows. It is mostly along the sodden creek-banks, and those quagmires of springs that you'll sometimes find even upon a mountain-top, that these fungous things are dangerously thick. Just as you found the leeches that made a bloody mess of your legs this afternoon. I suppose the fungus breeds or grows everywhere throughout the scrubs during a heavy Wet, when the wrigglers lie up in their hide-outs, of course."

"That fungus must kill a lot of snakes."

"Oh, I don't know. No one has investigated it. Probably it may do so, when a cycle season comes around when it is very bad. But of course instinct teaches them to avoid the dangerous places. And then, when they do get caught, the victim tries to work out his own remedy. Every living thing will put up a fight for life, you know, plants fight for their lives, too. I've seen a snake, in this particular case a scrub python also, working with might and main and no little common sense in cleaning himself of the fungus. He'd coiled himself tightly round and round the limb of a rough-barked tree and was slowly and heavily dragging himself round it, actually scraping the fungus from his scales. Then he writhed himself round the trunk of the tree and dragged himself to a higher branch, and there went through the same process."

As he began knocking out his pipe I asked, "Why?"

"So that he'd have a clean limb to scrape off the remainder of the fungus, of course. If he kept to the same limb he'd only begin to dirty himself again with the fungus he's already rubbed off."

"H'm."

"You don't believe me again." He smiled good-humouredly. "I wonder what you'd say, or rather think, if I told you of some of the real deep secrets vividly alive here in this vast womb of life called the scrubs. Never mind. Now look here, you did not believe me when I told you about the dancing worms. Would you believe that in this scrub there are worms that grow as long as a man?"

He grinned at my disbelief. "I'll show you plenty tomorrow," he said quite amiably. "We'll be walking over a lot of creek-head country. These worms really only average three feet long, but I'll find you quite a few at five feet, and I've really seen them grow to over six feet, as round as a broomstick. For good measure, I'll show them to you in their gaudy uniforms. One fellow in deep blue, another in pale. His cousin in red, his uncle in deep purple, his nephews in green. And if you like to sit up tomorrow night upon some chilly creek-bank I'll guarantee you see them in their night attire—a dull glow of colour phosphorus as they crawl in their five-foot lengths along the creek-bank. And now we'd better turn in."

Lying there in the firelit coolness, slow water drips sighing down on the tent-fly, the black breath of the jungle all around, for some time I could not sleep. It was the too sudden opening of a new world to a lad. The jungle! That awful scrub owl! Dancing worms! Worms five feet long! Phosphorescent pythons! This hidden creek which sang a lovely lullaby of haunting voices. How much of all of it was true? What far greater truths might lie hidden here?

Thoughts wandered away with the lulling rhythm of the creek waters singing by—what was that about some Boatman's Song? No boatman here, except a trapped insect on a fallen leaf being fast carried away—abandon hope—he would be dashed to pieces over the falls—it was a three-thousand-foot drop between here and the distant sea—yes, the creek was singing its travelling song—the leaf floating away ever a little faster into whispering night—the creek was changing note—the leaf and I were floating along—floating. . . .

CHAPTER XXXII

THE OGRE

NEXT midday we boiled the billy in a Glade of the Fairies, a dell of wondrous beauty.

"A carpet of moss," I exclaimed, "green as an emerald! No Sultan's palace could be as beautiful as this."

"I should say not."

He was gazing at tendrils of orchids drooping from statuesque palms, like delicate pink bells with tongues of gold—the first orchids I'd seen in the scrub. This most unusual space was nearly as large as a ballroom, draped all around by curtains of flowering creepers hanging from branches. There was a delicate green light throughout this glade, and the smoke of our fire coiled slowly up in a pale-blue spiral to merge in greenery amongst the leafy canopy above.

With a johnny-cake in one hand and cold boiled pigeon in the other I said, grinning, "How strangely that smoke coils! If we were in the Arabian Nights I could easily imagine some long, skinny old genie taking shape in it."

"Yes," he answered dreamily.

Through a mouthful of johnny-cake I went on, "If we stayed perfectly quiet, fairies might come gliding out from those ferny bowers and dance upon the moss."

"Why not?" he replied.

Swallowing the johnny-cake, I gazed at him a moment. "You're joking. Surely you don't believe in fairies, and little men in green?"

"Maybe not, though many folk throughout the world do. And *you* did not believe in some strange things I've already shown you, remember. However, there *is* an ogre in this dell." He was gazing straight across at a mighty spider-web spun from branch to branch and right down to the mossy carpet.

271

"What on earth do you mean?"

"Come and I'll show you." And he stood up and strolled across to the web, a silvered masterpiece that the world's most artistic jeweller could never have imitated.

"What a mighty web!" I said. "And what a hideous thing he is!"

"*She*—as you'll know if we have a little luck."

"What do you mean?"

"That spider in the web centre is a lady spider. And this is the season and perfect day when she is liable to expect a visitor."

"But how do you know?"

"Oh," he answered somewhat shortly, "I've been travelling through and through these scrubs for quite a time now." His eyes seemed searching the grass around.

"But what an awful-looking thing!" I said in disgust.

"Yes," he said absently, "but don't touch the web or she might spring on the instant. Otherwise, she can't see you, she's near blind."

"How on earth do you know?"

"Because I've tested them, of course." He was staring down at his feet, staring all around.

"What are you searching for?"

"Her visitor."

"What sort of visitor?"

"Her boy-friend, of course."

"But he won't be able to see her," I said stupidly.

"Of course he will. He can see, he is the one who *must* see. But how about boiling the billy again? May as well put on those turkey eggs while you're at it—I'm feeling extra peckish. Sing out when they're boiled—I'll watch here."

I walked away, not much interested. To think that that awful-looking, huge, hunched-up, blacky-brownish, hairy-looking thing should have a "boy-friend visitor"—ugh! It just left me cold. Yet again I wondered at my strange friend.

When the billy was boiled he took his two eggs and pannikin and johnny-cake and sat down by the foot of that web. With cheerful appetite, I set to where I was—those eggs and that billy tea tasted great; certainly we were living surprisingly well. Even old Mick and Jim, away back at Nigger Creek, wherever *that* was now, would not be dining on cold turkey and fresh boiled turkey eggs.

I was drinking the last of the tea when he whistled and beckoned, pointing with a twig at the roots below the web.

"There he is! Just squat quietly on your haunches, not too close. He's too agitated, and too anxious, to notice *us*."

"What is he anxious about?"

"You'll see presently!" he replied grimly.

"Are you sure this is the one? He's not a third her size. Not nearly as ugly, either."

"Just watch and see."

I stared down on that spider boy, who certainly did seem agitated, standing now on little hind legs, timidly reaching up at the web whose strands towered so mightily before him. Delicately he touched a strand. Away up, she seemed to freeze, and he leapt back a full six inches, crouching, ready to flee. I peered closely down, quite interested now. A soft chuckle came from the man beside me. The timid visitor crept forward, reached up and his tiny outstretched leg touched the strand again, only to leap back. The third time he hung on; she, away up there in the centre, seemed quiescent, a hunched bundle of ugliness. Standing up on his short hind legs now, most cautiously he shook that strand.

"He is vibrating it," whispered the man beside me, "in a certain way. He's really sending her a love telegram; she can't see him, but he is vibrating that strand telling her she's the loveliest thing he's ever seen, and would she mind if he climbs up to kiss her good day."

"That'll be the day!" I grinned.

"Yes," he murmured, "the one and *only* day!"

Gingerly, very gingerly, the little spider began climbing that strand, clinging to it while vibrating it now and then, only to pause, fearfully watching up. Even I could tell now that he was ready to drop instantly to the ground and run for his life.

"She can drop down on him fast as lightning if she's annoyed," murmured my mate.

"Why *should* she?" I asked.

"The course of true love seldom runs smoothly," he chuckled, "in the jungles as elsewhere. Just watch how young Lochinvar climbs up to his lady's boudoir."

Lochinvar climbed most hesitantly, I could never have imagined such an uneasy lover. But she merely waited, all hunched up, glaring down upon the intruder. Looking up, I could now detect her eyes gleaming like pin-points of luminous green.

"Is she really blind?" I whispered.

"Not quite. She can focus on him now—and he's not too happy about it, either!"

Slowly indeed now Lochinvar climbed or rather crawled up, until he was within three inches of her. He hung delicately there quite a time, then with the greatest care began to edge across the web right around behind her.

"Did you ever see such a frightened lover?" chuckled my mate.

"But what on earth has he got to be scared of?"

"Wouldn't *you* be?"

"You've got a queer sense of humour."

Lochinvar was right behind her now, most delicately he crept down to her, reached out a gentle foreleg, stroked her, snatched back his little "arm". She had not moved.

He tried again, with quick movement sidled up beside her.

My mate stood up. "It's all right now," he said, "he's clicked. They're only interested in one another, and I can assure you he won't know another thing—but for one awful second!"

Standing thus, we had the centre of the web before our eyes. They were motionless for quite a while.

Then, with a delicately terrified caution, he began stretching out a hind leg behind him, as if groping for a strand. His foot, or claw, or whatever it was, touched a strand, slowly fastened to it.

"Watch!" hissed my mate. "He is getting ready to jump for his life!"

Another little leg crept out, fastened to a strand. Then—

As the spider leapt free a flurry of outspread claws wheeled round and fastened all over him. The web rocked violently; he was overwhelmed under a fat hairy body that was with fierce energy spinning a web round him.

"She is lashing him to the web," said my mate's voice calmly, "as securely as a dozen men could lash a terrified prisoner to a post."

"But what for?"

"You'll see soon!"

The big web grew still as she crouched back, she seemed to be quietly licking hairy forepaws and what seemed like fangs. I saw that indeed he was lashed helpless with unbreakable security to the web. Then she crept forward, gloated over him a moment, snapped at him, began to—

"But she's *eating* him!" I protested.

"That's so."

"But why?"

"Why not? His job is finished. She'll lay scores and scores of eggs in a few days, there'll be plenty of young spiders, she may as well eat him. After all, she'll have to feed *them*!"

"She's a *beast* of a thing!" I said with utter loathing. "Come on! I've seen enough of your spider lovers."

He laughed softly as we slipped on our swags.

"Have you never seen the praying mantis?" he asked. "They do the same thing."

"No," I replied. "Never heard of it."

"Well, they do. But we'd better step out—we've wasted too much time studying the love story of a spider. However, other species manage with happier endings, if you feel any consolation."

But I only grunted, my eyes glancing up at a white myrtle flower glowing like a star in the gloom. We'd gone quite a way before I realized I'd missed enjoying that beautiful thing. A rifle-bird flashed by and was gone in a shimmer of colour and I knew we were near a creek. Birds are plentiful along a creek, for there they have space to fly up and down above the creek, the only place in the big scrubs where you can see a ribbon of blue far above. Of course, there are many birds, a multitude in fact, that feast upon the berries on that sea of tree-tops, but they can rarely be seen from below. And yet there are plenty of birds "down below", too, within the scrub itself. What a lot I had to learn!

I learnt a bit right at this very creek.

"What if we try this creek?" I asked grumpily, and while glancing round was sorry I spoke.

"Right-oh," he replied cheerfully, "but let us cross over first."

As sure-stepping as a cat, he walked over the slippery, moss-grown boulders while I clumsily followed. As surely, too, he had picked the one place where we could step up onto the bank without having to force our way through undergrowth. A mighty green frog with a waistcoat like a purple lily flopped on the rock between my feet.

"He's wondering what strange thing this is that he sees," chuckled the Jungle Man from the bank.

"I've a good mind to boot him in the belly." I glowered down at that squatting giant gaping up. "He dashed near scared me into the water."

"Don't hurt the old boy, I suppose he thinks we're some harmless sort of water toad. If we looked like a crane or a snake or a water-rat he'd dive for his life."

As I stepped up beside him he was frowning at the creek, saying, "That fool of a butterfly! Curiosity can teach you things, but it can kill, too!"

A large butterfly, gorgeous wings outspread, hung almost motionless in the air a man's height above the frog.

"Quick! Notice Old Greenback's haunches—and his eyes!" he murmured.

The frog crouched, his eyes protruding, gleaming.

"Will he get him?"

"Not in *that* position. If the butterfly flies higher, or darts swiftly away he will be safe. If not, it will be touch and go. But it will mean a mighty leap, whether or no."

For a moment or two I thought the butterfly was going to hover down upon what must have seemed a succulent, strange green leaf to it. Hesitantly though, it began to flutter away. Almost instantly the frog leapt; he was bounding up in the air with legs outstretched, looking ever so much longer and thinner now. The butterfly made one frantic wing-beat, then one wing was gripped in the frog's mouth and they were plunging down to splash in the water and vanish.

"Oh well," said the Jungle Man, "a pity the butterfly was not half a second quicker. But that sort of thing is going on every moment of the day and night in these places. *We* would have thought it much worse if that frog had been a crocodile."

"But why?" I asked.

"Just think it out!"

"You have the queerest ideas," I said slowly.

"Not so. That could easily have happened had we incautiously been crossing a coastal jungle stream farther up north. Men have actually been known to step upon a crocodile up there, thinking it was a log. As you'll hear all about if you persist in your idea of wandering in those places. Well now, here is the pick and dish, choose your own place and the creek and try it out. I'm going to enjoy a smoke."

And he did.

Quietly smoked, silently teaching me a lesson while I made an ass of myself. Ignorance is bliss, until you find out that you're the goat. Eventually I waded out of the icy water, threw down that baby pick and dish, sat down and glumly pulled on my boots.

"Satisfied?" he asked quietly.

"Yes," I answered shortly, "impossible to prospect any creek here without proper tools."

"Not impossible," he said. "I'll show you how when we come to some more likely looking creek. However, we could not add those 'proper tools' to our load, the trip would become a laborious misery and—we would not go far. And now we'd better be moving. The going has changed, as you'll soon find out. We must step out to reach the comfy camp I wish to make tonight."

I followed with mixed feelings as he slipped a cane-knife from his swag. Not the usual heavy scrub-knife—trust him.

In years fast coming I was often to be grateful for learning even about such a knife. It was lightly humming now, just light strokes slashing through cane and vine as he stepped along as if sliding his way through the bad patches while I clumsily followed, soon scratched and torn while he effortlessly kept going, though clearing a track.

Gone was the soft, clean floor of the scrub between the tree-trunks. This was a tangle of vine and creeper, lianas like the hawsers of ships drooping down from the branches, undergrowth that clung and tripped the tiring legs.

And then even he was slowed up in a maze of lawyer-cane that gripped the ankles and legs like writhing snakes, the hooks of the come-back-quicks ripping through pants and shirt to hook in the ribs and pull a man back. Pushing the leaves of the wretched things aside, step by step lifting the legs up out of the grip of the canes, forced to put them gingerly down amongst the snappy, clinging canes again, was misery. Itching and burning legs and arms became smothered with loathsome, blood-sucking leeches. It slowed him, but I could never have got through had he not waited again and again.

"Keep going," he encouraged, "but take it steady, don't exhaust yourself. We cannot work our way round this patch, but we'll be through it before long."

"Just as well," I breathed. "My legs feel like lead already, but they're burning from scratches. I can hardly drag my ankles up through these blasted clinging canes, my arms and ribs and legs are torn to shreds, I feel like biting these come-back-quicks each time they hook me back. Much more of this and a man would flop down and to hell with it all."

"A comfy camp you'd enjoy," he said, grinning, "smothered in these leaves, tangled up in the canes like a grasshopper that's kicked its way into a loose ball of prickly string. What if a hungry old wild boar came snuffling along in the night and shoved a tusk into your ribs?"

"Oh, carry on," I grumbled. "Lead the way out of this green hell quick as you can." And the knife hummed as it slashed on in earnest now.

Great bundles of these canes grew out from the butts of each palm-like plant to coil out among their fellows, only to stretch up a come-back-quick, hook itself up onto a tree branch, then go climbing on and up, branch by branch, to disappear in the foliage. Thousands of these canes reaching from the ground into the highest branches locked tree to tree in a wild confusion of elastic-like ropes. And the strength of little things was presently apparent in an acre-wide tangle of straining scrub. For a big tree had fallen, yet could not fall because thousands of tautened ropes of canes held its dragging weight to the straining tops of its brothers. Among the torn-away branches up there there was even a little blue glimpse of sky. No wonder these canes are the practically unbreakable ropes of the aborigines. Soon, farther north, I was to see them with these canes lashed to trees, hold maddened crocodiles.

What men the early pathfinders were to force a way through country like this, let alone find direction! It was not only they had the heart of lions, they must have possessed some sixth sense as well.

I was just about done when he cut our way through, but he kept on going. No fear of my falling behind, though I'd have given anything to flop down for a spell. How on earth was he finding his way? Sighting from tree to tree? But this seemed ridiculous, for visibility was only a few yards. And yet there was no chance of seeing the sky and I knew he prided himself on never carrying a compass—not that it would be much use here. Yet he seemed to know exactly where he was going. Such bushmanship amazed me. As when he lifted the rifle to fire straight up into that green roof, and down came softly falling a plump body, a beautiful pigeon green as a leaf with a purple breast, larger than the domestic pigeon. Five times more the little rifle cracked. I just could not see a thing for that impenetrable canopy of leaves.

"We'll enjoy a tasty supper tonight," he said as picked up the pigeons, "but come along—we must keep moving."

And we moved. The scrub was growing ominously dark when he halted and turned around.

"Hear anything?"

But only the murmurous breath of a million trees gave answer.

"Smell anything?"

But to my questing nostrils came only a faint dampness and the elusive tang of a sea of greenery.

"Lie down there in that clear place, there's just about room. Smell about a foot above the loam."

When I'd filled my lungs with just about all the mouldy leaf matter on earth his voice came: "Now run your nostrils slowly along that big damp root—about six inches above it—inhale slowly, but deeply."

I did so, and when just about tired of it glanced up.

"What do you smell?"

"I'm not sure, but there seems to be a faint tang of smoke."

"You're learning."

"But there's no fire in the scrubs!" I said, puzzled though pleased.

"You can never be certain *what* is in the scrubs," he replied, and I jumped erect like a startled hare to a sharp, rhythmic clap of drumming. Silence a moment, then in perfect unison that sharp clap of drums muffled by trees, yet strangely reverberating.

"Natives?" I whispered.

He nodded.

Again those challenging drums. Silence.

"It is their salute to the setting sun," he said. "We'll hear no more. Come on."

I followed, bewildered. He was making straight towards where that sound had come; I would have hurried in exactly the opposite direction. Surely there were no real wild natives left in these ranges! But then I vaguely remembered hearing an old-timer by Old Mick's campfire declaring, "There's still a little tribe or two of the wild 'uns left hidden away out in the big scrubs."

Old Mick's camp seemed a desirable place to be in right now.

CHAPTER XXXIII

WILD LIFE IN THE SCRUBS

QUITE suddenly, the jungle grew noticeably light, almost like mild daylight. Then we stepped out into a blaze of late afternoon sunlight.

An open forest pocket ringed by dense black jungle, a natural clearing large enough even to feed a handful of sheep. Squatting just out from the scrub edge right opposite were a hundred or more naked aborigines, the warriors vividly painted and feathered, women and children staring silently towards us, smoke from their cooking fires wafting lazily upward. Leaning against the gunyahs were bundles of hideously barbed spears.

"Light a fire while I fill the billies."

I did so, in a moment he was back and the billies were on, he was already plucking a pigeon. I started on another, gazing across the clearing. Here and there a forest tree was beautiful in its bath of fading sunlight. The grass in the centre of the clearing had been pulled up, the red earth showing as if brushed with a broom, considerable labour here. And all over this huge red earth clearing was built a maze of queer designs as if carved out of white stone. They were stones, whitewashed with pipeclay. Paths, straight, circular and semicircular were running throughout the designs, a few of which seemed hauntingly familiar, most were strange. In the very centre stood a raised dais of stone which queerly reminded me of a mighty starfish.

"All those designs are symbolical," he explained, "some too are totem and animistic symbols. Those big rounded heaps to right and left of the star represent two sacred mountains, womanhood also. That long zigzag design represents lightning and what it brings to earth, including the connecting of sky with earth, as do those long 'coils' of stone-work, which represent thunder. Several of those crossed symbols represent human and superhuman descent and identity with star, plant, animal, reptile, fish. Others are symbols of the gods."

"The gods!" I said wonderingly. "But aboriginals know nothing about the gods."

"Out there are symbolic representations of the gods," he replied evenly. "Call them supermen if you like, just as ancient people in other countries did. And so does the Australian aboriginal, just the same. Those beliefs may have all come from the one source when humanity was young. You see that large circle, with a fiery red centre and long white rays? That represents the sun, and the life it brings to earth. Those little groups of stones within the little circle represent their group-marriage system, and it is intricate, believe me. Others are spirit symbols; it is not allowed that I point them out to you, but I can see the symbol of the demon spirits of the swamps, the forest spirits too, the jungle and gorge, river and mountain spirits, others also. There is a lot of nature and spirit worship in these people's secret beliefs. Spirits are believed to be lurking everywhere, in the whispering breeze, plentiful among the spirit trees and spirit waterholes, among the spirit rocks. They can hear their voices, or such is their belief, can be helped or persecuted by them. They believe they are in touch with the dead. The witch-doctor is their close link between them, the spirits, and the superhuman beings, otherwise the gods. You won't see the Dance of the Spirits, unfortunately, it is not allowed. But if you saw the witch-doctor in action out there, dancing with his spirit partners, I don't think you'd sleep well for a night or two."

"I don't want to see him!"

"It's not allowed!" He smiled. And smiled in a strange sort of way, staring out there across the symbolic grounds to the gunyahs with their now shadowy groups of people. In surprise I noticed for the first time how straight and clearly defined were his eyebrows, those cold grey eyes now animated with life.

"What are those two big circles?" I asked a bit hastily. "That big circle of white stones around that altar thing, and that whopper circle enclosing all the grounds?"

"Why," he answered in slight surprise, "those are the spirit circles to keep out unwanted spirits. They were erected at the very last. The witch-doctor and his assistants 'danced' all spirits away from what you call 'that altar thing', which was then enclosed by the circle. No spirit forms, neither from the air, from the earth's surface, nor from up out of the earth, can now enter that circle. Then he 'danced' all spirits away from all the ground which similarly was fenced in while he was still dancing."

"H'm!" I said.

He brought us both back to earth with a gruff, "Better get a move on with these pigeons."

Even as he spoke the last rays of sunlight faded away down into the dark crown of the scrub facing us. That maze of symbols faded into blurs of whiteness. Then it was quite dark.

"Do you know these people?" I asked.

"Of course. Otherwise, do you think I would have led you into a trap like this?"

"Of course not," I answered. "And now I remember you smelt them—or smelt their fires."

"You remembered just in time." His face wore a cynical grin in the firelight. "Your mind is all 'het up' at present—do you remember, too, that I can do a little mind-reading?"

"You win," I replied. "And what do we do now?"

"Eat, then let the fire die down. Rest and smoke. The tableau opens when the moon rises."

For several hours we sat there smoking, hemmed in by that circle black as the pit, the clearing faintly lighted by the open sky, stars above seemingly just overhead and made of bronze gold, glorious to gaze at after the pitch-black nights of the scrubs. The few trees in the clearing were still as if carved from mottled ivory.

"I did not know there were places like this in the scrubs," I murmured.

"Yes. Every here and there, some larger than this, others so small you could hardly build a house upon them. Natural forest, forest trees, forest grasses in the hearts of the scrubs. Strange indeed that the scrubs have not overwhelmed such oases of daylight thousands of years ago. But then, the sea does not overwhelm its little islands. These forest pockets are the secret of the scrub blacks' continued existence, for these are impenetrable hide-outs. There were, and are, but few tribes of scrub blacks, compared to those of the open country. But for these open forests deep in the scrubs, there would be no scrub blacks. To the open-forest men, these scrubs are full of demons, spirits, particularly at night. They are, too, in the night, to the scrub blacks. The forest men, in daylight, will penetrate the edge of the scrub only a very short distance, whereas the scrub men can emerge and hunt and make their forays out into the open forest whenever they like. When in danger they simply vanish into the scrubs. They are quite safe then. They make their way to some hidden forest pocket like this and camp in security, both from human enemies and spirit terrors, until danger is past."

"I can easily understand that now," I said, "once you've explained it and I see this clearing. What were those 'white-fellows' painted with?"

"Some with a white ochrous pipeclay, others with snow-white down from cockatoo breasts, stuck on with their own blood. All are aids to illusion. Some have the down plastered all over them. Others, only upon certain parts of the body, some on one leg and not on another, others with circular bands, others with long stripes. You'll see with what weird effect soon."

I did!

There was not one solitary glow of coals, not one sound, not one movement from away across the clearing. Just a haze of sky light and an eerie feeling as if the jungle were holding its breath to listen.

From black sky behind us a silver searchlight stole out over the forest pocket, growing stronger every second until suddenly the pocket was a blaze of silver light in which silver trees stood beautifully towering above silver grass; those symbolic mazes suddenly were silver, the "dais" was actually gleaming. Away behind by the bright scrub edge even the gunyahs were silvered. I noted the spears had gone. By the farther side of the maze, squatting in a semicircle with their legs bent under them, were motionless ebony figures of women and children silvered by moonlight. As one, their clasped hands rose and came sharply down between their thighs, and the human drum in a startling crash reverberated throughout the clearing again and again and again. From behind them, within the black jungle, a sudden roar of voices was sustained in an animal savagery as out glided ghosts—some, I could swear, were floating—ghosts that were living skeletons, ghosts all white and seeming almost shapeless, others with but one ghostly arm, one ghostly leg, others all white but headless, others all body but legless. The howl in those voices, which now all merged into one, fairly made my hair stand on end as they came gliding past the human drum that now was fairly crashing with sound as the oncoming phalanx, with stamping feet, added thunder to the sound. I actually felt the earth vibrate as with one shuddering roar they came bounding straight towards us, waving spears and clubs and those mighty swords. I snatched at the rifle, but a grip of steel held my wrist as the Jungle Man said, "Sit quiet, you fool!" Above the now tumultuous drumming, piercing screams from the women froze my blood, and the savages were upon us in a frenzy of glaring eyes and gleaming teeth, some chewing their beards in maniacal rage as I leapt up and back to ward off those frightful weapons. I reached the scrub and vanished into it, to an awful roar I only realized was laughter when it was joined by the shrieking howls of those wretched women and children. Clinging round a tree in the darkness there, I listened with a thumping heart; it was quite a time before I could believe the whole mob were in nearly hysterical laughter. At my mate's reassuring shout, I groped my way back, feeling as mad as a March hare and much smaller.

Still howling with laughter, they pranced their way back to their silly women as grumpily I sat down by my grinning mate. I was still shivering

"They *can* be frighteningly realistic," he said placatingly as he pulled out the pipe. "However, it was all a joke, just their way of saying, 'Welcome'."

"I wish they'd all broken their stupid necks," I replied hotly.

"After all," he said, "we *are* poachers, you know, encroaching on their sacred dancing grounds."

"Then why didn't they tell us to clear out?"

"We will—tomorrow. Tonight is really only the opening night, they'll be dancing, and going through the ceremonies for a week yet."

"Anyway," I said, still a bit angrily, "what do the fools think they could do with those stupid swords? They couldn't cut a man's head off with a wooden sword!"

"They are actually frightful weapons," he replied grimly, "in a surprise attack at close quarters. They don't dream of cutting a man in half, of course. But just imagine the weight in those huge hardwood double-handed weapons swung with the maniacal strength you've just witnessed. A victim would throw up his arms as you did, but the sword would swing around and under, and both your ankles would snap like carrots while the impact of the blow would throw the body yards away. A body blow would break a man's back. He is finished by even a blow down on the shoulder. Just imagine the numbing effect of a blow hurled down like that —a man simply crumples up, paralysed."

"They're nice brutes!" I said soberly.

"Oh no, quite natural. I might mention that with our superior civilization we've thought out some pretty frightful weapons ourselves."

In coming years, under the horrors of shellfire, crouching into the very earth under the hail of exploding bombs, the showers of machine-gun bullets, I was to think of those very words. And, believe me, how passionately I then wished I were back within that peaceful forest pocket sheltered by the million trees of that great scrub!

CHAPTER XXXIV

THE JUNGLE SPEAKS

EERILY beautiful now was the chanting, changing to a haunting melancholy, dying away into the whispering bush, then softly rising in rapid crescendo to a savage roaring of men's voices, above which the shrill wailing of the women was hair-raising, accompanied by the clapping thunder of human drum and stamping feet. That moon-flooded circle walled in by black jungle presently seemed rolling with vibration, whirling sound around and around the clearing, holding it to vibrating earth and jungle wall until in softening dance and song it was slowly absorbed into the jungle and the skies. In my stirred-up imagination I could actually feel these waves of sound beating around us to be softly drawn away by timber and sky. To this very day I am not sure it was imagination either, certainly not the vibrations from the earth upon which we were actually sitting.

Piece after piece they danced, re-forming out behind the drummer after each silence, to come marching back chanting into that stone maze again and stamp out into the patterns partitioned off by the silvered rockeries. Solid figures they appeared at times, then, eerily separating out, some appeared as half bodies of men floating, others as legs, others headless. This was due not only to the painting, but also to the grouping and movement and their expert use of the moonlight. The Jungle Man stared as I was staring, absorbed by it all, only occasionally would he growl an explanatory word on this age-old symbolism.

"Obeisance to the moon, the mother of life, which brings the tides to the waters, the things of earth, and to man."

"The Serpent Dance—this goes far back to the Dream Time, the creation of things."

"Dance to the Spirit World. This dance expresses their age-old

287

beliefs in reincarnation, in a spirit world upon earth, and in spirit worlds up among the stars. Impossible to follow it, even in part; we are watching the beliefs of Ancient Man, beliefs that were born ages ago, maybe we are watching the beliefs of worlds come and gone. I cannot understand it all myself. But watch, this is a big gathering, and they are rare now. Civilization has thinned out both the natives and their beliefs. You may be watching one of the very last of the seasonal sacred ceremonies—in this district, anyway." And his mouth set in a grim line as he gave all attention to this fascinating thing happening out in this clearing now fairly ablaze with silver light from the great moon so low above. And now that stone dais in the centre seemed gleaming silver. In later years, with slightly increased knowledge, I've wondered whether their paints were dusted with flakes of mica, for under that molten moon the illusion of gleaming silver designs throughout the dance-field was perfect.

They chanted until slowly, unwillingly it almost seemed, the last of the moonlight died away over the black westward scrub, and their figures and voices died with the vanishing moon.

"It is all over—for tonight," said my jungle mate, and I could swear he sighed. "We had better turn in."

And he rolled out his blanket and coiled it round him, turning his back on me without another word.

I know now that wild scene was a book of primitive life to him.

For hours I seemed to toss there, ears ringing with the chanting, the stamping, the drumming, the haunting weirdness of it all. To a roar of triumph, a thunder of stamping and drumming, I sat bolt upright, and the sun was pouring into the clearing, bathing the dais with fire.

"I thought *that* would wake you!" came a cynical voice.

"Good Heavens! Sunrise!"

"As you see."

"What is it all about now?" I asked in sleepy bewilderment.

"A triumph song to the sun god who brings light and warmth raining down upon the path of the moon, who showered fertility down over the earth as she went before. But it is the light and warmth of the sun that awakens that fertility into life. So, another day is born—all is well."

With the sun cosily risen, the dancers returned to their gunyahs. The lubras coaxed at the cooking fires, thin coils of smoke wispily arose. The Jungle Man already had the billy on.

"There will be no more today," he said. "They will rest and hunt until tonight. By then we will be camping quite a distance from here. Eat up!"

As he spoke, two gnarled old greybeards came strolling along to grin down at him. He offered them a smoke and a share of our breakfast. They gravely accepted, squatted down, and began eating as if this invitation were fully expected.

To my surprise, tinged with envy, he spoke throughout the meal in native language. He seemed to know it as well as they.

Swags on backs, we entered the scrub again, the cane-knife singing, but he did deign to say, "Those old warriors were two of Christy Palmerston's boys, the only two left. And they are not long for this world."

And his mouth shut like a clam as he pushed forcefully on. The undergrowth was not so bad as yesterday, but obstructive enough as we pressed on through this cathedral-like coolness of greenery. A startled croak ahead as a turkey indignantly scuttled away, to foolishly rise in clumsy flight at my mate's loud, insistent, "*Hisss! Hisss! Hisss!*" Peering eagerly, I saw the purplescarlet head and neck as it alighted on a low branch to gape back towards us. To the crack of the rifle the bird came thudding heavily down, and a moment later I wheeled round to a distant, muffled drumming. His face was expressionless as I exclaimed, "Aboriginals again!"

"No. Cassowary." He grinned as if amused. "I see you don't quite catch on," he said evenly to my silence. "That drumming is made by a male cassowary, a jungle bird, the emu of the scrubs."

Quietly he described this amazing bird, as vividly as he was to describe many another of the creatures of the wonder life in the scrubs.

"Then what is the silly ass drumming about?" I asked as again, muffled through the timber, came that drumming.

"Is that him again?"

"Yes."

"I never could have believed it. Why, there almost seems something *challenging* in it."

He almost smiled. "You really are learning," he said quietly.

"H'm! Well then, what is he challenging?"

"Us."

"Us?"

"Yes, disbeliever. He is answering the muffled report of the rifle. For he thinks it was the drumming of some rival on the war-path for his lady love. So that you see even things of the wild can be mistaken, can make fools of themselves right in their own natural environment. But we'd better get moving."

By midday the undergrowth was thinning out, but I was jolly glad when he called a halt.

"You can light a fire from those yellowish sticks." He pointed. "Then you'd better clean the turkey so it will keep fresh for to-night."

He picked up both billy-cans and strode towards the tinkling of water over rocks. I'd plucked and cleaned the turkey by the time he returned; you learn to do things simply and quickly when living in the rough.

He was preparing to set both billies on the fire, and I glanced curiously into the larger.

It was full of big, fat green crayfish, in a kicking indignation at their strange quarters. Oh, what a tasty dish this would be!

"Where on earth did you get them?" I asked incredulously.

"In the creek."

"How did you catch them?"

"With my fingers."

Go to hell! I thought. If you don't like to tell me, then do the other thing.

He was telling the simple truth. I was to learn, too, that he could even catch fish with his hands.

But then, he knew secrets much more strange.

He chose to camp that night under the pillared shelter of a grotesque monster. In his own tight-lipped way he admired it. This strangler was a wholesale tree-killer, it had taken full possession of the jungle right here over an area the size of a large house and had strangled out everything for its own mighty roots, which formed an unshakable base in great twisted roots that grew *upward* far into the air to support the gigantic trunk. Those roots grew far down into the earth of course, but also upward in a maze of lattice-work high as the lower branches of other trees, where they all grew into one another and formed the trunk. These weird monsters, like the gigantic strangling fig with buttresses large enough to shelter a tent, constantly intrigued me.

"He's a beauty," said my mate. "Each root is a tree in itself— writhing pythons of an age long past, now all frozen into one another, petrified but alive."

"What strange thoughts you do get!"

"Can you describe the base of this tree better?"

I couldn't. Let alone the effect when the playful campfire flickered those terraced "pythons" to life, a fantastic scene.

"I wouldn't camp alone here for all the tea in China," I said as we lit the pipes.

"Why not?"

"Who would? What with blood-curdling owls, fiery pythons, howling savages, trees that eat one another while their cannibal roots grow like writhing snakes—not on your life!"

He laughed softly, that rare laugh of his.

"There's one man camped alone somewhere in the scrub right now," he said soberly, "or rather, he's probably got a couple of blackboys with him."

"What's he doing? Prospecting?"

"No. We are the only prospectors in this scrub at present. He is cutting a track from Ravenshoe to Chilverton—or is just about to start on the job."

"What for?"

"To help open up the country, of course. How would you expect settlers to travel through places like this unless there is a track cut ready for them?"

"They wouldn't dream of attempting it," I replied. "What's his name?"

"George Rankine. And he's got sixty miles of jungle country to hack his way through."

"Good Heavens! How on earth will he find a way?"

"Because he's a good enough man to do it," he replied.

"H'm! Then he's a better man than I am, Gunga Din."

"And it will not be a track such as I have slashed a way through for us two now and then. It must be wide enough for a loaded pack-horse."

"But how on earth will he do that, when there is not even grass in the scrubs to feed a horse?"

"He must first scout out the country from forest pocket to forest pocket. If he can find a chain of them, those pockets will be his camps. As he battles on with the job, it will grow into a green tunnel leading from open forest pocket to pocket."

"What a job!"

"I'll say. But it is the one and only way in which the scrub-jungles have been, and will be, opened up."

To me, this chance little bit of news was quite a thrill. To think that a pathfinder was actually now at work in this very scrub!

Involuntarily I glanced around. But all was impenetrable blackness, the only sign of life the firelight dancing on those writhing roots that towered up into darkness. In that deathly silence the weird thought struck me that the jungle was listening to our talk. Uneasily I glanced at my companion, now staring moodily at the fire.

He must be much older than he looks, I thought. He has seen so much, knows so much. He is young—yet he must be old. No, he is young—

Abruptly I stood up to throw more wood on the fire. Strange thoughts come seeping into a man's mind when he is working deep below in an ancient river-bed, and yet stranger thoughts by night in the womb of a jungle.

CHAPTER XXXV

HE CALLS UP THE ANTS!

CAME afternoon, then sunlight filtering through the trees ahead. How glorious to step from the gloom into sunlight of open forest country with grass underfoot and sky overhead! Even more so when on the very rim of a mountain-top to gaze away out and over where mists merged into distance. Ranges, valleys, sunlit forests, mountains seeming black with scrub, streams glinting like silvered wire. The whisperings seeping up along grassy slopes, swelling up from rock-bound valley and gorge. At our very feet this mountain fell precipitously to join a massive ridge upon which grasses and tree-tops were swaying. The majestic beauty of everything fairly raised a lump in my throat.

"I *thought* that would get you!"

He was sitting there on the very rim of this mountain-top, pulling his pipe from his belt.

"I promised I would show you Christy Palmerston's track." He stretched out an arm. "There it is—right before your eyes."

His words held no meaning for me. I sat down beside him. Near by, a bird was singing as if his little heart would burst. My mate's thoughts were elsewhere, his gaze had been wandering over the mountains. Dreamily he turned to me, and it seemed as if the light faded from his eyes.

To hell with him! I thought. He can't stand his fellow man!

His face turned eastward again as he said abruptly, "I promised I'd show you Palmerston's Track. Roughly speaking, we are sitting facing Mourilyan Harbour, forty miles straight away out over there past where the mists and horizon meet. The track—in part it is developing into a road now, of course—goes from the coast to Innisfail, already rich in sugar-cane lands, and spreading rapidly. From there Christy cut a winding track all the way to near here, Millaa Millaa. A track carries on to Cedar Creek, which they now call Ravenshoe, only a few miles from here. Christy carried on the track through the ranges north to Herberton. Through all that—" he pointed—"and what is north behind us."

"It's a bit too big for me to grasp. He must have been a dozen men rolled into one."

"He was," he agreed emphatically, and he seemed pleased.

"But all those huge patches of scrub lands stretching away out there ahead of us! Surely there's no one there yet?"

"No," he answered. "You are gazing out over the Tully Scrubs. The axe has not reached there yet!" There was deep satisfaction in his voice.

"Surely it never will," I said. "It hardly seems possible. Not for years and years and years, anyway." And instinctively I felt I'd said the right thing.

Within twenty-five years the axes would be ringing in those primeval depths.

"Do these range and scrub and forest lands stretch from here right north to Cairns?"

"Yes, and farther north, too. This country is vast."

"You know it well!"

"I love it!" and the fierceness in his voice startled me.

"Come!" He stood up abruptly. "We've a few miles yet to go—it will soon be sunset."

"Just a moment longer," I begged. "That big stream gleaming down in the valley away out there—is that a river and where does it flow?"

"The Tully," he said, "flowing eastward to the coast. They all do. This country is wonderfully well watered." He sat down again. "Ten thousand creeks that are roaring rivers in the Wet. Then the rivers themselves. The Burdekin, Herbert, Johnstone, Tully, Russell, Mulgrave, Barron, Daintree—rain is measured in feet and even yards along the coast, pouring a sea of fresh water into the ocean every year."

"Rain in yards," I murmured. "No wonder there are strange things in this country."

A boyish smile lit up his sombre face as he sat back and gazed again out over space. Clasping hands over knees, he murmured, "You still don't believe me! You won't believe in the dancing worms, though I've shown you worms as long as a man. You won't believe in a bird that grows a helmet so he can race through the scrubs, that can beat his body into a living drum. You won't believe in a flower and a fruit that grow underneath the loam—you certainly would not believe in the very essence of life contained in that fruit! Why, I don't believe you'd believe in a kangaroo that climbs trees!"

"Of course I wouldn't!" I laughed.

"But in these scrubs, generally clinging to edge of scrub and forest lands, there is a tree-climbing kangaroo."

Again I laughed. A bush lad whose thrill for years past had been in hunting the poor old wallaby, the bandicoot, the euro and 'roo! Of course I knew all about the kangaroo. A kangaroo that climbed trees! Unable to stop, I laughed and laughed. A curious smile began to play at the corners of his mouth, I had the impression he was gazing round at the hard red earth upon which we were sitting.

In an amused voice for him he asked, "Would you believe in a tree that changes its mind?"

"How on earth can a tree change its mind?" I replied warily.

"By growing into a vine instead. It grows bravely up into a tree, only to suddenly change its mind and turn itself into a vine."

"No, I wouldn't believe. Would you?"

"Of course. I've seen them. Well then, would you believe in a fern tree that grows upside down?"

"No!" I answered, a bit sulkily.

"I'm not trying to pull your leg," he said evenly. "Well then, would you believe I can call up the ants?"

I gazed at him, feeling a bit chilly. After all, I was alone with this man. At the "end of the world". Neither I nor any other man but he knew where I was.

"Would you believe?"

"No," I answered cautiously.

"Would you believe," he said patiently, "that there are ants which call up one another with a signal, just as a telegraph operator calls up a station with a Morse signal? Would you believe that I can call up ants with a signal?"

"No," I answered defiantly.

He reached out, picked up a stout stick and struck the hard earth before him five sharp blows, then again, this time calling, "Dot! Dot! Dot! Dot! Dot!" then, "Dash! Dash! Dash! Dash!" and again, "Dash!"

I saw a big ant, antennae outspread, come hurrying out from a grass tuft. Then another one. Hair beginning to rise on end, I gazed around. Here came others—why—I sprang up! Big ants were hurrying towards us from everywhere!

Fairly trembling, I jumped back. He laughed as I had not heard him laugh before. Picking up his swag, he chuckled.

"Come along. We've got a few miles to go yet."

Snatching up my swag, I hurried after him back into a further scrub. I'd received a nasty shock.

The scrub was growing ominously dark as a deep murmur steadily swelled into a harsh roar barely muffled by the timber.

"The Tully Falls," he said. "You'll see them at daylight. We'd better camp or we'll be rolling down over into the gorge in the dark."

Another sound, like the swelling waves of an incoming sea rising to a howl.

"The wind moaning up the gorge," he said as he lit the fire. "It's a bit blowy out there tonight. And the rains are pouring more water over the falls."

It sounded to me like a thunderous storm striving to break free from somewhere deep under the earth. Eagerly I looked forward to the dawn.

As we settled back for the evening smoke I asked, "Where's Ravenshoe from here?"

"Oh, about twenty-five miles northward."

I was silent. So he had, as I'd begun to suspect, worked his way round and by-passed the tiny settlement. What cussed streak was it in this man that urged him to keep away from the haunts of his fellow men? And I had been so keen—

"Aren't you going to call in there?"

"No!"

Well, then, do the other thing, you surly cow! I thought. But presently I asked, "How did Ravenshoe start?"

"Oh, the usual way," he answered absently. "The prospectors and cattle-men pushing up from south and central Queensland. A lot of that country south-west of us and right back north to the Evelyn was taken up by Frank Stubley as Evelyn Station. Later, Bill Mazlin found magnificent cedars along a creek they christened Cedar Creek. It became a cedar camp of John Moffat's, now called Ravenshoe."

"Why?"

"Oh, maybe because there are many 'cedar creeks'. Anyway, surveyors working on the Evelyn Station came upon some forgotten campfire, and in the fork of a tree the tattered remains of Kingsley's novel *Ravenshoe*. Those same surveyors have surveyed Cedar Creek for the township that is to be, and renamed it Ravenshoe."

"Is that how Innisfail away back on the coast got its name, too?"

"Not exactly. It was first named Nind's Camp after one of the early pioneers. It became a favourite camping place as settlers came to the Johnstone, and it was named Geraldton. But when Henry Fitzgerald, who I suppose could be called the father of the sugar industry in the north, established a successful plantation which he called Innisfail, the township was then called Innisfail. And, believe me, that district will spread and prosper, and grow and grow."

I am positive that not even the Jungle Man could have visualized the fabulously rich Innisfail district of today.

"The origin of many names," he resumed in a more maty way, "is sometimes quite interesting. 'Way back there where the natives entertained us—" and he half smiled across the firelight— "you thought I was pulling your leg about their spirit beliefs. You've got to learn, of course. Oh well, little Yungaburra is named after the spirits—it means 'the spirit people'. So there is a good Australian name for you, signifying a world you are not aware of."

I remained warily silent. "Very well then," he said, "here's another surprise. You know Almaden?"

"I've only passed through it."

"Do you know that it is named after a famous Spanish town?"

"I certainly do not!"

"Well, it is. After Almaden in Spain, where they have been mining quicksilver for centuries, I believe."

"You've surprised me."

"I thought so," he said in a satisfied sort of way. "From spirit people to a historic Spanish town and back to the Cairns hinterland is an interesting mixture. Think it out for yourself. Oh well, you know Chillagoe?"

"Hardly at all. I've only travelled through and back again."

"Oh well, you know the end chorus of that old music-hall ditty:

> "Hikey, Tikey, Sikey, Crikey,
> Chillagoe, Warrabedory!"

"Don't think I've ever heard it," I replied doubtfully.

"You *must* have! Where's your memory? Anyway, Chillagoe was named after the word in that chorus. So John Atherton told me, anyway, and he also says he named a station of his 'Warrabedory', from that refrain, too."

"Surely some of these places have been given Australian names!"

"Oh yes, and right from the earliest days. You've heard of Smithfield?"

"Plenty. Named after Bill Smith, who found a track from the Hodgkinson to the Barron."

"Yes, he was one of the great band—Hall, Mulligan, Smith, Douglas, Warner, Oswald, Robson, Johnstone, Palmerston, Dalrymple, Atherton—two score or so of wonder men. Oh well, Smithfield was named after Smith. And surely you, who dream of gold, know of Bill Smith's golden horseshoes!"

I was puzzled. And unbelieving.

"I see you don't believe me again," he said, "but it is fact. Bill Smith had his horse shod with shoes of gold. Eddy Crossland the blacksmith made the shoes for him, from gold Smith had won on the Hodgkinson."

"I've heard of several flash diggers shoeing their horses with gold on the Victorian goldfields," I said doubtfully, "but never in Queensland."

"But look at all the things you haven't heard of that's happened right under your nose," he replied good-humouredly. "Anyway, you've only been here five minutes, remember. Bill Smith derived much pleasure in riding his horse with the golden horseshoes along those so-called streets of Smithfield."

"But golden horseshoes would so soon wear out," I said doubtfully.

"Not upon Smithfield streets," he replied. "Not upon that loam, and often slush."

"He must have won plenty of gold," I said enviously.

"Not so much. It was the gold he was always *going* to win that counted with Bill."

"Did he win it?"

"No. His life ended suddenly, tragically. Just as he had done big things, and appeared set to do bigger. And soon afterwards the Barron came down in flood and wiped Smithfield itself off the map."

"How did Smith die?" I asked.

But he sat frowning at the fire, growing into one of those moods of his again. I threw on a couple of logs to try brighten things up.

"Shall I put on the billy?" I suggested.

"An idea!" he agreed.

I'd found out one way to sweeten him up. As we were supping the steaming hot tea he said amiably, "Mareeba is going to grow into a good-sized town. And they're going to name their streets after Tableland men who've done things."

"Good idea," I said, "and I hope they will at Ravenshoe, too."

"I suppose they will," he said absently. "That country will be settled now that the railway has arrived at Herberton, and rumour has it that it may continue on through the Tumoulin and Evelyn to Ravenshoe. Moffat sold his sawmill to Robinson and Perrott a year or so back. Evelyn Station is now being cut up into blocks, the settlers are arriving from the south, mostly from Charters Towers, by buggy and wagon and cart and pack-horse."

"Do you mean to say that beyond all this timber ahead of us settlers are trekking to take up land just as they did in early settlement days?"

"Yes, of course. In what other way could they come?"

"I dunno," I answered lamely.

"That is only because you do not think!" he replied amiably. "The first crowd have already arrived, and with a few head of cattle, too, a month or two ago, so I've heard in Herberton. Charters Towers men. The Rankine and Witherspoon brothers, Charlie Kerr and Peter Strang. Some have their women-folk with them. I've heard that a Norman and Bolton family are coming, too, and other Towers people, the Merrin and Major families, are preparing for the track." And that tight-lipped mouth of his closed on his pipe-stem. By now I knew the signs. I suspected he was dodging civilization again, even such tiny outposts in this world of ranges, forests, and scrubs. What *was* the urge that made this man shun these brave little "civilizations", that made him hug the places of the wild only?

"Wouldn't you rather see places like this?" He waved his arm towards the gorge and the falls. Abruptly again he had broken in on my very thoughts! "You have already *seen* Ravenshoe. Primitive scrub lands, the smoke from the sawmill boiler, the whine of the circular saw. Teamsters on a dusty track hauling the logs to Herberton—for the sea. The ring of the axes of the first selectors who dream that their clearings in the scrubs will develop into rich farms, that a railway may come with the years, that this frontier hamlet of Cedar Creek may actually grow into a town of Ravenshoe. Which it will!" he added bitterly. "Nothing can stop it. But already you have seen it occurring in a dozen places now since you landed at Cairns."

I had, too; I was seeing those places even as he spoke. But to me, there was, and always had been, a thrill of warmest interest at seeing men and women gamely setting out to carve a home from the wild bush—the bush that can give great reward, but can also, alas, break hearts.

"What about Mount Garnet then?"

"You've 'seen' Mount Garnet, too. It lies away to the nor'-west of us, sou'-west of Ravenshoe. Different, much drier country than the Ravenshoe scrubs, of course. But you've seen it all before. It's been worked for some years now. Mount Garnet, Return Creek which runs into the Herbert River, Glutton Creek—mining camps scattered over a wide area, men working just as you've seen by my camp along the Dry River. The country is tin-bearing all the way to the Mount Albion silver mines. Isolation and transport awful, of course, until after Vollenvider struck a rich copper show. Then John Moffat opened up. For John Moffat scented business, interested capital, and built a smelters. You'll find the hand of John Moffat in anything big anywhere throughout this vast Tableland and even beyond into the poorly watered country. Quite often Moffat has got that hand of his burnt. But for his pluck and enterprise much of this country would still be as it was twenty years back. Perhaps much more. Anyway, you've already seen all that sort of work, surely you'd rather see sights that you've never seen before—as you will tomorrow. And now I'll turn in."

And he rolled up in his blanket, leaving me smoking, gazing up at those wonderful stars, the triumph song of the gorge thundering up from those great falls close by somewhere out there in the night.

CHAPTER XXXVI

SHE MUST OBEY

TRUST him to do the thing properly. He had me on the lip of the world thrilled to a maelstrom of sound just as a golden ball arose and in moments the world was on fire. Where there had been a roaring blackness was now thick green water breaking in seething turmoil far below on a mighty ledge to shoot down again in clouds of foam and rainbow sprays, while far away down along the black gorge filmy mists came rising in wispy clouds of lace. The longer a man gazed and listened the more the grandeur and music filled him with awe and wonder. Yet again I understood something of the deep primal quality of the Jungle Man's love for these wild, primitive lands.

Several nights later we camped to the song of the Millstream Falls, a "happy" song quite different to the triumphant thunder of the Tully, the roaring power of the Barron.

As I gazed at the Millstream Falls in their setting of beauty I hoped fervently that when settlement did come it would not tarnish such priceless gems as this. I was to see a score and more cf these beautiful waterfalls and each brought me a surge of sympathy with the Jungle Man.

The Millstream is a fairyland cascade, a vast curtain of sunlit water and sparkling foam gaily tumbling down into a pretty little lake.

There are many falls in that district, the Little Millstream, the Millaa Millaa, the Beatrice. We roamed a week and more among them, my mate in the most companionable humour I'd yet known. I did not realize until long afterwards that it was because I was so obviously entranced by these things he loved.

And one evening I took advantage of it.

"Tell me, how did you call up those ants?"

He glanced at me a moment, then laughed up at his precious stars.

"No need to have been worried about it," he replied in the best humour I had yet seen him in. "I'm not Old Nick calling up his naughty fantods, nor some Arabian seer conjuring up his all-powerful genie. Worse luck, maybe.

"The ants are simple. They only breed true to kind, like everything else. This particular kind possesses some sense or intelligence apparently not born in us, though it may only be 'sleeping'. They send and receive vibratory signals when in quest of food, building materials, warnings of the presence of enemies, of coming sudden changes in weather, of coming fire or flood or other causes which might bring disaster to their nest and colony. These few things I've learnt only from observation, and from aboriginal friends. Some at least among these ants have 'hammer heads'. Regulated by weather, of course, scouts hurry out in all directions with the dawn, prospecting for food. A scout stumbles upon some little gold-mine in the food line. Immediately he hammers his head upon the hard earth, and from far and wide his fellow ants lift up questing antennae, as do those also down below in the nest. They catch the vibratory message in those antennae of theirs and all hurry to the spot; those still down below come pouring up from the nest. For, you see, they must cut that food into fragments and hurry it back to their storerooms down below in the nest before other hungry creatures of the bush find and devour it, the birds and lizards and insects, and foreign ants, also. For everything in the bush is constantly seeking tucker, remember, everything is constantly hungry and ever on the move for food."

And then until far into the night, in that dreamy voice of his, he talked about ants, telling me fascinating things that I'd never dreamt of, and introduced me to a new world, that restless, pulsating, virile, fiercely energetic, frightening World of the Ants.

By now we had run out of flour, the only food I would actually miss. For effortlessly he could find food as we walked along, animal, bird, fish or plant, secrets the aborigines had taught this old-young man. On the faint hope of directing his steps towards the settlement I suggested, "If we had some flour, I'd make a damper."

"You're sitting on flour now," he replied.

I stared stupidly. By now, if he'd said I was sitting on a castle in Spain I should have hesitated to contradict. We were sitting upon a grassy spur enjoying a smoke-oh. He pointed to a barely perceptible twig sticking up from the earth by my boot.

"Dig there!"

I did so—and at eighteen inches' depth came upon a large tuber. And another and another.

"There is your flour," he said. "Boil them in the billy tonight."

And those floury yams *did* make a good substitute.

"How on earth did you know they were there?" I asked. "The dried stem of that vine was sticking up only half an inch amongst the grass. No sign of a vine, let alone leaves."

"The leaves were lying there," he said, "shrivelled up and fallen aside as the vine died and withered away. Train yourself to observe and memorize until it becomes second nature, which will bring secrets of nature to you."

He explained then the native process to make actual flour from that same yam.

"You can make johnny-cakes from it—damper, too. Just as you can with our own flour," he said casually, "with the same addition of cream of tartar and soda. But—don't experiment with plant foods until you've learnt which are wholesome, and those that are poisonous. Otherwise you'll never find your Golden Palmer."

I wasn't much interested, could hardly have cared less.

In the silence he casually suggested, "Why don't you ask your own storekeeper about the Tumoulin and Evelyn and Ravenshoe when you are so interested in new lands and settlers?"

"What do you mean?" I stupidly asked, feeling he had read my thoughts again.

"All that information is yours for the asking, and a great deal more besides, right at Nigger Creek."

"How so?" I asked, thoroughly puzzled.

"Ask Grigg the storekeeper."

"What on earth does *he* know about it?"

His half-smile changed to outright laughter as he looked up at the sky, clasping hands across his knee.

"Men are blind!" he exclaimed good-humouredly. "Often what they desire is right before them, yet they see nothing. Grigg is an enthusiast upon the possibilities of all these scrubs right to Ravenshoe. He is crazy on development he swears must take place there as yet more settlers come. He is right, too," he added soberly, "and so enthusiastic about it I'm certain he will take a big hand in it himself."

What prophetic words!

It is only within very recent years that I have learnt what a big hand that quiet, far-seeing, industrious storekeeper had in the development of a rich district. But now, in the heart of primal bush, I could only sit and wonder. At the man at my side, who knew so much. At my own ignorance. At the hard-working young storekeeper whom I saw quite often, suddenly presented in such a new light. Yes, I agreed to myself, I was blind, and dumb, too. Pure ivory from the head up. In a mood of sulky self-pity I wondered if *ever* I would "learn things".

"You must train yourself," said a soft voice and I almost jumped. "It grows easier after a time, you begin learning subconsciously, as it were. You notice things, without noticing. Something like breathing. We are breathing every moment of the night and day. But we don't notice it."

"H'm," I said doubtfully, while sourly thinking that knowledge *must* come easily to a man who could read thoughts.

From a creeper-clad ravine down below us came the happy "tinkle-tinkle" of a bell-bird. Dreamily my mate was gazing out into blue distance.

"Bellenden Ker lies away out there," he said, "nor'-east away out beyond those blue mists, towards the coast. Maybe we'll go walkabout out there some time, unless you're tired of chasing the golden rainbow—and tired of me! I wouldn't be surprised if there *is* gold away up on those old mountain crowns somewhere or other. Just the same, it is very likely looking country. A stiff climb, over five thousand feet, but worth it. Between here and there are plenty of waterfalls, too; some are known to only half a dozen white men, at most. Plenty of country, too, that has not heard the ring of even a prospector's pick, let alone the axe. Your river of gold could be awaiting you somewhere in there. What might interest you, too, is that away down there on the coast is a little cove called Bingle Bay, quite near to where natives in the early days massacred a goodly number of the castaways from the wreck of the *Maria*. She had sixty-eight men aboard sailing to try their luck in New Guinea. They never got there. Anyway, at Bingle Bay another crowd of your friends the settlers are already taking up land just as they are away back here at Ravenshoe and the Evelyn and Tumoulin and elsewhere. There is wonderful land in that Bingle Bay area also, and I think they'll make a do of it."

They certainly have—as witness El Arish, and the rapid expansion of a "new" district.

"They'll be carving a home and rich farm out of the scrubs while you are still looking for gold. However, you might drop onto another Palmer one of these days—who knows? But we won't find it by sitting here dreaming."

He had reached for his swag. We were on the move again.

During all this walkabout he led me to "civilization" but once —to a lonely settler's hut.

Stepping out from the scrub into the rosy brightness of sunset, I gaped at a towering kauri pine stretching up in beauty to the sky, its massive trunk now a rosy gold from sunset rays. And there towered a beautiful maple, and just across there a walnut, and just past it a veritable beauty of a hickory—eight gigantic trees in a lovely nakedness. For a moment I blinked to realize that all scrub had been cleared from around these statuesque giants. For weeks past now we had seen many such, but only some little portion of each mighty bulk, for all the rest was hidden by fellow trees, undergrowth and foliage. Here was the beginning of a man-made clearing, and these beauties had been allowed to stand in their unobstructed glory. Seen thus, they commanded attention, even though there was a panorama of beauty all around. These magnificent giants, supreme accomplishment of vegetable Nature, stood proudly awaiting the axe.

I stole a glance at the Jungle Man's face and saw how he loved trees.

To step out from the scrub and thus see those splendid victims standing naked, the remains of their thousand fallen brethren smouldering away in great heaps, the selector's hut with smoke slowly curling up from the chimney down at the farthest edge of the clearing, was to look upon a vivid picture of what must ultimately happen to all these seemingly unperishable scrubs. For where a settler's hut stood now a township could spring up. In many places it had happened already.

As we picked our way over fallen logs down to the hut I glanced away ahead. Just a vista of forest hills, now brightly lit with sunset, merging into hazy blue distances, black patches of scrubs, suggestions of valleys, and rocky peaks in sunset distance with a deep, murmurous sighing from some near-by gorge.

And then we were at the hut, roughly but comfortably built of sheets of messmate bark, the musical splash of a little mountain-top waterfall just behind it. The selector hurried out to welcome us with unfeigned pleasure. Yes, we *must* camp there tonight. He seemed old to me, a lad, but he would have been surprised to know it, believing himself in his prime, despite his grizzled whiskers. Certainly he was all gristle and bone and sinew, capable of doing the work of a horse.

Bustling about at the simple cooking, he was just dying for a yarn. Yes, those "sticks" outside would bring him in a few hundred pounds, a fortune, when the bullockies had time to "come up on in" and haul them out. He could not say when that would be. There was so much more easily accessible timber down below around Ravenshoe, and other places " below the range". But time would bring the teams up to these parts. Meanwhile he was felling scrub, and burning off. Already he'd planted a garden to help keep the tucker-bags filled. "This land will grow *anything!*" he declared proudly. "Any blessed thing will grow up while you look at it; it's growing while I sleep, just like the wool grows on the sheep's back while the squatter sleeps." His grey eyes twinkled as his gnarled hands lifted off the billy.

"I guess no squatter would think much of *this* show," he chuckled as he reached for a damper in the camp oven. "He'd just sniff and ride by. But I'll knock a cosy little home out of this scrub within a very few years."

And by his voice I knew his heart was in the land, as the Jungle Man's was in trees.

I made a hog of myself with those fresh-grown vegetables, those papaws, bananas, soursops and five-fingers.

"Eat up!" he kept insisting. "They're growin' faster than a whole family could eat. I'll go out and pick you a bucketful more when you've finished those—there's plenty out there, there's only the birds to eat 'em."

"Those" included a huge bunch of golden-red bananas suspended from a rafter.

Easing myself down on the blanket, leaning back against the bark wall too full to talk, I merely listened, gazing round the hut. His bunk of boards he had sawn from a log was stoutly built along one side of the hut, with a "mattress" of plaited lawyer-cane over which were neatly spread blankets. Two guns—with boyish enthusiasm I noted they were muzzle-loaders—were on pegs just above the bunk. They would be ready loaded; he could awake in the night, reach up his hand, and in a second his gun muzzle would be pointing at the slab and bark door. Obviously he was a "homely" man, for he had gone to the trouble of knocking up some home-made furniture from rich red cedar. Around the hut were cedar shelves neatly fitted upon wooden pegs; wonderingly I saw that one shelf held a neat row of books. There were weavils in his flour, I knew by the damper; he had simply boiled them in the doughboy, too, with salt water. Little *I* cared—I'd enjoyed that doughboy. Anyway, it must be a laborious job to pack a few bags of flour up here. Besides, he wouldn't have the time to be fussy; there were too many trees to chop down. Brown sugar in his tea, and now he reached for a black cake of fig tobacco. I knew the smoke would smell strong indeed; I'd last seen such fig tobacco smoked by other settlers when a toddler in the bush in New South Wales. And here it was all over again. Yes, and here he was now lighting a slush lamp, a home-made wick floating in fat within a dish. I'd used one myself when a boundary rider far away from here, but I'd thought those pioneering days were done. How many lonely nights did he spend lying here dreaming of his farm to be, or poring over those well-thumbed books by this slush lamp's dull, wobbly flame! Yes, a real settler's hut—there were the hobble chains hanging from the wall, a "home-made" branding iron, too, that well-kept axe hanging in its greenhide loop. . . .

Nearly asleep, I almost missed a yarn that has intrigued me to this day. Their talk, of course, had drifted on to aborigines, and the settler was telling of an early settler's wife, in a hut such as this in a clearing such as this. Looking after the place—alone. The husband had taken the pack-horses and ridden away for rations, and would not be back for another day at the earliest.

She was tending the garden when a young lubra raced out from the scrub, screaming for help, a pack of warriors running at her heels.

The woman rushed into the hut, pulling the girl with her, slammed the door and dropped the heavy bar into place. The young lubra crouched sobbing, with her arms round the knees of the white woman, who thrust a gun through a loophole and called out that she would fire.

The avengers stopped in a group before the hut. They were led by a witch-doctor. He turned and harangued them. They were chewing their beards in rage, rattling their weapons towards the hut, yelling demands for their lubra to come out. They could easily have rushed the hut, though not without loss. The husband had taught the wife how to handle firearms, she was a cool shot and could reload as quickly as a man. She had two guns, she could have shot at least two before they burst in. After that—well there were two axes, and if both women had snatched those they might have lasted a moment or two longer.

However, the witch-doctor marched his men sullenly back to the scrub edge. Then he turned back towards the hut, raised his arms to the sky, and cried out in a long-drawn, piercing wail. The settler's wife said afterward that that awful cry froze her very blood. The lubra sprang up, eyes staring from her head, face awful. She opened her mouth, screamed, and kept screaming—one long, long scream. She snatched up the bar, hurled it aside. As she tore open the door the startled white woman threw herself upon her, but the lubra threw her aside as if she had been a child. She ran out into the open, still screaming, and with arms outflung raced straight to her tribesmen. They cut her to pieces before the white woman's eyes. Then they vanished back into the scrub.

I lay awake after the other two had turned in, wondering at this story, which I later learnt was fairly well known. The hut was lit by glowing logs in the big open hearth, but it was black as pitch outside, and the wind was moaning up from the gorge.

We were miles away from the settler's hut by midday, in wild forest country, a sea of crags. We boiled the billy below a granite tor nearly the size of a castle.

As we lit the pipes before moving on I said, "I'm puzzled about that story of the lubra last night. Why *did* she rush out to be slaughtered while there was still a chance of life? The settler's wife was determined to defend her, and she could shoot! They had only to hold out until next day, or night, and the settler would return. After all, the avenger's party was only a small band of picked men, and they might not have dared to rush the hut. If they had, two at least would have been shot dead. The white woman was determined and used to the bush, and she would have been fighting for her life and for her home. Then, with the axe, she would have chopped off a hand or two, and some fingers, before they could have broken through that strong door. The lubra chopping with the other axe, would have fought like a wildcat for her life, as you say they can, and do. There would have been four or five dead men before the others could have smashed into the women with spear and club—a loss that would have made a much stronger party think twice. And yet when the witch-doctor howled for her to come the lubra went mad, threw open the door, and rushed out to certain death. Why?"

"There are transgressions of a law which go even beyond the fear of death," he answered slowly. "I cannot put into our words, I can only *feel* the meaning of it myself. The aboriginal definitely believes in life after death. Maybe he believes also that for some deep crime against the tribe, or some sacred tribal law, punishment could follow him even in the after life. I'm not sure. You may have felt just a little of these strange things when you watched that preparatory dance to the moon in the forest pocket back there. That wail of the witch-doctor calling out the errant lubra from the settler's hut was primal, it was not a call for man-made vengeance, it was the spirit-call of the tribe going back throughout the ages. No wild aboriginal dare resist that command —neither man nor woman would have the power to do so. That call is answered by something as deep within them as the mystery of life and death. I do not know any words that could explain this thing. We'd better move on."

He stood up, slung on his swag, and moved off. As I followed, a harsh, mournful cry fairly startled me. Wheeling round, I saw high above the Tully Gorge a black cockatoo in heavy, lonesome flight. Lonesome indeed is the cry of those heavy black birds above the gorges of the lovely north, and above the gorges of the wild Kimberleys far to the west.

CHAPTER XXXVII

COPPER FROM WATER, OPAL FROM THE SEA

WE HEADED back north over forest country, my mate immediately reverting to his quiet moods, seldom speaking either by day or night unless spoken to. Trudging mile after mile behind him, in boyish impatience I thought, He should never leave the jungles, the only place where he's human. But then I'd think over in growing surprise the many things he had taught me, some of which I only began to realize as the hours trudged by. Of strange facts of scrub and forest and water-torn gorge, of animal and plant, bird, reptile, and insect. My thoughts would then drift on to amazing information on the properties of metals I'd never heard of, not even in mining camps, not even in the Silver City now so far away. Little thoughts of resentment at his moody ways would be quite lost as I pondered over those strange things about humans —"us" and "primitive" men—he'd half told, half hinted at. And I'd wonder and wonder how much more he knew, until with a shiver I'd suddenly remember his thought-reading and say something abruptly, say anything, just to try to start a conversation.

In the hills near the head of the Walsh River we struck the coach road to Herberton. And eventually at Watsonville, a lively mining camp, I rebelled, eager to greet my fellow-men again. Besides, I'd heard many stories past and present of the glories of Watsonville, the fortunes won from its rich tin lodes and rich copper.

"Very well." He shrugged. "I'll camp down by the creek, so please yourself. I'll give you until midday tomorrow. Then I'm moving off—I'm going to be in Herberton by midafternoon."

As he strode away I felt a bit sorry, I had half expected him to move on without me. I walked on into the dusty little township. Men, burnt brown as the hills, were knocking off work and stroll-

313

ing to camp, or to one of the tiny pubs to wash the dust and copper fumes from their throats, I was eager to spy out Gibbs's hotel, for he was the prospector who had found Irvinebank, and a prospector who had found a rich mineral field was a hero. I would only be able to gaze from afar, not being able to afford more than two beers at the most. Difficult indeed to realize today the value of a shilling those days to those who did not have it! However, the "hail-fellow-well-met" of the mining camps was wonderful, and I spent an entrancing evening so far as shyness would permit. The little notebooks being long since filled up, there was no drudgery here, interesting facts and yarns being committed to the light-hearted mercies of a happy-go-lucky memory. Much too happy-go-lucky, as I was to realize with regret in coming years.

Watsonville was named after Bob Watson, who with Connelly and Doherty pushed out from Herberton in the early years and found these hills rich in minerals. In the rush that followed a few men were killed by the blacks, but rich claims were quickly found; the Great Western was still going strong, the King of the Ranges, the fabulously rich North Australian—the boys that evening reeled off the names of a score of shows, the returns from which fairly made my mouth water. I used to wonder when the wretched wars came at the fabulous fortunes the hard-toiling men who found those little mines would have made had they found them during the war years, and after. At this time a rich new show, the Plum, had been found, and was destined to produce some wonderful returns. The first battery was built by an ingenious Tasmanian named Dempster and was powered by the waters of the Walsh River by a Pelton wheel; it had crushed thousands of tons of stone for the early mines. I wished the Jungle Man had been there to hear that, but then remembered he must know all about it. By now I would have been surprised to hear of anything that was strange to him. It did not surprise me, though, to hear John Moffat constantly mentioned, now working the North Australian on a big scale. Here again were many tales of luck and fortune, of dogged perseverance and heartbreak that are the very life of every mining field. How I longed to try my luck for a few months at least among these hills! Came the sudden realization that just a few short trips with the Jungle Man had taught me how impossible was this constant longing.

"A man would have to possess as many lives as a cat!" I thought despondently. "Even Methuselah would grow old trying to prospect all this district."

And the same old problem was here, too. It was only the very lucky ones who found the rich shows. The big majority were barely scratching out a living, many were working outright for wages. To go farther afield meant transport—pack-horses, saddlery, tools, tucker, money.

With my head full of local mining yarns, I found my mate's lonely camp at midnight, agreeably surprised to find he had a billy of tea on the simmer. A hunched-up shadow wrapped in his blanket on the creek sand, he was sound asleep.

Or was he?

But that tea went down well.

Breakfast was scanty. We could not whip out the rifle here and bring down game as we walked along. This was civilization. Feeling a bit peckish, and guilty, too, at almost forcing him to camp the night, I was ready to move off with him. But he nodded back towards the township.

"Better make the most of your time," he said quietly. "Have a look around the North Australian. Get them to show you how they extract pure copper from water."

"From water!" I said blankly.

"Yes, water. You don't believe me, but they'll prove it. I'll meet you outside the pub at midday. I've got enough to shout us both a feed before we move off."

And, pulling out his pipe, he half turned to gaze across at the hills. Eagerly I started walking towards the poppet heads high above the big dumps.

And they *did* show me how to extract pure copper from water. Not only that, but they showed me shovels and picks and spiders of copper—handsome, they were. Showed me horseshoes and old billy-cans and tins and all manner of things, once old iron, now transformed into bright copper. Like most other things, simple of course, when you know how.

This mine was very rich in copper. The water which seeped from it and which had collected in disused shafts was highly impregnated with copper in solution. Throw iron into that water and in the course of time the iron was "eaten away" and copper was precipitated upon it in its place. As to the shovels, they had been left by oversight for some time in a drive. The drip of copper-impregnated water upon them, and upon two picks and iron spiders, had eaten away a film of the iron and precipitated copper in its stead. It is a purely chemical action. Where mine water is so rich in copper as this, the copper can, with time, be simply recovered by running the water into boxes packed with any old scraps of iron. The iron is eaten away and in its place is practically pure copper. Live and learn.

Suddenly I remembered the far away opal-fields, and something even more startling. There, deep under solid rock, we quite often dug out shells that once—how many millions of years ago?—had been live shellfish. Opal had taken the place of the shell, in some instances forming a perfectly opalized shell. In rarer instances we found fish—deposits of opal on the bones had formed "opalized fish".

Yes. Live and learn. But, as the Jungle Man would say, "You must memorize to learn! Otherwise you could grow old as Methu-saleh and merely be a living fossil."

Walking back along the dusty road to Herberton beside my quiet mate, I was thinking on how much I'd learnt during the short time I'd known him. Amazing! And I knew that I didn't even know him.

Pleasant indeed to sight the "Seven Hills of Herberton" again, the little town gleaming under the sunlight that showers down through the exhilarating air far over that "top o' the world". Little wonder the citizens justly claim the old-timers refuse to die until their whiskers sprout into feathers.

Lightly dismounting, several horsemen were tethering their horses outside Jack and Newell's store as my mate half turned towards me and drawled, "Well, I suppose you'll be making back to your camp now. Regards to Old Mick and your friends. I hope you enjoyed your walkabout. Will be seeing you. So long." And with a nod he turned and was strolling along the road in the direction of the Dry River.

I stared after him a bit disappointedly, then turned and stepped out along the road by the Wild River. With a cheery greeting from some passer-by I'd come to know, each step taking me more eagerly towards Nigger Creek. How different this freedom of road and open country and sky and sunlight, quiet bustle and cheery talk of friendly people, to the gloomy depths, the breathless silence, the overpowering hostility of vegetable life of the big scrub! I could hardly get to Nigger Creek quick enough to be greeted by the chuckling grin of Old Mick, the saturnine welcome of Jim Bell, the lumbering friendliness of big Old Brookes, the excited, boyish welcome of Garnet Aitchison, the chirpy welcome of little Tommy Turley, the slow smile of Long Stewart, the cheery welcome of Mrs Reynolds and the girls and Grigg the storekeeper and the whole tiny camp. There'd be a smile, too, from the nice girl in the creeper-clad cottage who had patted the fat duck. The Wild River was singing beside me as again I caught first glimpse of the little cottages clinging around Wondecla, the Meeting of the Waters, right there at Nigger Creek.

At my tiny camp all alone on the ridge the tent was a bit windblown, a whopping big goanna scuttled out and hissed violently as I opened my own tent door, and it was obvious that the possums had been holding nightly parties there. But Old Mick had seen to it that everything was "all right"!

At Old Mick's campfire all were in great form. Mick and Jim had struck a patch that looked like developing into "good dirt", and were toiling like galley slaves to prove it one way or the other. Even Old Mick was talking learnedly of so many pounds to the yard, and all hands were anxious that these promising prospects would "make" and yield the two hard-bitten mates a hundred pounds or two or more in a short time. In all the mining fields this enthusiasm for other people's luck was a help to everyone.

The boys were curious to hear of my little adventures, of course, especially Garnet. I said little of the Jungle Man, having fully realized by now that, like me, they simply did not understand him. Because of some undefined feeling I felt anxious to "protect" him —how he would have grinned had he known! He was a man who would never be popular, he would always be a lonely man. I felt relieved when they asked only a very few questions about him.

"Well now," I said brightly, "there's tons and tons of fortunes 'way back in them thar hills, though we didn't find any. They're lying there only awaiting you experienced mineral-chasers. And now, Mick, have you written any new poems since I've been away? Or a love-letter or two maybe? Don't tell me your pen has gone rusty just because you've found a whopping big tin-mine!"

At the grins on all their firelit faces, Jim Bell frowned. "For once in his life he's been using the pick instead of the pen. First time he's been of use since I've known him."

"You don't make allowance for Mick's romantic nature," said Garnet. "After all, Jim, life is not all pick and shovel."

"No, and it's not all soft soap and poetry, either," answered Jim, "and there's such a thing as a pub handy and an empty pocket when a man is perishing of thirst, and an empty belly when he can't pay the storekeeper's bill!"

"That's only because you're not one of the early settlers," said Mick mildly.

"What the hell have the early settlers got to do with it?" snapped Jim. "What do you mean by an early settler?"

"An early settler pays his bill on the first of every month," said Mick.

Jim's long moustache fairly twiched, but before he could think up a reply Garnet said, laughing, "I believe you *have* written something, Mick! I can see it in that grizzled old face of yours— like the cat that's swallowed the canary."

"Like a gorilla that's swallowed a hot boiled egg!" growled Jim.

"I *have* found time for a little composition," Old Mick murmured angelically.

"I thought so!" cried Garnet triumphantly. "I saw it in that battered countenance of yours. Out with it! Is it a 'pome'?"

"No," answered Mick modestly, "merely an epistle."

"Who to?"

"Mrs ——."

In the momentary silence Garnet gasped, "Oh Heavens, no, Mick!"

But Mick just grinned at the fire.

"Tell me," I asked eagerly, "who is the lady?"

"She was member of a more or less official party from Cairns, in connection with the opening of a little school for the Tumoulin settlers' children," explained the troubled Garnet. "All bigwigs. She is the young wife of one of them—they've only been married a couple of years. She is a most charming person. They did me the courtesy of paying me a visit on their way to the Tumoulin. This prize idiot happened to stroll along, and I was fool enough to introduce him—as a local curiosity!" and Garnet glared at the complacent Mick.

"A *world* curiosity!" declared Jim Bell, as he grinned from ear to ear. "And did you hear what the schoolmaster just called you?"

CHAPTER XXXVIII

JIM BELL LAUGHS LOUDEST

"Garnet was ever a flatterer," replied the cunning Mick.

"If I said what I really mean!" threatened Garnet. "Look here, you grinning old heathen, you have not *really* posted that lady one of those asinine letters of yours, surely?"

"No." Mick smirked.

"Ah!" breathed Garnet relievedly.

"I've been waiting for Jack to return before I posted it," grinned Mick.

"You wretched old fox!" declared Garnet. "I shall certainly censor that poisonous epistle of yours!"

"Good boy, Mick!" I laughed. "Have you got it there? Read it out!" Which was echoed by all hands, except the schoolmaster.

As Mick retired to some secret hide-out within the camp Jim grinned at Garnet.

"Well, there now! You and Jack have been encouraging this prize goat for quite a time past. And just what do you think of him horning in now?"

"There's no telling *what* repercussions one of those awful letters of Mick's might start in this case," replied Garnet uneasily. "Remember, these are very nice people."

"They're all *nice* to Mick," replied Jim in a satisfied sort of way. "Anyway, serves you jolly well right for encouraging him. I only wish he'd drop a line to Jack's lady friend."

"She'd think I'd gone nuts in May." I grinned. "Anyway, mine is one of those hopeless sorts of love—she won't have me!"

"Who would?" laughed Garnet as Mick reappeared, tenderly nursing his precious scribbling pad. The grizzled old ganger was obviously well pleased with himself. Taking his time, he made himself quite comfortable, then with sundry sighs and "ahs" slowly began to drone out his epistle.

" 'Wondecla, via Herberton. Full moon.' " He paused for us to admire this touch. " 'Dearest,' " he went on, " 'In hopeless longing I can but pen my deepest thoughts to you. As a star seen from afar, you can but ever appear as a beautiful vision to me. And thus I have gazed upon you, my heart breaking that you did not—could *never* know. Alas! Could I but wield the magic wand with the perfection of poor Goldsmith to convey to you my poor heart's yearnings! For, forced by the irony of cruel Fate to live among rough, uncouth men as I am—' "

"Yah!" grunted Jim Bell with startling loudness. "And *that* from a buck navvy! A ganger, too! A *nigger*-driver!"

"For Heaven's sake let the ass finish," implored Garnet. "Let's get this over!" But the others of us were impishly amused. I was delighted, the more I sympathized with Garnet.

Old Mick smoothed his wrinkled brow, sniffed a time or two, drew a deep, contemplative breath, then started again. " 'For, living among rough, uncouth men as I am I fly to secret thoughts of you to fill the heart with ambrosial sweetness. Alas, that I must ever awake to the loud laugh, the vacant mind, the coarseness around me—' "

"Well, I'll go hopping to hell!" declared Jim Bell. Old Brookes laughed like a rumbling old bull. Little Tommy Turley chuckled like a chattering possum. I laughed heartily at the anguished expression on the young schoolmaster's face.

With an uplifted, aggravating composure Old Mick finally consented to carry on again.

" 'Dearest, please write me but one little line, that the sweetness of your thoughts cause my soul to soar unstained to the heights of heavenly delight. Yours in longing, Harold Hawthorne.' "

Garnet joined in the laughter eventually, but most definitely not in the congratulations.

"You all know where you stand now with your precious poet!" declared Jim Bell with keen satisfaction. "Your most valued lady friend is not safe with him—from the old baboon's silly pen, I mean—and serve you all damn' well right! And you just know where you all stand, too! 'Rough, uncouth men'—'the loud laugh' —our 'vacant' minds—our 'coarseness' bogging down this honey-hearted poet while he scribbles his sweet nothings to his lady fair! While his coarse mate is swinging the pick and shovel down in the creek up to his bowyangs in muck and slush!"

But Jim's criticism made it seem all the funnier, while Old Mick smirked there with his irresistible old grin.

"Of course, you are not going to post that letter." Garnet smiled ingratiatingly.

"Sure," replied Mick, "but *not* in little old Nigger Creek!" He smirked meaningly at Garnet. "I'm going into Herberton to-morrow!"

"Like hell you are!" declared Jim. "It's a solid day on the windlass for you tomorrow, my horny-handed poet."

"But, Mick," protested Garnet earnestly, "just look what trouble a letter like that would cause! Two people, *important* people, too, only recently married, deeply in love with one another, and *that* bombshell drops into the happy home."

"It will help make it all the happier," replied Mick virtuously. "This epistle from some longing, unknown hand will surprise her, take her breath away. Then fill her with a delightful curiosity. At last, after changing her mind a dozen times, she'll show it to *him*. After wanting to pull the place to pieces, he'll grow convinced she knows nothing whatever about the unknown lover, and they'll love one another better than ever. Each secretly interested, too, in knowing there is some unknown rival pining to come between them from afar. It will bind them all the tighter together, I assure you—he'll hurry home all the earlier, she'll wait all the more eagerly to hear his footsteps coming up the garden path."

"I'd like to twist your wretched old neck! There's no telling what *any* woman would do!" broke in Garnet. "You should be growing a forked tail and hoofs and horns, you old devil."

"I've told you so all along," declared Jim Bell in a satisfied voice.

"Just because from afar my pen has tried to bring a little more happiness into the lives of two nice people," said Mick in injured tones.

"Look here, Mick," declared Garnet energetically, "you'd better burn that precious letter! That gentleman is no fool and he could be a pretty tough customer—you can measure up men, you've seen him, you know enough about men to realize *that* much, anyway. If he comes raging up here to get his hands on the man who wrote that letter then it will be my great pleasure to lead him straight to you! And I'll clap hands heartily when he wrings you out like a dishcloth and hurls your remains into the Wild River!"

A widening grin spread over Old Mick's face from ear to ear.

"Oh boy," he said mildly, "you delight me. To think that a humble epistle from my pen could produce such a flurry amidst the Intelligent Circles. At last, I have not written in vain!"

At which Garnet, with a final scorching reprimand, joined in the laughter.

"You just can't do anything with him," said Long Stewart. 'He'll post that letter in Herberton for sure. The lady will probably burn it and say nothing about it. If not—well, then we'll promise Mick a Christian burial."

"Unless he starts out for the hills first!" laughed Tommy Turley.

"He'd better get a flying start," said Garnet grimly, "if I know anything about the gentleman concerned."

Again, how different all this was to the big scrubs—these light-hearted evenings under the Milky Way to the uneasy loneliness, the inky blackness! No such thing as laughter in the night there.

So it was toil again by day, Mick and Jim stepping out lively to work now that they were "on good dirt". Floating across the road from the tiny school, a chorus of childish voices as Schoolmaster Aitchison conducted a singing lesson. Old Brookes up on the dump at his windlass, Tommy Turley hauling mullock, too. Muffled thunder rolling over the hills—they were shooting again at the Great Northern, maybe the Rainbow. Sounds like the Bradlaugh now. Wondering whether the shots would bring down rich stone or only worthless mullock, I climb down the shaft again. Light the candle, crawl into the drive, pick up the pick and delve into the old river-bed—with little hope indeed that I might strike a patch here, but a man must knock out tucker money somehow. As to where a man was to get the money to buy those horses and twelve months' tucker before he could ride away to seek a new field—!

Times were when I longed to be able to travel and live in scrub or forest as the Jungle Man could. And where was he now?

Life did seem hard at times, in those wonderful days. I'd hope that Garnet would not be studying tonight or putting young Gallogoly through his paces, that he'd be able to stroll across for a laugh at Old Mick's campfire. "Pick! Pick! Thud! Thud!" I'd wonder what the Jungle Man was doing, and think how independent he was, what a strange life he led—almost frighteningly interesting—he was not a bad sort of a bloke when you came to understand him—if only you *ever* could understand him. Queer chap—moody—queer ideas—can smell snakes and things and hear the trees talk—"Pick! Pick! Thud! Thud!"—can read men's thoughts—"Pick! Pick! Thud!"

CHAPTER XXXIX

DISTANT HILLS

THE time came when I made a break.

Such a time comes to most of us, fairly often to some.

"Farther north" kept beckoning—irresistibly.

I had just the few pounds necessary to pay the boat fare north to Cooktown, and a month's tucker money over. I'd carry the swag out to gold- or tin-fields that I was assured somewhat vaguely were "out back of Cooktown". And chance it.

To stay here meant that I would turn the windlass handle for ever and ever, like little Tommy Turley. Or so it seemed to despondent me.

Somewhere in that great Peninsula "farther north" there surely was country that had never been gone over, surely some areas at least that had not yet known the prospector's pick. That parts of it were still "wild" was well enough known, for occasionally four or five lines in some newspaper or other told how some wanderer had been speared by the blacks. In country such as that there could well be "another Palmer".

I would chance it, anyway.

And thought of the Jungle Man. Would he come too? Be drawn as by a magnet to new country, as had Christy Palmerston to the Cairns hinterland, then the jungles of Malaya?

If only the Jungle Man would come! There would not be the loneliness of going alone.

Down below, in that deathly quietness in the old river-bed, in the lonely tent at night after the Council Fire, the more I thought of it the more it seemed he might come. I wished I'd guardedly mentioned the idea before. We had made quite a number of short trips by now, we could put up with each other's company, fairly well, anyway.

Ah! If he *did* agree, he would certainly bring his horses. Ever so much the better. Only the very best of bushmen could find their way overland to Cooktown, so I had been told. Well, the Jungle Man was all that, I was quite certain. He only had two horses, but—he could find gold! We should very soon have the needed team.

One evening, saying nothing to anybody, I walked into Herberton, and next morning at dawn was walking out towards the Dry River.

His camp was gone.

No litter even, let alone rubbish anywhere. Just the bare ground where the tent had stood.

I inquired of men working a claim farther up-river. But they knew nothing. He was here today, gone tomorrow, without a word to a soul. Had left no message.

Woefully disappointed, I trudged back to Herberton, surprised at realizing how keenly I had wished he would come.

Neither at Jack and Newell's nor at the post office had he left a message. Simply squared up his accounts, and gone. Had not even mentioned that he was leaving the Dry River.

I worked a week longer at Nigger Creek, hoping for a message. But the Jungle Man had vanished.

It came hard indeed to say good-bye to good friends. To Old Mick and Jim Bell, Old Brookes and little Tommy Turley and Long Stewart and other friends I'd made. And to Garnet Aitchison.

How strange is life! We little knew that within a few years Garnet and I were to meet again—under the shadow of the Turkish guns before Beersheba.